SPMG Scottish Primary Mathematics Group

Infant Mathematics

A development through activity

First Stage

Teacher's Notes

Heinemann Educational Books

Heinemann Educational Books Ltd
22 Bedford Square, London WC1B 3HH

LONDON EDINBURGH MELBOURNE AUCKLAND
HONG-KONG SINGAPORE KUALA LUMPUR NEW DELHI
IBADAN NAIROBI JOHANNESBURG
EXETER (NH) KINGSTON PORT OF SPAIN

ISBN 0 435 02941 X

© Scottish Primary Mathematics Group 1980
First published 1980
Reprinted 1981

British Library Cataloguing in Publication Data

Scottish Primary Mathematics Group
  Infant mathematics.
  Stage 1: Teacher's notes
  1. Mathematics – Juvenile literature
  I. Title
  510   QA107

ISBN 0–435–02941–X

Typeset by Interprint, Malta, and printed
in Great Britain by Spottiswoode Ballantyne Ltd,
Colchester and London.

Contents

	Page
Outline development of the First Stage	iv-v
General introduction to the course	1
Workbook 1 Sorting; Matching; 1 and 2	7
Workbook 2 Counting to 4	28
Workbook 3 Counting to 8	46
Workbook 4 Counting to 10; Concept of addition	59
Cards 1 to 14 Counting to 10	68
Workbook 5 Addition to 6	78
Workbook 6 Subtraction within 6	96
Workbook 7 Addition to 8	110
Workbook 8 Addition to 10; Number names	129
Cards 25 to 38 Addition to 10	143
Workbook 9 Subtraction within 10	164
Cards 49 to 60 Subtraction within 10	177
Cards 61 to 70 Miscellaneous addition and subtraction	179
Shape, Length, Time Workbook	183
Cards 15 to 24 Solid shapes	186
Cards 39 to 48 Flat shapes	199
Appendix 1 Free play	221
Appendix 2 Number and time rhymes	231

Outline development

	Number		
Workbook 1	Sorting	Sorting of concrete objects into sets. Sorting by colour, type, size, and shape. Recording of sorting by colouring or drawing rings.
	Matching	Matching of concrete objects. Matching pictures of objects one-to-one. Finding which set has 'more'.
	1 and 2	Sets of 1 and 2 objects by inspection. Reading and writing numerals 1 and 2.
Workbook 2	Counting to 4	Reading and writing numerals 1 to 4. Counting to 4. Sequence of numbers 1, 2, 3, 4.
Workbook 3	Counting to 8	Reading and writing numerals to 8. Counting 5, 6, 7, 8 objects.
Workbook 4 **Cards 1 to 14**	Counting to 10	Counting 9, 10 objects. Reading and writing numerals to 10. Counting to 10. Shopping using 1p coins. Sequence of numbers 1 to 10.
	Concept of addition	Combining sets of objects including 1p coins. Totals to 10 by counting. Adding on 1.
Workbook 5	Addition to 6	Introduction of + and = signs. 'Stories' of 2, 3, 4, 5, 6 using concrete material. Commutative idea, e.g. $3+4=4+3$. Addition of money to 6p. Mapping diagrams:
Workbook 6	Subtraction within 6	Taking away—removal or covering of concrete material. Introduction of − sign and of 0. Subtraction 'stories'—Taking from 1, 2, 3, 4, 5, 6. Subtraction of money within 6p. Mapping diagrams.

iv

of the First Stage

		Number (continued)	
Workbook 7	Addition to 8		Revision of addition to 6. Addition 'stories' of 7, 8, including stories with 0. 'Doubles' from $1+1$ to $5+5$. Commutative idea, mapping diagrams, simple problems. Addition of money to 8p.
Workbook 8 Cards 25 to 38	Addition to 10		Addition 'stories' of 9, 10; money to 10p. Commutative idea, mapping diagrams, problems. Addition of three numbers—totals to 10.
	Number names		Reading and writing of number names one to ten. Sequence of number names one to ten. First, second, and third.
Workbook 9 Cards 49 to 60	Subtraction within 10		Revision of subtraction within 6. Subtraction 'stories'—taking from 7, 8, 9, 10. Subtraction of money within 10p. Miscellaneous examples and problems.
Cards 61 to 70	Miscellaneous addition and subtraction		Practice examples and problems to 10.
		Shape, Length, Time	
Shape, Length Time Workbook Cards 15 to 24 Cards 39 to 48	Solid shapes		Model making, sorting, matching with cones, cylinders, cubes, and cuboids.
	Length		Language and sorting activities—long, short, thick, thin, tall, etc.
	Flat shapes		Making pictures, sorting, matching with circles, triangles, squares and rectangles.
	Time		Vocabulary and time sequences. Telling the time—o'clocks.
	Length		Language and sorting activities—longer, shorter, etc.

Informal 'free play' activities involving weight, area, volume, sequence, pattern, etc., are described in Appendix 1 of the *Teachers' Notes*. Appendix 2 contains a selection of number and time rhymes. These appendices are intended for use throughout the year.

General Introduction to the Course

Background

The course *Primary Mathematics—A development through activity* had its origins in a Working Party which was formed to examine the structure and content of a Mathematics course for children in Scottish Primary Schools. The Working Party recommendations provided the framework for *Curriculum Paper 13, Primary Education in Scotland: Mathematics*, which was published by the Scottish Education Department and which '... serves as a handbook of guidance to the teacher in the primary school ...'.

The Working Party also produced material for children aged from seven to twelve years. This material was tried out in schools throughout Scotland, and was assessed by the teachers, and by the Working Party members who visited classrooms on a regular basis and who subsequently revised the material. Stages 1 to 5 of *Primary Mathematics—A development through activity*, suitable for children aged seven to twelve years, was published as a result of this project.

The authors of this series, the 'Scottish Primary Mathematics Group', recognized the need to write and assess material for children aged five to seven years, which would lead directly into Stage 1 of the existing series. This material, *Infant Mathematics: First Stage* and *Second Stage*, was piloted in a wide variety of Scottish Primary schools. During the course of the piloting the authors regularly visited the schools. As a result of this and of assessments from the infant teachers involved the material was revised and rewritten for publication.

List of the authors of *Infant Mathematics*: First Stage

Craigie College of Education, Ayr

Archie MacCallum, Principal Lecturer in Mathematics
David McCulloch, Formerly Lecturer in Mathematics
Ian K. Clark, Lecturer in Mathematics
Peter S. Henderson, Formerly Principal Lecturer in Mathematics

Callendar Park College of Education, Falkirk

Catherine D. J. Preston, Principal Lecturer in Mathematics
John Mackinlay, Lecturer in Mathematics

William W. R. Tait, Senior Primary Adviser, Tayside

2 General Introduction to the Course

Introduction to *Infant Mathematics: First Stage*

The material provides a course on Number, Money, Measure, and Shape for children in their first year at school. It consists of ten expendable **Workbooks**, a set of **Workcards, Teacher's Notes**, and a **Teacher's Materials Pack**.

Throughout the whole course, emphasis is placed on the use of material to introduce concepts and new ideas. Many practical activities are detailed in the **Teacher's Notes**, and the Workbook pages and Workcards should only be used after the children have had sufficient experience with the material. Indeed, some topics are to be found only in the **Teacher's Notes**, which also contain Appendices on Free Play and Number and Time Rhymes.

The Number work includes sorting, matching, counting to 10, and addition and subtraction experiences within 10. Money is integrated with the Number work and involves only the use of the 1p coin.

Informal Measure work is referred to in the Appendix on Free Play in the **Teacher's Notes**. More specific activities involving the language of Length appear in one of the Workbooks, which also includes work on Time and Shape.

Workbooks

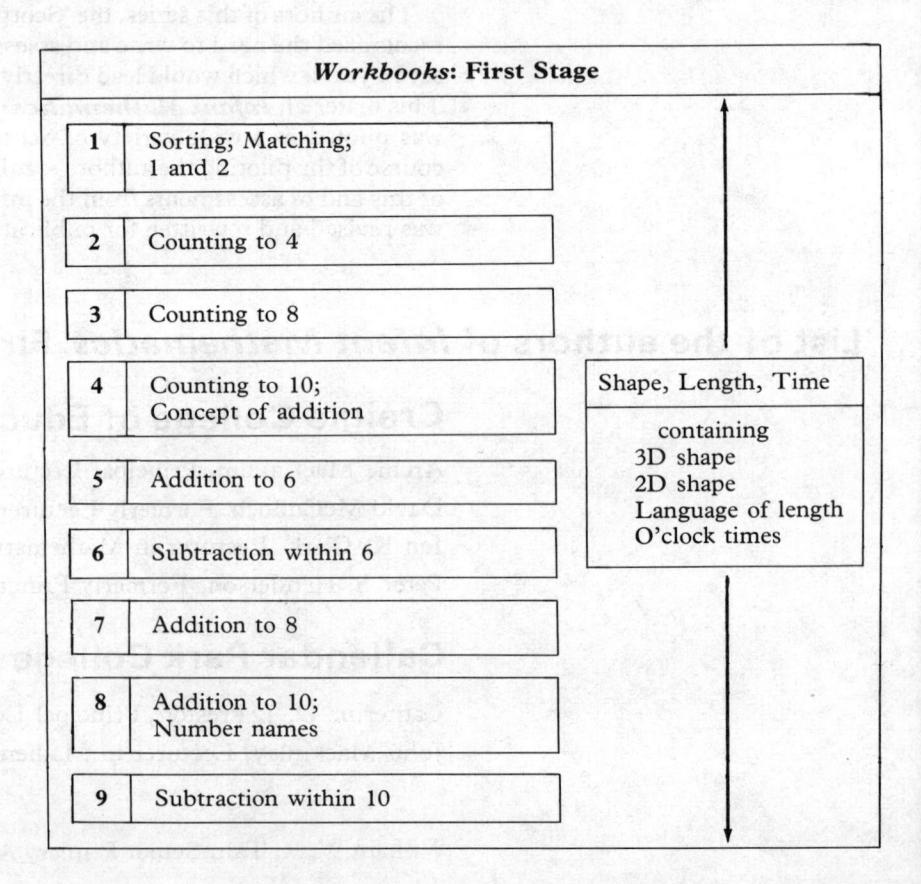

Workbooks: First Stage

1	Sorting; Matching; 1 and 2
2	Counting to 4
3	Counting to 8
4	Counting to 10; Concept of addition
5	Addition to 6
6	Subtraction within 6
7	Addition to 8
8	Addition to 10; Number names
9	Subtraction within 10

Shape, Length, Time

containing
3D shape
2D shape
Language of length
O'clock times

General Introduction to the Course 3

There are nine expendable Workbooks providing a sequence of work on Number and Money. Each Workbook contains only fifteen pages and is thus completed in a fairly short time. This means that the children are being presented with new booklets at regular intervals throughout the year, which in itself helps to maintain the children's interest.

The remaining expendable Workbook deals with Shape, Length, and Time. This Workbook should be used at fairly regular intervals throughout the session to ensure that the children have varied mathematical experiences.

Some Workbook pages contain references to Workcards. Cards to be done before a specific Workbook page are referenced at the *top* of the appropriate Workbook page. Workcards which could follow a Workbook page are referenced from the *bottom* of the appropriate Workbook page.

Workcards

There are thirty-five double-sided non-expendable cards, numbered on each side from 1 to 70. They have been grouped together to provide a reasonable number of cards on six sections of the work, as listed below.

Workcards	*Section of work*	*Referenced from*
1 to 14	Counting to 10	***Workbook 4***, page 10
15 to 24	Solid shapes	***Shape, Length, Time*** page 1
25 to 38	Addition to 10	***Workbook 8***, page 8
39 to 48	Flat shapes	***Shape, Length, Time*** page 10
49 to 60	Subtraction within 10	***Workbook 9***, page 15
61 to 70	Miscellaneous addition and subtraction	***Workbook 9***, page 15

Guidance on the use of these cards is given in this section on 'Using the Course' on page 4. More detailed suggestions for their use are also given at appropriate points in the ***Teacher's Notes*** for each separate Workbook.

Teacher's Notes

The ***Teacher's Notes*** form an essential part of this course. They contain many suggestions for practical activities which should precede most of the Workbook pages and the Workcards. They also describe additional activities, oral work, games, extra cards, and worksheets which could easily be made by the teacher.

4 General Introduction to the Course

Lists of contents and materials are given for each Workbook, together with detailed notes relating to individual Workbook pages.

Teaching notes for the Workcards appear at the point at which they are referenced from a Workbook. Reference is also made at appropriate points in the *Teacher's Notes* to the *Teacher's Materials Pack*.

Teacher's Materials Pack

The *Teacher's Materials Pack*, which contains cardboard shapes, games, and teaching aids closely related to the content of the *First Stage*, is an optional extra, but should provide useful and desirable resource material for the classroom.

Using the course

Two essential features of the course are practical activities using materials and discussion of these activities. Suggestions for such work are contained in the *Teacher's Notes*. Teachers should select from these suggestions as there are often too many to be attempted in the time likely to be available. On the other hand, these activities may be supplemented or replaced by other ideas which the individual teacher prefers and which achieve the same aims. The *Teacher's Notes* also contain advice about using each Workbook page and Workcard.

The written work supplied in the Workbooks and Workcards should not be attempted until the children have had sufficient experience with practical materials and the opportunity of discussing these activities with the teacher. The pages and cards are intended as follow-up practice in using ideas already taught through activity and discussion.

Workbooks 1 to 9 contain a sequence of work in Number and Money covering ideas of cardinal and ordinal number, and addition and subtraction to 10. The *Workbooks* on addition and subtraction are arranged alternately as follows:

Workbook 5: Addition to 6
Workbook 6: Subtraction within 6
Workbook 7: Addition to 8
Workbook 8: Addition to 10
Workbook 9: Subtraction within 10

This order is flexible in that teachers may wish to

(a) use the books in this order;
or (b) tackle addition and subtraction simultaneously;
or (c) do all the work on addition (*Workbooks 5, 7, 8*) first before starting subtraction.

The remaining *Shape, Length, Time Workbook* contains five separate sections of work which should be interspersed with the Number work from *Workbooks 1 to 9*. The teacher should choose when to use one of its units, 'lifting and laying' the book throughout

General Introduction to the Course

the year. It is *not* recommended that all the Number work should be completed before tackling these other topics. The five sections on Shape, Length, and Time need not be used in strict order. Further advice about this is given at the start of the teaching notes for this **Workbook** (page 183).

The page headings of the Workbook pages include a description of the type of work covered on that page. This appears in a rectangular box and is intended for the teacher.

| Counting to 10 | How many? | 10 |

The other title or instruction on the page is for pupils who may require to have it read to them.

The activities on the **Workcards** are intended for use at the teacher's discretion. They are referenced from particular pages in the Workbooks, and advice about how, when, and with whom they might be used is contained in the *Teacher's Notes*. The references look like this:

▼ Cards 1 to 14 (Counting to 10)

The cards about Number topics provide, for the most part, further practice, problems, and revision. Some are intended as 'stretching material', while others provide straight-forward practice. Cards about solid and flat shapes are referenced from the start of the appropriate sections in the **Shape, Length, Time Workbook**. They should be used for practical work in handling and fitting shapes before the children attempt the Workbook pages on these topics.

Not all of the Workbook pages and Workcards should necessarily be attempted by all of the children. Some pages and cards are more suited to able pupils and should be omitted by the others. Practice examples which many pupils of average ability will need might be omitted by more able pupils who have mastered the technique involved. The least able pupils will progress at a slower rate and will be unable to cope with written work without constant reference to 'concrete' material. The pages and cards which they do should be carefully selected by the teacher. This course is not intended as a 'programmed text'. Teachers should select from it or supplement it from other sources as they see fit.

The *Teacher's Notes* contain lists of **materials** required for each Workbook and its associated cards. These should help teachers to gather together bits and pieces before they are needed. There is also a list of the material needed for each individual page or card at the start of the teaching note for that page or card. Most of the material is of the type likely to be found already in schools—counters, beads, cubes, etc.

The *Teacher's Materials Pack* for the First Stage contains simple cardboard apparatus, games, shapes, etc., which provide supplemen-

6 General Introduction to the Course

tary activities for children to fit in with the course. There are references to appropriate Teacher's Pack cards at various places in the *Teacher's Notes*. The Pack also has its own set of notes which describe how it can be used with children. Although an optional extra, teachers should find the Pack a useful source of additional activities. There are many other materials produced commercially which have not been specifically mentioned in the *Teacher's Notes* but which would also be most valuable.

At various places in the teaching notes there are suggestions for **Additional activities** which can be used to enrich the work of a particular section. **Cards and worksheets for the teacher to make** also appear in the Notes in such a way that teachers could quickly select from them and produce extra activities for the children.

Some activities do not appear in written form at all; for example, regular oral practice and informal discussion. Such activities should, however, become a regular and important feature of the work in mathematics, although they cannot be satisfactorily provided in worksheet or workcard form.

The **course** has been written in such a way that, if used flexibly, it should suit individual, group, or class teaching. There is no single 'best' way of using it as this will depend on the teacher, the children, and the topic. An outline development which corresponds to the *Workbooks* and *Workcards* is given on pages iv and v.

Workbook 1

Sorting; Matching; 1 and 2

Contents

Colouring sets	Pages 1 and 2
Drawing and colouring sets	Page 3
Drawing rings round sets	Pages 4 and 5
Sorting sets by colouring	Page 6
Drawing lines to match	Page 7
Drawing objects to match one-to-one	Page 8
Matching to find set with more	Page 9
Writing 2	Page 10
Drawing 2 objects in a set	Pages 11 and 12
Drawing to make 2 in a set	Page 13
Colouring and ringing sets of 2	Page 14
Writing 1 or 2	Page 15

Materials

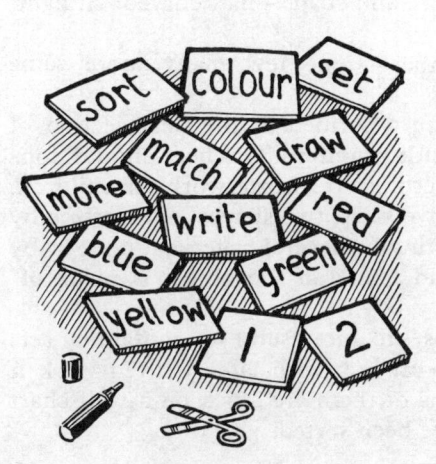

A variety of materials would be needed to cover a wide range of properties associated with matching ideas and one-to-one correspondence:

    beads, buttons, counters, coins, building bricks, coloured rods, toy animals, cars, boats, aeroplanes, soldiers, gummed paper shapes, cardboard and plastic shapes, attribute blocks, playing cards, crayons, pencils, pens, tins, straws, nails, screws, marbles, wool, ribbon, string, streamers, embroidery threads, coloured elastic bands, plasticine, shells, bottle tops, coloured plastic pegs, cutlery, cotton reels, etc.

Hoops, sorting trays, boxes, lids of tins or boxes, etc., are useful for containing the materials being sorted. 'Pictures' of objects are extremely useful for making wallcharts, etc., to record the result of a sorting activity.

There are many other equally suitable materials not mentioned in these Notes which teachers may prefer to use for sorting activities.

Although teachers may not be formally teaching the vocabulary associated with sorting and matching, it would be desirable to have flashcards for display.

Workbook 1: Sorting; Matching; 1 and 2

Sorting (Pages 1 to 6)

Development

This section gives suggestions for a great deal of oral and practical work where children sort out actual objects and discuss the ways in which they sort them. The aims of this work are to develop children's ability to sort out sets of objects with a common property and to decide if a particular object belongs to a set.

The Workbook pages are intended to follow up such sorting activities by asking the children to colour and ring sets. The children at this stage are not expected to read the words on the pages. The teacher should give the work orally.

Practical activities and teaching

General points about sorting activities

1. Some activities are suitable for children just starting school but others should be offered much later in the year.
2. Only some of the sorting activities should be attempted by the children. The teacher should choose these to suit the children's needs. The work with actual objects is the important experience. The pages in the Workbook should only be attempted by children who have had considerable practice in sorting actual objects.
3. The most important aspect of these sorting activities is the discussion and language development which take place. Discussion would introduce a lot of vocabulary:
   (a) names of objects—beads, pegs, bricks, etc.;
   (b) words associated with sorting by size—big, small, long, short, etc.;
   (c) names of colours—red, blue, green, yellow, etc.;
   (d) words associated with texture and shape—flat, curved, straight, rough, smooth, etc.;
   (e) words associated with number—some, few, many, more, same number, etc.
4. The sorting activities which are described in the next section of these Notes **are in no particular order**. Teachers should consider these possibilities when setting up sorting work for children.
5. In general, sorting two kinds, two sizes, two shapes, and sorting by colour are 'early' activities. Sorting by several criteria at once or by properties such as 'texture' and 'material the object is made of' should come later.
6. Sorting trays, boxes, lids, hoops, etc., are useful for containing sets during sorting. It is also a useful link with later written work if actual objects or representations of them are stuck on a wall-chart diagram to show sets which have been sorted.

Workbook 1: Sorting; Matching; 1 and 2

Preliminary sorting activities

The following section contains a number of suggestions for sorting work involving concrete materials. Teachers should choose activities suitable to the children in their class and to the materials available.

Children should experience many of these activities before attempting *Workbook 1*, Pages 1 to 6.

Sorting mixed collections
Materials Mixed collections of things: beads, buttons, pegs, counters, toy animals, cars, aeroplanes, etc.

Possible activities
1 Sorting out the different objects by separately collecting all the beads, all the buttons, all the pegs, etc. This might be the first type of sorting activity.
2 Pick out all the toy animals, say, from a mixed collection of things. Afterwards the different animals might be separated out.
3 A more difficult type of sorting is to ask the children to pick out a property which different kinds of objects have.
   e.g. 'Put all the red things in that tray.'
   or 'Put all the things with holes through them in that tray'.
   or 'Collect all the wooden things in that tray.'
   or 'Separate things which float/sink; are shiny/dull; are rough/smooth; etc.'

Note It is important in all sorting work to ask questions to make sure that the children can
   (a) state the common property of objects in a set;
   (b) decide if a 'new' object belongs to the set or not.

Sorting beads
Materials A collection of threading beads of different colours, sizes, shapes, and materials; string or cord.

Possible activities
1 A child could be given a string which has one bead threaded on it and asked to thread all the beads of this kind (same shape, size, colour, and material). All beads of another kind could be threaded on another string, and so on until all the beads had been threaded. Perhaps 3 to 5 beads on each of 4 to 5 strings would be reasonable. The ablest children might be asked which string (a) has most beads, (b) has fewest beads.
2 Beads could be sorted by colour by threading all beads of a particular colour on one string.
3 Separate strings could be used for different kinds of bead regardless of colour, e.g. long beads, plastic beads, wooden beads, etc.
4 (a) Less able children could be given a simple string of beads to copy.
   (b) Children could be given a string with two similar beads of different colours and asked to continue the pattern.

Workbook 1: Sorting; Matching; 1 and 2

Sorting buttons

Materials A collection of buttons of different types, sizes, colours, materials, designs.

Possible activities
1 Buttons of two different sizes could be sorted into 'large' and 'small'. This could be extended to three sizes.
2 The beads might be sorted by colour.
3 Suitable buttons could be sorted by texture into 'rough' ones and 'smooth' ones.
4 A mixed collection could be sorted by type into coat buttons, shirt buttons, etc.
5 Some children might be able to sort buttons with two holes from those with four holes.
6 Buttons could also be sorted by considering the material they are made of: plastic, metal, wood, etc.

Sorting bricks

Materials Collection of building bricks of different colours; or interlocking cubes of different colours; or cotton reels of different types.

Possible activities
1 Children could make towers or rows of each colour. The number of each colour could be chosen so that the children could be asked which colour had (a) most, (b) least, and (c) the same number of bricks.
2 An activity like this could be recorded by children sticking gummed paper squares on to a sheet of paper.

Workbook 1: Sorting; Matching; 1 and 2   11

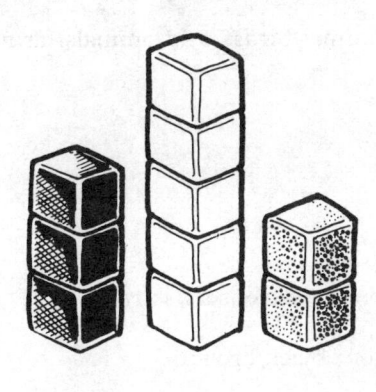

3   Children could be asked which towers were the same height (or rows the same length). Bricks could be taken off to make pairs of towers or rows the same height or length.

4   Cotton reels could be piled according to type.

Sorting cards

Materials   Playing cards with pictures of the 'Happy Families' or 'Old Maid' types; ordinary playing cards; home-made cards using rubber stamps or stencils.

Possible activities

1   Sets of cards which contain identical pictures can be sorted by 'type'. 'Old Maid' cards and 'Snap' cards can be sorted into identical pairs.

2   'Happy Families' cards can be sorted in a number of ways: those showing parents/children; fathers/mothers/sons/daughters; different families; etc.

3   Particular 'types' of ordinary playing cards, e.g. 'Kings', could be picked out of a pack (or part of a pack). Cards could be sorted by colour black/red or by suit (by shape) spades/clubs/diamonds/hearts.

4 Cards may suit different sortings: animal/birds; wild animals/farm animals; 4 legs/2 legs, etc.

Sorting children
Materials The children in the class.

Possible activities
1 Sorting into boys/girls.
2 Sorting by clothes into short trousers/long trousers/skirts.
3 Those wearing spectacles/those not.
4 Different types of shoe: lacing/slip-on; black/brown.
5 Sorting by hair colour.
   Such activities can be done by having different sets of children lined up in rows.

Sorting counters
Materials Collection of counters of two sizes, two or more colours, perhaps made of different materials; trays or plastic bags as containers.

Possible activities
1 A child could be given a plastic bag or tray with one counter in it and asked to put in all the counters which are the same (size, colour, and material).
2 Separate bags or trays could be used for each kind of counter.
3 Sorting might be by size (large and small regardless of colour) or by colour (regardless of size).
4 Able children could arrange counters in rows and decide which row has more (most).

Sorting coins
Materials Actual $\frac{1}{2}$p, 1p, 2p, 5p, 10p coins; plastic or cardboard coins.

Possible activities
1 A collection of the two types of 'silver' coins can be sorted by size. Similarly the 'copper' coins can be sorted by size.
2 Coins could be sorted by colour into 'copper' ones and 'silver' ones.
3 Plastic, cardboard, and metal coins could be sorted by the type of material.

Sorting gummed paper shapes
Materials Jollycraft mosaic, play shapes, gummed paper shapes.

Possible activities
1 A child could be given separate pieces of paper with a different sample shape stuck on each. He would then stick on shapes identical to the given one.
2 Another way of sorting by shape is to provide an outline picture made of shapes where children have to stick on shapes which fit.
3 Shapes could also be sorted by colour, recording by sticking each colour (regardless of shape) on its own sheet of paper which had a colour code.

Workbook 1: Sorting; Matching; 1 and 2

Sorting 3-D shapes

Materials Empty cartons, boxes, tins, balls (perhaps 3 to 6 examples of each), including shapes such as Toblerone packets, Smartie tubes, etc.

Possible activities
1 Children could be given trays or lids with a sample shape in each. They have to put the same kind of shape on each tray.
2 Shapes of one kind might be sorted into large/small.
3 Children could be asked to pick out the shapes with a curved surface (or which roll easily).
4 Children might use plasticine to make shapes like these.
5 Further work using 3-D shapes is described in these **Teacher's Notes**, Appendix 1: Free Play, and the **Shape, Length, Time Workbook**.

Sorting 2-D shapes

Materials Plastic shapes, attribute blocks, cardboard shapes, gummed paper shapes.

Possible activities
1 Shapes come in sets of squares, rectangles, circles, triangles, etc., which are designed to be sorted by shape, colour, size (large/small) and thickness (thick/thin).
2 Attributes which might be used for sorting:
   (a) curved/straight edges;
   (b) colour;
   (c) size (large/small);
   (d) kind of shape, e.g. 'all shapes like this one'. Eventually names such as circle, square, etc., would be used.
   (e) fitting shapes to outline pictures.
3 Further work using 2-D shapes (flat shapes) is described in the **Teacher's Notes** for **Shape, Length, Time Workbook**.

Introducing colour

Before attempting Pages 1 and 2 of **Workbook 1** children would have to have had a considerable experience involving colour. The concept of colour as a property of things is quite difficult for some young children. Every opportunity should be taken to check on individual children's understanding of colour.

A good early experience is to make a collection of, say, **red things**, one week followed by, say, **blue things**, and so on.

Each collection could be labelled with a card showing a coloured disc and the name of the colour. This could lead to a poster display of red things or even to a hanging mobile of red things.

Children could be given outline pictures or shapes to colour. Rubber stamps or stencils could be used and a spirit duplicator could give the sample colour. Later a sheet could require two colours, for example to colour different football jerseys.

Workbook 1: Sorting; Matching; 1 and 2

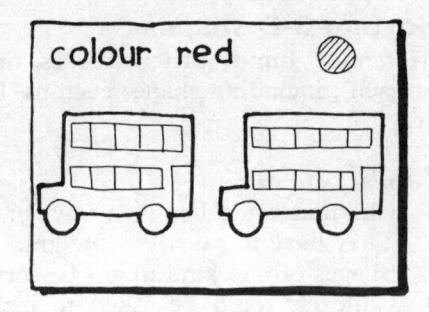

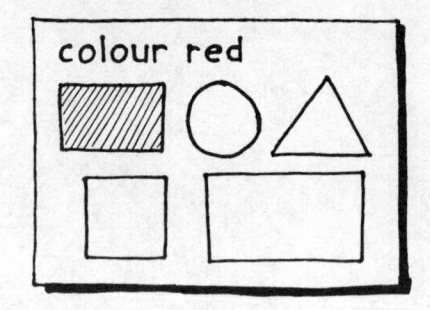

Following these experiences, and the use of flashcards, children should gradually get to know, at least orally, the words 'colour', 'red', 'blue', 'green', 'yellow', and should then be able to attempt Pages 1 and 2 of **Workbook 1**.

Pages 1 and 2

Colour

 Sorting

Materials   Red, blue, green, and yellow pencils or crayons.

Children have to colour in pictures using a specified colour: red and blue on Page 1; green and yellow on Page 2.

Adult standards are not to be expected. The important thing is that children use the correct colour in each set.

When Pages 1 and 2 have been coloured, reference could be made to the 'set of red pictures' or 'a red set'. Children could be asked to name the things in each set.

Teaching suggestions for Page 3

The work on this page is quite difficult for children, although adult standards cannot be expected. Children have to think of two attributes (colour and kind).
1   They will need to be given a lot of practical work to pick out a set of red beads; a set of blue pegs; a set of round beads; a set of yellow squares; etc.
2   They should have experience of creating sets of coloured things on paper—coloured pictures or shapes.
3   A blackboard demonstration of creating a set of red flags; a set of green apples; etc., should be given.

Extra worksheets for the teacher to make

Worksheets could be made, similar to those on the left, showing objects in a set (rubber stamps or stencils could be used) which the children have to colour.

Workbook 1: Sorting; Matching; 1 and 2   **15**

| Page 3 | **Draw sets** | Sorting |

Materials Red and blue pencils or crayons.

Children are expected to draw one or two more apples and balloons then colour them in. Adult standards should not be required, but the colours should be correct.

Some children might be able to discuss their work and even consider questions such as:

'Have your sets got the same number of things in them?'
'Which set has more things?'

Additional worksheets for the teacher to make

Here are two examples. Teachers might wish to make several sheets of this type.

Note A selection of children's work would make a worthwhile classroom display and lead to helpful discussion; for example:
'John has drawn a lot of cars in his set'; 'Tom and Ann have the same number of cats in their sets'; and so on.

Teaching suggestions for Pages 4 and 5

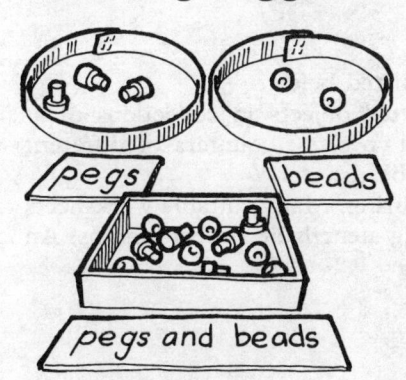

Before attempting these pages, children should have sorted collections of things into two sets by placing them inside hoops, stapled paper or cardboard rings, lids, or sorting trays.

A blackboard illustration could be used. The teacher should discuss and then ring each set. In some cases the rings should be one above the other.

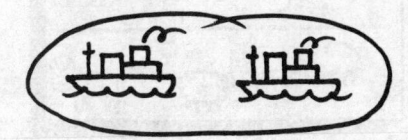

16   Workbook 1: Sorting; Matching; 1 and 2

Simpler worksheets for the teacher to make

Here is an example of the type of sheet which could be made.

| Pages 4 and 5 | Draw rings to sort | Sorting |

Materials   Pencils or crayons.

Following the teaching suggestions, children should be able to attempt Pages 4 and 5.

They could be asked to identify the things pictured. When they have found all the things of one kind, they should draw a ring or loop around them. They should see the need for two rings in each collection. It might be helpful to suggest that different coloured rings are used in case children make them overlap. It might also reinforce the idea if they coloured the things in each set (two colours).

Every opportunity should be taken to encourage the use of language such as 'a set of flowers' and number words such as 'some', 'few', 'more', 'less', etc.

Teaching suggestions for Page 6

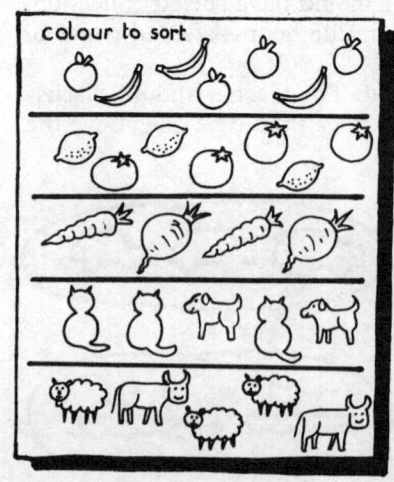

Some possible practical activities are listed below.
1. Practical experience of sorting actual objects in collections of at least two kinds, e.g. counters of two sizes; counters of different colours; pegs of different colours; beads; etc.
2. Prior experience of sorting by colouring. Many suitable worksheets could be made by the teacher using stencils or rubber stamps. An example is given here.

Workbook 1: Sorting; Matching; 1 and 2

| Page 6 | **Colour to sort** | Sorting |

Materials Coloured pencils or crayons.

Children should be asked to look at the pictures to identify the objects. They should then colour all those of the same kind—all the boats with sails—using the same colour. They should then find and colour differently the other kind of object pictured. The dolls and teddy bears may cause difficulty because they face in different directions but if children are asked to colour all the dolls they should be able to complete this satisfactorily.

Matching (Pages 7 to 9)

Development

This section introduces the idea of matching. Matching the members of a set one-to-one with the members of another set is a necessary preliminary to the counting activities of **Workbooks 2, 3, and 4**, where a number name is 'matched' to each object in a set.

The children should have a lot of experience of matching actual objects before attempting the Workbook pages of this section, which deal with matching pictures of objects in two sets by joining them with lines. At first the sets have an equal number of objects, but later one set has more objects than the other set. The children also draw one straw for each glass, etc. Vocabulary such as 'more', 'less', 'same number', 'match', etc., would be introduced orally.

Practical activities and teaching

Preliminary matching activities

1 Matching actual objects

Many opportunities for 'natural' matching should be provided.

Wendy House (see Appendix 1 Free Play—Home Corner, page 225). Activities here are rich in these matchings, for example:
cups to saucers; knives to forks; spoons to plates; teaspoons to saucers; lids to pans; persons to seats; etc.

Dressing a doll Here a child matches socks to feet; shoes to feet; hat to head; dress to doll; buttons to button-holes; etc.

18 Workbook 1: Sorting; Matching; 1 and 2

The classroom This gives an opportunity for matching boys to girls; children to seats; seats to desks; coats to pegs; pencils to children; straws to milk bottles; toggles or buttons to buttonholes; etc.

At this informal stage, teachers should ask, 'Are there enough?'; 'Do you need more?'; 'Has each got one?'; 'Is there a cup for each saucer?', and so on.

2 Joining to match

The written recording of matching by joining with a line can be simulated by the children using straws or strips of cardboard or pieces of ribbon to join the actual objects matched.

3 Matching picture cards

A set of cards showing pictures of things which form obvious pairs could be made and used by the children to find pairs.

4 Matching pictures of objects by drawing a line between

Worksheets could be made by drawing pictures of matching pairs.

Workbook 1: Sorting; Matching; 1 and 2

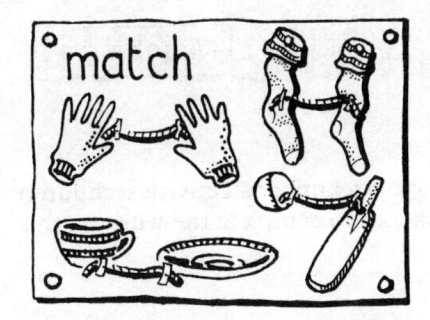

5 Classroom display

A wall display could be made, in discussion with the children, by sticking on pictures of matching pairs of objects and joining them with felt pen lines or lengths of wool or string.

Page 7 — Match — Matching

Materials Pencil or crayon.

Children who have experienced preliminary activities like those listed above should be able to attempt the work on Page 7. The teacher should discuss drawing a line joining the first matching pair of spade and pail. Vocabulary used should include 'has a' and 'match', e.g. 'Each pot (pan) *has a* lid', and '*match* a knife to a fork'.

Some children will realise that these one-to-one matchings (with no objects unmatched) mean that there is the same number in each set.

Teaching suggestions for Page 8

The children should do appropriate practical work before attempting Page 8. Some possible activities are:
1. Set out a row of bottles or jars and a supply of straws and ask the children to put one straw in each.
2. Ask a child to give one pencil to each of a group of children.
3. Ask children to give
   (a) each cup a saucer;
   (b) each saucer a spoon; and so on.
4. Cut out several cardboard mice and supply lengths of wool or string as tails. Then ask children to stick a tail on each mouse.
5. Supply egg-cups and imitation eggs and ask the children to put an egg in each egg-cup.
   This activity can be simulated as a wall display with slots cut to insert cardboard eggs.

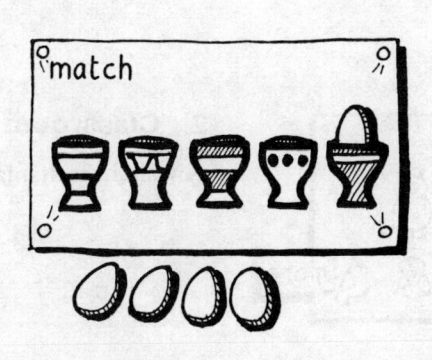

Workbook 1: Sorting; Matching; 1 and 2

Page 8 — Match — Matching

Materials Pencil or crayon.

After experiencing some of the above preliminary activities children should be able, with minimal explanation, to complete the work on this page.

Teaching suggestions for Page 9

Considerable practical experience of comparing the number of things in two sets is necessary before children should attempt this page. To minimize the tendency to count the objects, each set should contain at least 7 things.

1 Matching objects

Collections of 2 things should be compared by one-to-one matching; e.g. boys and girls; pegs of 2 colours; counters of 2 colours or 2 sizes; beads of 2 colours or 2 shapes; cubes of 2 colours; etc.

The teacher should show the children how to match pairs of objects to find which set has **more**. Children could place a flashcard with the correct set. For example:

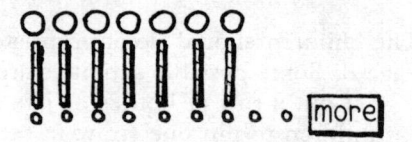

There are more small counters than large counters.

A pegboard could be used to pair off the pegs:

There are more white pegs than black pegs.

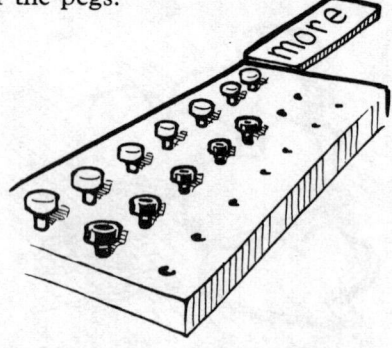

2 Classroom display

A wallchart display could show this type of matching.

Workbook 1: Sorting; Matching; 1 and 2   **21**

| **Page 9** | **Which has more?** | Matching |

Materials Pencil or crayon.

The work on this page is intended to be done by one-to-one matching rather than by counting. The number of things in each set is probably beyond the children's ability to count.

Children who have experienced some of the above preliminary activities should require only a little help with the work on this page.

When they have completed one-to-one matching between two sets they could be told to colour the set which has 'more' things in it.

Additional activities

1. Children given two sets could be asked to match one-to-one then place flashcards more and perhaps also less with the correct set.
2. Teachers could use rubber stamps or stencils to make further worksheets.
3. Some children might be able to attempt work requiring them to draw a set with 'more' or 'the same number' of objects.

Cardinal numbers 1 and 2 (Pages 10 to 15)

Development

This section deals with recognition of sets of 2 and 1 by inspection or by one-to-one matching with familiar sets. This leads to writing the numerals 1 and 2 which are then used to record the number of objects in the sets.

Workbook 1: Sorting; Matching; 1 and 2

The Workbook pages provide practice in drawing and colouring sets of 2 as well as in writing 1 and 2. The associated vocabulary includes 'write', 'draw', 'make', 'colour', and the names of objects pictured on the pages. Although it is intended that the work will be given orally to the children who are not expected to read these words at this stage it could be helpful to display the key words on flashcards.

Practical activities and teaching

Preliminary activities

1 Number rhymes, songs, and stories are a useful contribution to this work (see Appendix 2 on page 231).
2 The 'two-ness of two' can be established by one-to-one matching with familiar sets of two, e.g. feet, legs, hands, arms, eyes, ears, shoes, socks, mittens, etc.
3 There are many practical activities related to this work:
 (a) Stringing beads in twos (2 red, 2 blue, 2 white, etc.). 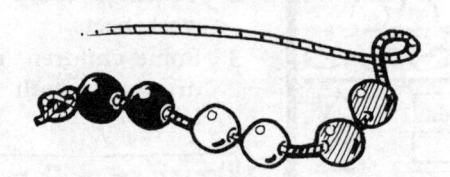 
 (b) Placing plastic animals, toys, etc., in twos.
 (c) Placing objects in hoops, rings, or trays in twos. 
 (d) Joining interlocking cubes, beads, etc., in twos.

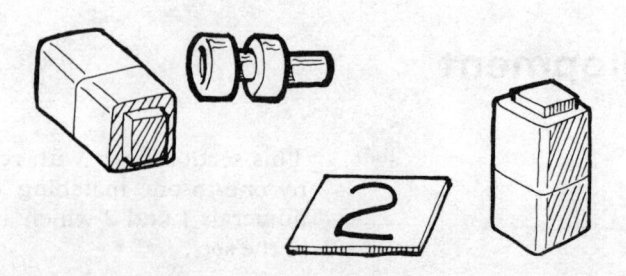

Workbook 1: Sorting; Matching; 1 and 2

(e) Activities involving the children, for example arranging in twos by taking a partner, clapping twice, taking 2 steps forward, backward or to the side, etc.
(f) Making pairs of things with plasticine, e.g. 2 snakes, 2 balls, etc.
(g) Making 'Our book of 2' as a group project.

4 Formation of numeral 2 This requires careful teaching and supervising. Some suggestions are:
(a) Finger writing in the air, in sand tray, in paint.
(b) Tracing over a large numeral with the point of a finger.
(c) Using tracing paper to trace over numeral 2.
(d) Worksheets could be made with dotted outlines which the children 'go over'.

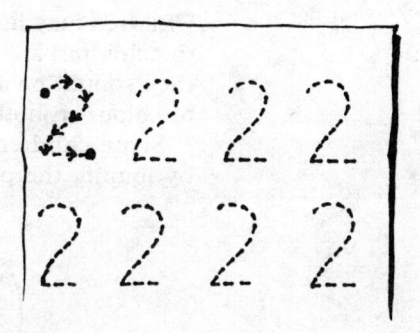

(e) Copying the numeral 2 on blank paper.
(f) A washable, wipeable workcard covered with clear plastic can be made. The children copy or trace over the numeral (perhaps dotted) on the card which can then be wiped clean for further use. This can also be done using a sheet of paper inside a clear plastic folder.

24   **Workbook 1:** Sorting; Matching; 1 and 2

| **Page 10** | **Write 2** | Sets of 2 |

Materials   Pencil or crayon.

Children who have experienced many of the preliminary activities should be able to attempt this work.

The writing of the numeral 2 should have been achieved by the children to a reasonable standard before they complete the top portion of the page.

The names of the things pictured—cats, dogs, trees, ducks—do not need to be read but some children may be motivated to try. They should be asked to say what the pictures show.

The children are expected to realize by simply looking at the pictures that there are 2 things in each set.

| **Page 11** | **Draw** | Sets of 2 |

Materials   Pencil or crayon.

Children may have to be told to draw the two things in each set. Again, the children are not expected to read any of the words on the page but they should be able to say what the pictures are. They could be asked to colour in both the given pictures and also their own drawings.

Some children may be helped by asking them to match one-to-one by joining the pictures with a line like this:

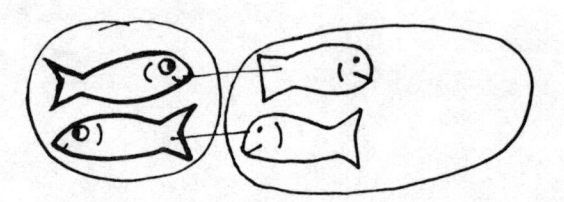

| **Page 12** | **Draw** | Sets of 2 |

Materials   Pencil or crayon.

Children are not expected to read all the instructions. Teachers will have to explain carefully what the children have to do, particularly by copying the given drawings of the objects (egg, flower, button, and boy). A blackboard illustration would help most children.

The pictures are intended to help the children with their drawings and to stimulate language work.

Children could be asked to colour the things on the page when they have done their drawings.

Workbook 1: Sorting; Matching; 1 and 2

Additional workcards for the teacher to make

This work could be supplemented by a series of simple workcards such as:

Teaching suggestions for Page 13

It is on this page that the idea of *one* object is introduced. Some teaching using concrete material will be needed.

Put out 1 cube. How many here?

Put out another one. How many now?

This should be repeated using other objects such as children, counters, pegs, beads, toys, etc.

| Page 13 | Make 2 | Sets of 2 |

Materials Pencil or crayon.

This page introduces a difficult idea and will therefore need to be explained carefully to the children. A blackboard demonstration is desirable. The children have to realize that there is only 1 object shown in each set and that they should draw another one (flower) to make a set of 2 flowers.

It is important to emphasize that the completed set must show 2 things. The pictures should be used both to help the children with their drawings and to encourage language development.

This page, and the preliminary activities, could be used to introduce the numeral 1 and to give the children practice in writing it.

26 Workbook 1: Sorting; Matching; 1 and 2

| Page 14 | **Sets of 2** | Sets of 2 |

Materials Pencil or crayon

This work will need to be explained very carefully to children. The words on the page are intended for teachers although some children may be able to recognize one or two of them.

In the bottom half of the page the children are expected to draw a loop or ring round pairs of dogs.

Many children will require a lot more practice at this work. More worksheets, of the type shown on Page 14, could be made using rubber stamps, stencils, or banda masters.

Additional worksheets for the teacher to make

1 Further worksheets similar to the top half of Page 14 are shown below.
2 Worksheets like the bottom half of Page 14 could also be made.

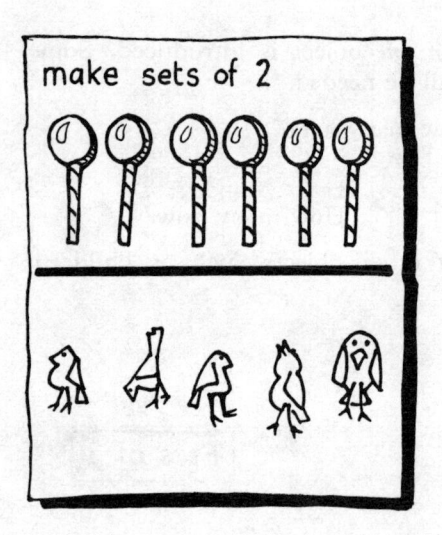

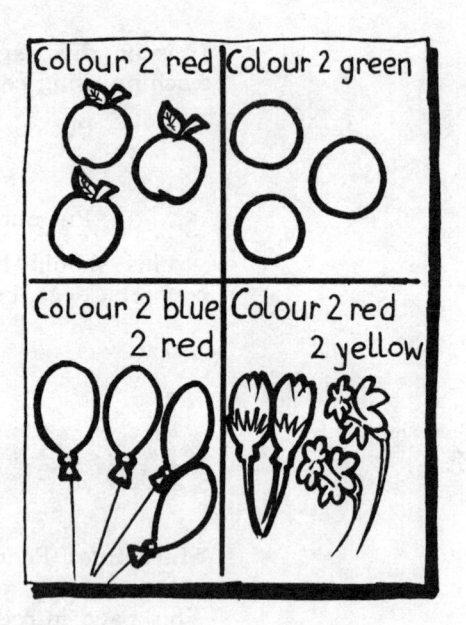

Formation of numeral 1

This requires careful teaching and supervising. It is important that children make the numeral in an acceptable way. Useful activities are:
(a) Finger writing in the air, in sand tray, in paint.
(b) Tracing over a large numeral with the point of the finger.
(c) Using tracing paper to trace over the numeral 1.
(d) Drawing over dotted outlines on worksheets.
(e) Copying the numeral 1 on paper.
(f) Using a washable (wipeable) workcard or plastic folder on which children draw over or copy a given outline.

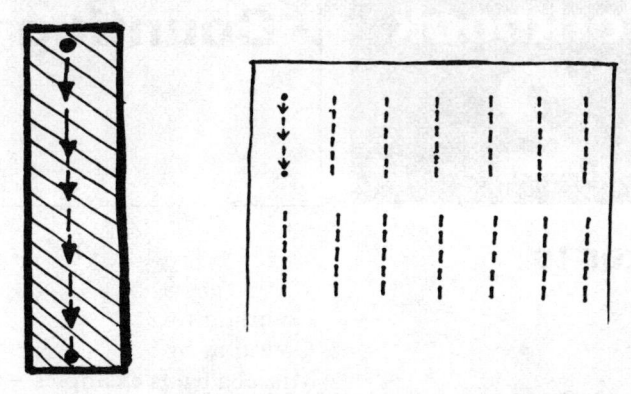

Workbook 1: Sorting; Matching; 1 and 2   **27**

| **Page 15** | **Write 1 or 2** | 1 and 2 |

Materials   Pencil or crayon.

Children are expected to tell just by looking at the pictures whether the answer is 1 or 2.

Filling in the answer in the 'box' will have to be stressed. This is probably best done by a blackboard example.

Some discussion to bring out the names of the objects pictured is desirable *before* the children start the page.

Extra workcards and worksheets for the teacher to make

1   Worksheets (or washable workcards) similar to Page 15 could be made.
2   Workcards similar to the following could be used:

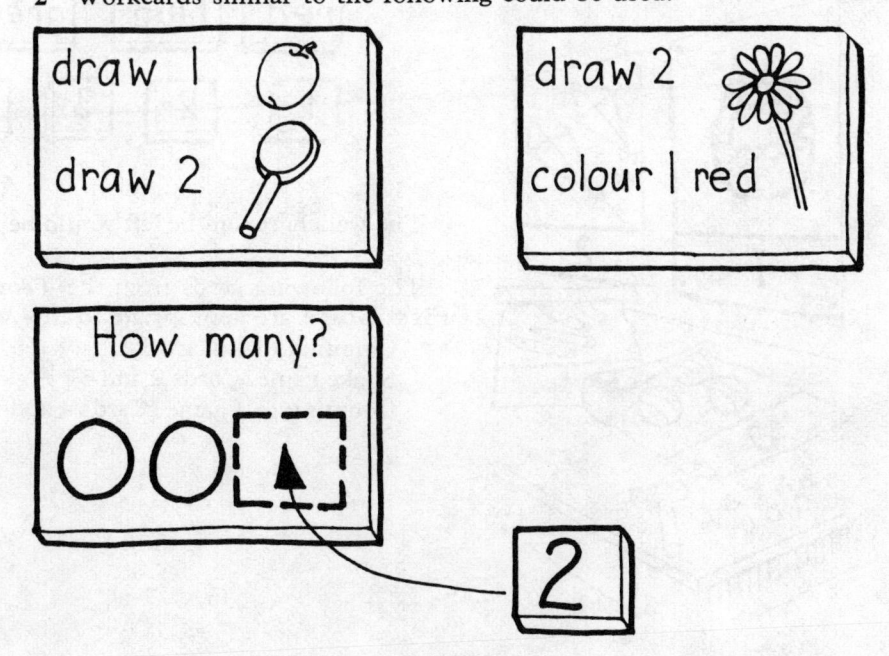

Workbook 2

Counting to 4

Contents

Counting to 2	Page 1
Counting to 3	Pages 2 to 6
Miscellaneous examples—counting up to 3	Page 7
Counting to 4	Pages 8 to 12
Miscellaneous examples—counting up to 4	Page 13
The sequence of numbers 1, 2, 3, 4	Pages 14 and 15

Materials

A selection from the following is required:
   interlocking cubes or pegs; beads; straws; pencils; farm animals; toy cars; counters; building bricks; pegs and pegboard.

The following would also be useful:
   coloured gummed shapes; sorting boxes; rubber stamps of toys; cubes to make special dice.

Coloured pencils or crayons are required.

The following flashcards would be useful:

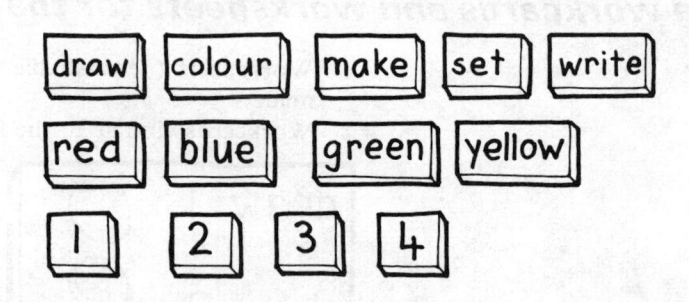

draw   colour   make   set   write

red   blue   green   yellow

1   2   3   4

The wallcharts on the left would be useful.

The following cards from the *Teacher's Materials Pack* for the **First Stage** are appropriate to this Workbook.
   Counting to 4 (Card 1)
   Snake game (Cards 2 and 3)
   Counting to 4 game (Cards 4 and 5)

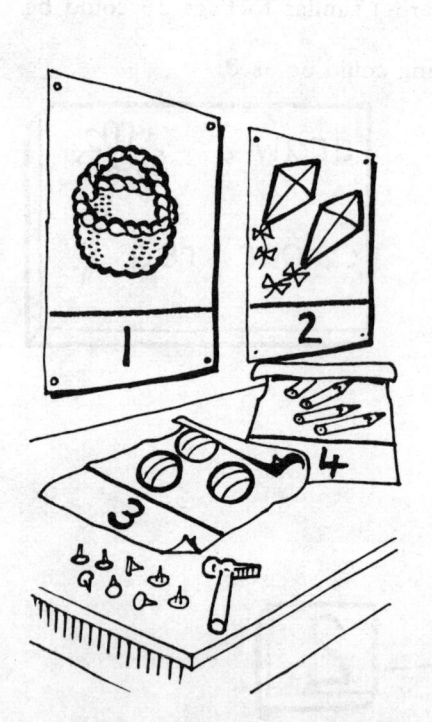

Counting to 4 (Pages 1 to 15)

Development

In *Workbook 1*, the cardinal aspect of the numbers 1 and 2 was introduced.

Workbook 2 introduces the 'counting' of objects in a set, the number of objects in each set being 1, 2, 3, or 4. Emphasis is placed on each number being 1 more than the preceding number. Associated activities include counting, drawing, colouring, and making sets of 1, 2, 3, and 4. Some work on the conservation of number is also included.

The counting process up to sets of 8 is continued in *Workbook 3*.

Practical activities and teaching

Before children are asked to complete pages in *Workbook 2*, much teaching and practical activity should take place. Suggestions for this work are now given in some detail.

Teaching suggestions

Sequence of number names

Children should, prior to receiving this booklet, have heard rhymes, songs, and stories involving number names.

Some further work should be done at this point. A choice from the following Number and Time Rhymes in Appendix 2 would be appropriate.

Rhymes 1 to 3: Rhymes involving 1 and 2
Rhymes 4 to 8: Rhymes about 3
Rhymes 9 to 12: Rhymes about 4

There would be no harm, however, in including number rhymes to ten at this point.

Introducing counting to 2

It is important to emphasize that 2 is 1 more than 1. Some practical work and discussion will be needed. One suggestion for such work is given below but, of course, there are many other ways in which teachers might choose to approach this.

30 Workbook 2: Counting to 4

The teacher could pick out 1 Unifix-type cube and ask the children 'How many cubes?', putting 1 beside it.

She could then take out another cube and place it beside the first one.

She could then ask a child to give her another cube, placing it on top of the first as shown in the diagram.

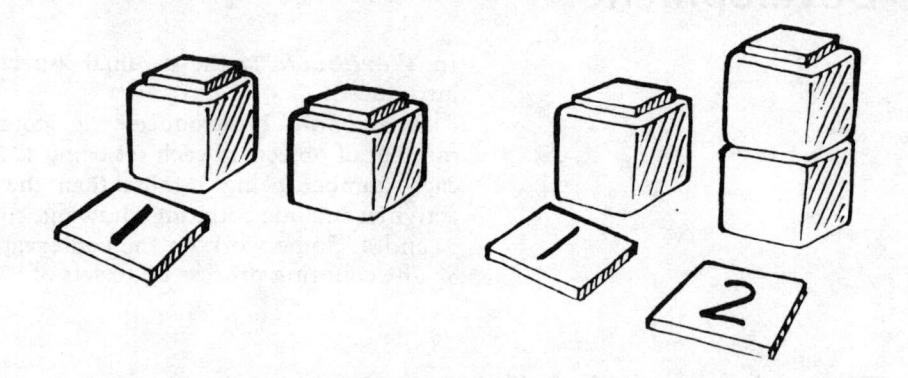

She could then ask, 'How many cubes in this column?', and *count* 'One, two'. By comparing the two columns, emphasis should be placed on the fact that 2 is 1 more than 1.

This activity could be repeated with building bricks, pegs on pegboard, farm animals, toy cars, or even the children themselves.

| Page 1 | 2 | Counting to 2 |

Materials   Coloured pencils (red, blue).

The teacher should demonstrate and discuss this page before the children complete it. For example, she could draw 1 apple on the blackboard and say 'one'. She could then get a child to 'draw 1 more', giving . She could then ask, 'How many apples?', encouraging the children to point and count, 'One, two,' and say, 'Two altogether'. '2' could then be written beside the drawing of the two apples.

This could, of course, be repeated several times.

The teacher could also demonstrate on the blackboard, or with a large sheet of paper, the idea outlined at the foot of Page 1 of **Workbook 2**.

The children could then try Page 1. In most cases, the teacher will have to read the instructions to the children.

The teacher may wish to prepare extra worksheets similar to Page 1 by using rubber stamps or simple outline drawings.

Colour 2 red.
Colour 2 blue.

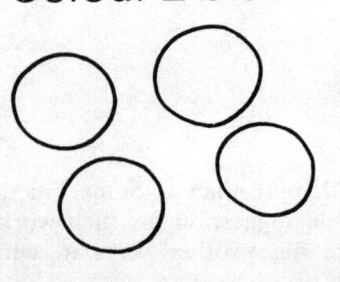

Workbook 2: Counting to 4   **31**

Teaching suggestions

Introducing counting to 3

1   It is important to emphasize that 3 is 1 more than 2. The following practical work and discussion is suggested.

   The teacher could build up a sequence of 1, 2, using Unifix-type cubes as outlined in 'Introducing counting to 2'.

   Another two cubes could then be taken and, by matching or by counting, it could be established that there are 2.

   By putting *one more* cube on top it could be established that there are now 3 cubes in the column. This column of cubes should be counted, 'one, two, three'. 'Three altogether'.

   This idea could be demonstrated several times using the Unifix-type cubes.

2   Other concrete material could be used in a similar fashion.
   (a) Beads on a string.
   (b) Pegs on a board.
   (c) Houses (or cars or children) in rows.

3   In all of this work it is essential to stress the sequence, 'one, two, three'; to practise counting 3 as 'one, two, three'; and to realize that each number is one more than the preceding number. The children should also appreciate that the last number name used gives the 'number' in the set. For example, three or 3 altogether.

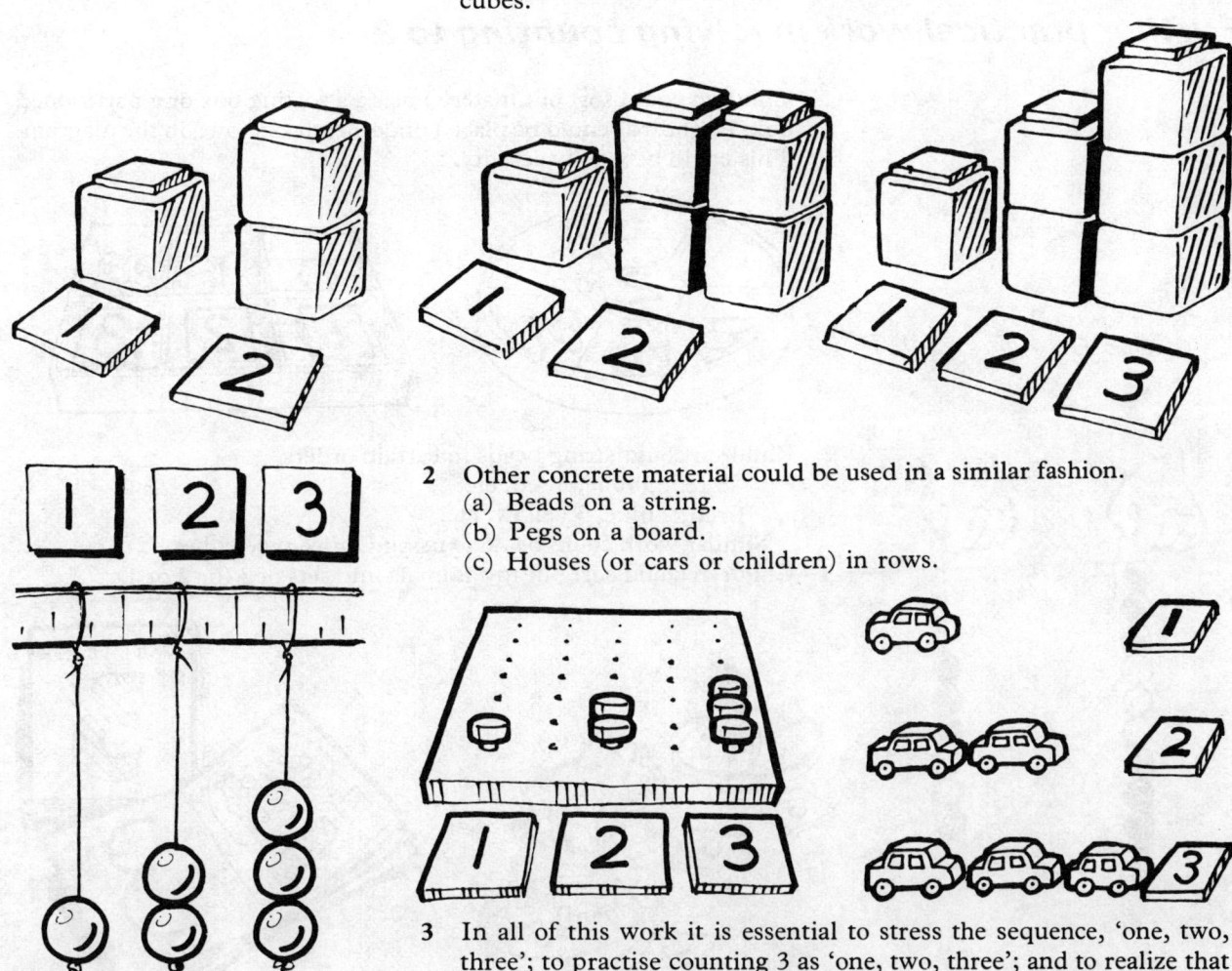

32   Workbook 2: Counting to 4

Oral work involving counting to 3

1. The teacher could ask for 2 beads from the box, and could then ask the child for 1 more. 'How many are there now?'
2. The teacher could put out 3 pencils and ask 'How many pencils?' The child could then be asked to give one back. 'How many are there now?'.
3. The teacher could hide 3 counters in one hand and then put one out at a time. The questions 'How many are there?', and 'How many are there now?' should be asked.
4. The teacher (or a child) could clap both hands together and ask 'How many claps?'
5. Children could be asked to clap, hop, skip, or jump '3'.
6. The children themselves could be counted.

Further practical work involving counting to 3

1. Children could sort out material using a sorting box or a partitioned box. Flashcards could be placed underneath as shown in the diagram. This could be a daily activity.

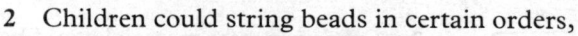

2. Children could string beads in certain orders,
   e.g.   3 red, 3 blue, 3 red, etc.
   or   1 red, 2 blue, 3 yellow, etc.
   Similar work could be done using Unifix-type cubes.
3. Children could sort out toy animals into sets of 3 (or 2 or 1).

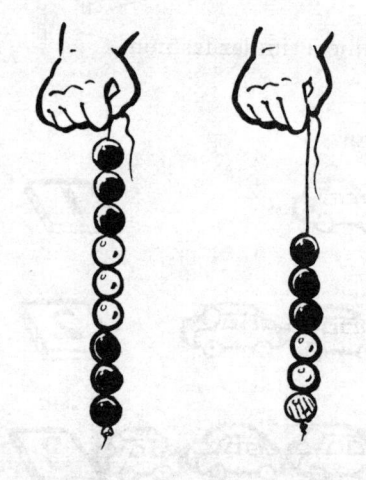

4. Children could contribute to 'Our book of 3' by drawing sets of 3 things, using cut-outs from magazines, or using coloured gummed shapes.

Workbook 2: Counting to 4   33

Conservation of 3

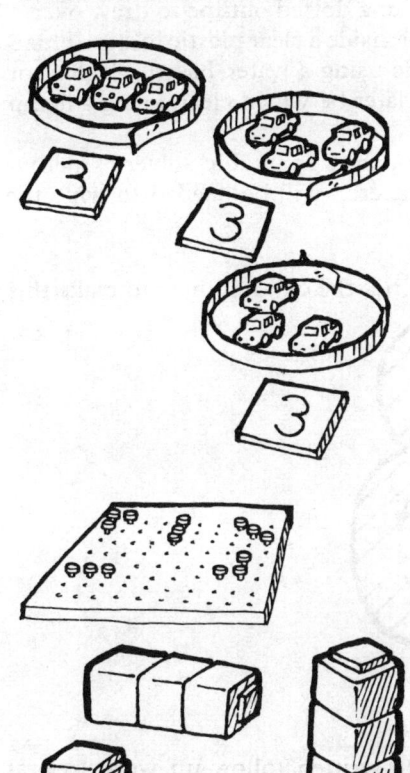

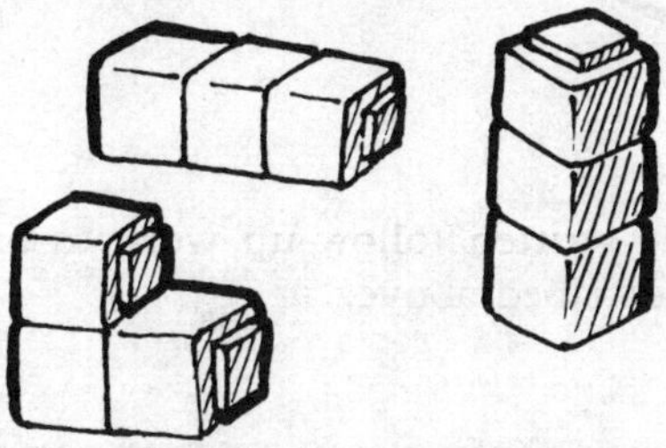

The teacher should be sure to incorporate practical work on the conservation of number with the children.
Some possible activities are given below.

1. Arrange sets of 3 toy cars in different ways and emphasize that there are 3 in each set, no matter how they are arranged.

    The child could be encouraged to have different 'starting' points when counting, for example

2. Arrange sets of 3 pegs on pegboard in different ways and arrange sets of 3 building bricks in different ways, including standing them on top of each other.

3. Draw sets of 3 things in different arrangements to contribute to a wall frieze or to 'Our book of 3'.

Formation of the numeral 3

Some suggestions for practising the formation of the numeral 3 are given below.
1. Draw '3' 'in the air'.
2. Feel the outline of a large rough figure, e.g. one made of sandpaper.
3. Make a '3' with plasticene.

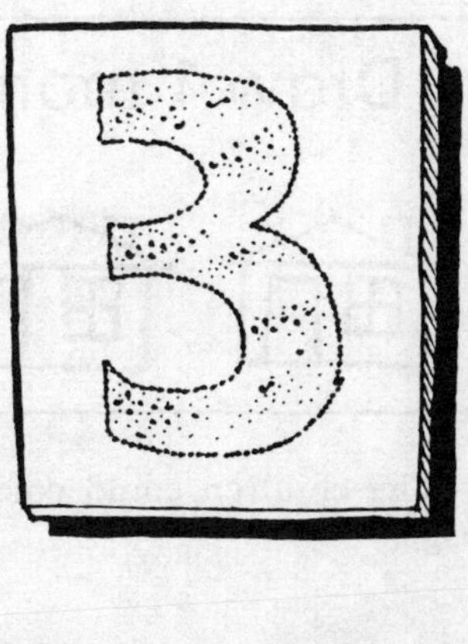

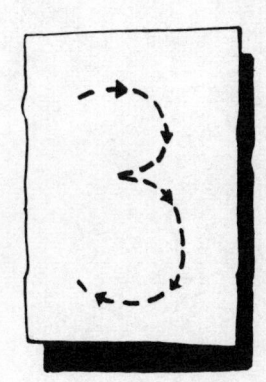

34 Workbook 2: Counting to 4

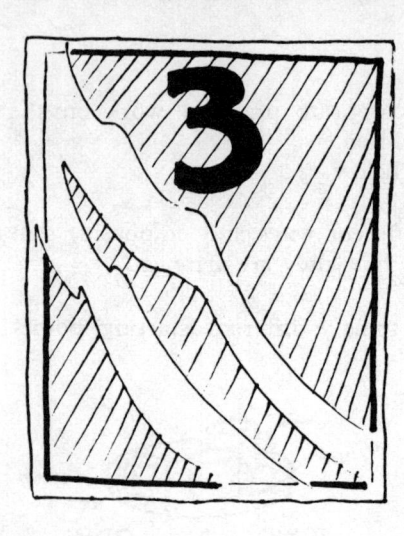

4 Finger-paint a '3'.
5 Draw a 3 on paper with and without a dotted outline to draw over.
6 Put a double-sided card with 3 on it inside a clear plastic folder. This 3 can then be traced onto the plastic using a water-based felt pen, or copied underneath. The card can later be wiped clean using a damp cloth or tissue.
   If a spirit-type felt pen is used, then a suitable solvent (methylated spirits, nail varnish remover, etc.) will be needed to wipe the surface clean.

It is important that the teacher teaches the children how to make this outline, i.e.

Pages 2 to 7

These pages are intended to provide written follow-up work to oral and practical activities of the type described above.

| Page 2 | 3 | Counting to 3 |

Materials Coloured pencils.

This page emphasizes that 3 is 1 more than 2. It is assumed that the teacher has already taught the children how to make the numeral 3 as outlined in the preceding section.
   What the children have to do should be demonstrated and discussed before they try the page on their own, e.g.

Draw 1 more.   How many now?

The children could colour the objects when they have finished the page.

Workbook 2: Counting to 4   35

| Page 3 | **Draw** | Counting to 3 |

Materials   Coloured pencils.

This page asks the children to *draw* 3 objects.

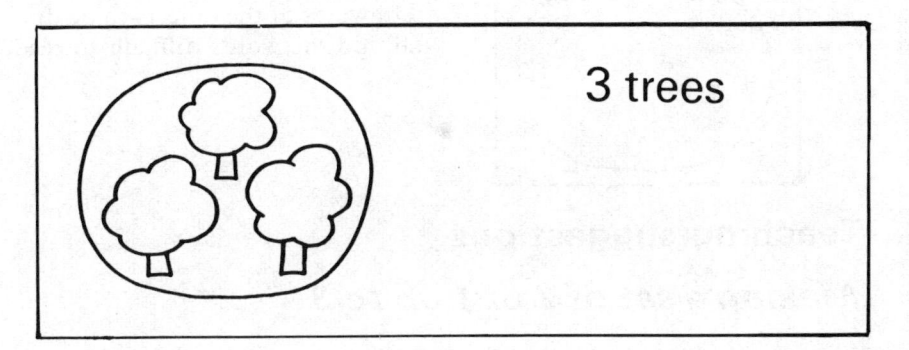

3 trees

The children are not expected to *read* the word 'tree'. This is why *drawings* of trees have been included.
The children could colour the objects if they wished.

| Page 4 | **Sets of 3** | Counting to 3 |

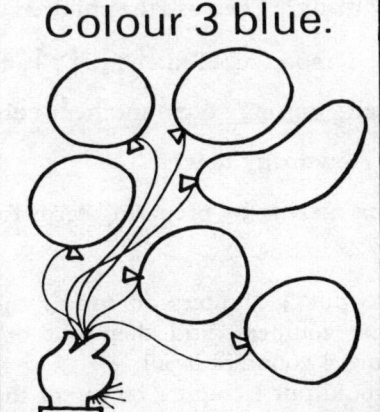

Materials   Coloured pencils.

The top half of the page asks children to *colour* 3 objects in a set containing more than 3 objects.
The bottom half of the page asks children to make sets of 3 from a set containing more than 3 objects.

Colour 3 red.
Colour 3 blue.

Make sets of 3.

The children are meant to ring sets of 3 using a pencil. Using different colours for the different rings or colouring each set of 3 objects might help some children.
The teacher will have to demonstrate both ideas contained in this page before the children try the page.
The children should also be encouraged to make a start towards recognizing the words
draw, colour, make, set

Workbook 2: Counting to 4

| Page 5 | Draw | Counting to 3 |

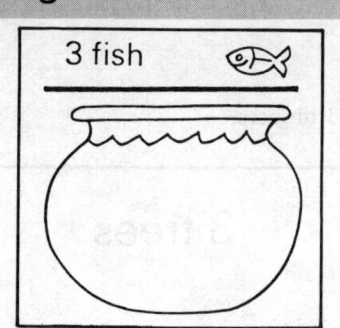

3 fish

Materials None.

This page asks the children to *draw* 3 objects.

Drawings of the objects to be drawn are given to help those children who find the words difficult to read, e.g. fish

Teaching suggestions

Making a set of 2 or 1 up to 3

Workbook Page 6 introduces a new idea which will require careful teaching. The children are (a) given a set of 2 which they have to make up to 3, or (b) given a set of 1 which they have to make up to 3.

The teacher might first of all demonstrate this idea using material in the following manner.

(a) Put out 2 cubes and ask 'How many?' Then ask the children to make this set up to 3. The children should be encouraged first to put out 1 more cube and then to count to see if they have 3.

(b) Put out 1 cube and ask 'How many?' Then ask the children to make this set up to 3 by putting 1 more cube out and asking 'How many?'; and then putting out another cube and asking 'How many now?'

(c) The teacher may wish to repeat this activity by preparing cards for individual children as shown.

The children would be expected to put 2 counters on top of the drawings on the first card, count the counters, and then put out another counter and count again, giving 3 counters in all.

For the second card, the children would put 1 counter on top of the drawing, put out another counter, count, put out another counter, count again, giving 3 counters in all.

This activity could be repeated with cubes, shapes, etc.

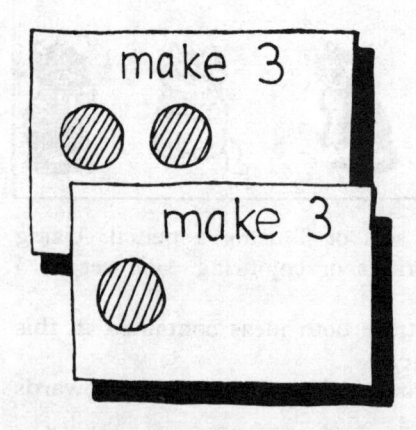

Workbook 2: Counting to 4   37

| Page 6 | Make 3 | Counting to 3 |

Materials   Coloured pencils.

This page should be preceded by activities of the type outlined above. The examples on the page are graded so that the top half of the page has examples of sets of 2 to be made up to 3. The bottom half has sets of 1 to be made up to sets of 3.

The children will probably find it easier to draw 1 more and then count to see if they have 3. If they do not have 3, then they should draw another one and count to see how many there now are.

The children could colour the page when they have finished and write '3' beside each set.

| Page 7 | Write 1 or 2 or 3 | Counting to 3 |

Materials   None.

This is a page of miscellaneous examples where the sets to be counted contain 1 or 2 or 3 objects.

The children should have had practical experience of matching numeral flash cards ☐1☐ ☐2☐ ☐3☐ to sets of objects, for example by using sorting boxes, before they try this page (see page 32).

The teacher should demonstrate the ideas contained in this page before the children try it.

38 Workbook 2: Counting to 4

Additional activity: wallchart

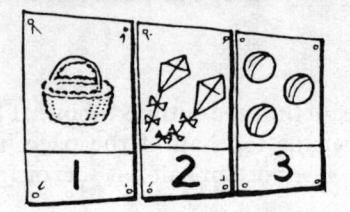

The teacher could now have the usual wall chart on display showing sets of 1, 2, and 3. This will be added to as the children gradually learn to count to 10.

Teaching suggestions

Introducing counting to 4

It is important to emphasize that 4 is one more than 3. The following practical work and discussion is suggested.

The teacher could build up a sequence of 1, 2, 3, using Unifix-type cubes as outlined on page 31, in 'Introducing counting to 3'.

Another 3 cubes could then be taken out and, by matching or by counting, it could be established that there are 3.

By putting *one more* cube on top, it could be established that there are now 4 cubes in the column. This column of cubes should be counted 'One, two, three, four'; 'Four altogether'.

This idea could be demonstrated several times using the Unifix-type cubes.

As explained on page 31, in 'Introducing counting to 3', other concrete material could be used in a similar fashion, for example
(a) beads on strings;
(b) animals in fields;
(c) houses in rows;
(d) children in rows; etc.

Oral work involving counting to 4

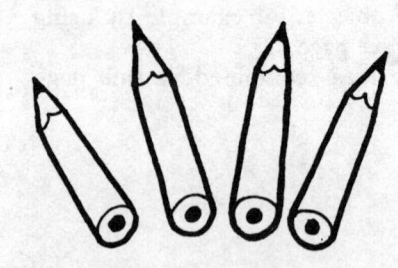

This essential work should follow the ideas given for oral work involving counting to 3, e.g.
(a) 'How many pencils are here?'
(b) 'Give me 4 pencils.'
(c) Clap or hop or skip 4 (or 3 or 2 or 1).
(d) 'What is the number before 4?'
(e) 'What is the number after 3?'
(f) Point to a set of 4 (on a wall chart or in the classroom).

Workbook 2: Counting to 4   39

Further practical work involving counting to 4

This should continue and be expanded as described on page 32.
(a) Using a sorting box.
(b) Stringing beads.

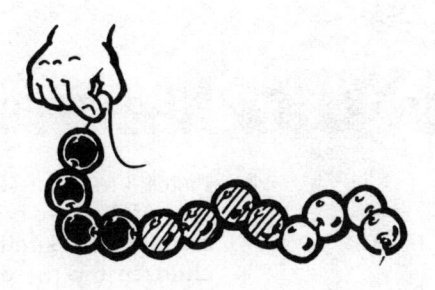

(c) Sorting out sets of 4 from larger sets.

(d) 'Our Book of 4' could include pictures of
  (i)   horses, cows, pigs, dogs, cats (4 legs);
  (ii) table, chair, stool (4 legs);
  (iii) gummed shapes grouped in sets of 4.

Conservation of 4

Practical work on the conservation of 4 should be done along similar lines to the 'conservation of 3', i.e. it should be emphasized that no matter how four counters are arranged, the set still contains 4.

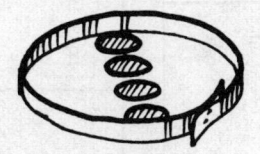

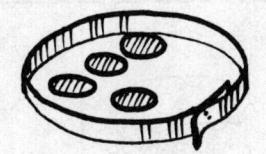

40 Workbook 2: Counting to 4

Formation of the numeral 4

Children should be taught how to make a 4.
The ideas given for the 'Formation of the numeral 3' would be appropriate here also.

Pages 8 to 13 — Counting to 4

Pages 8 to 13 of **Workbook 2** are follow-up pages on counting to 4. They follow a very similar pattern to Pages 2 to 7 on counting to 3 and should have similar practical experience and pre-teaching before the children try the pages.

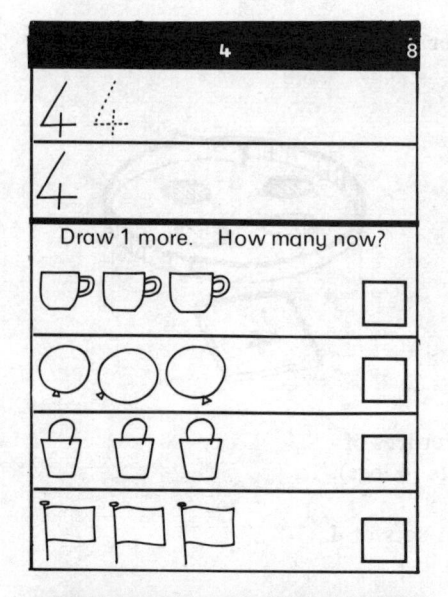

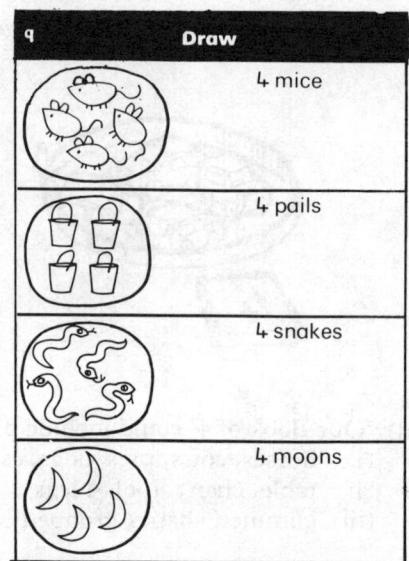

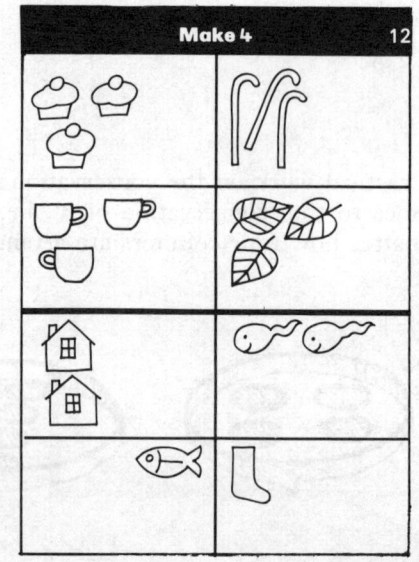

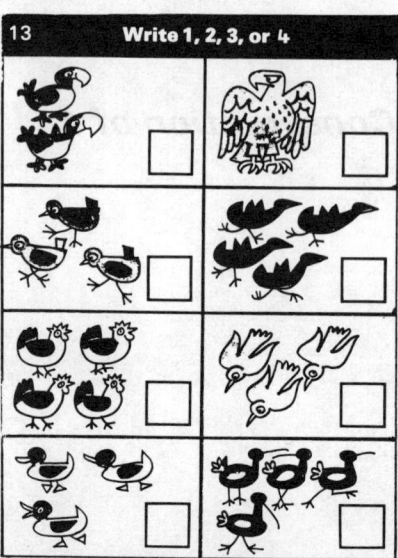

Workbook 2: Counting to 4   41

Cards for the teacher to make

The teacher may wish to supplement work on counting to 4 by making similar cards to the following sample cards.

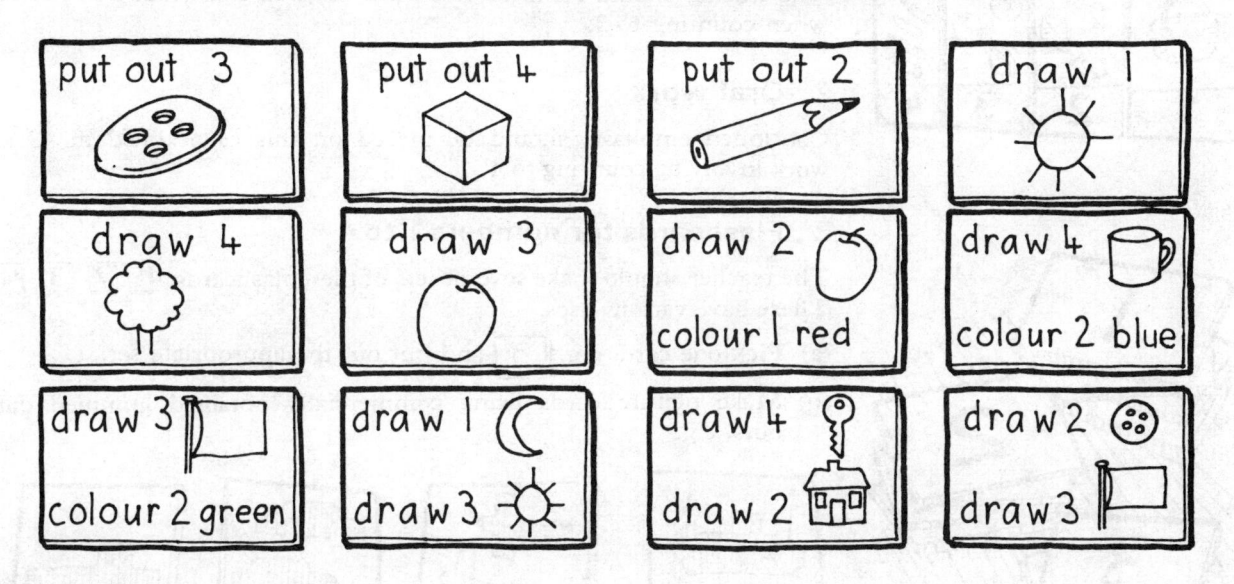

put out 3	put out 4	put out 2	draw 1
draw 4	draw 3	draw 2 colour 1 red	draw 4 colour 2 blue
draw 3 colour 2 green	draw 1 draw 3	draw 4 draw 2	draw 2 draw 3

Worksheets for the teacher to make

The teacher could use the usual commercially obtainable rubber stamps to make worksheets similar to the following examples.

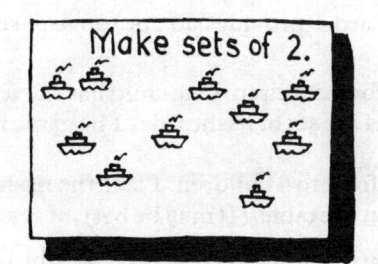

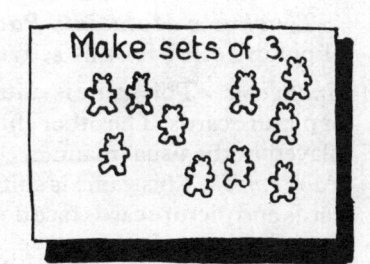

Make sets of 2.

Make sets of 3.

Make sets of 4.

The children could ring sets of 2, 3, or 4 as appropriate.

Draw 1 more	How many?

Draw 2 more	How many?

Workbook 2: Counting to 4

Additional activities

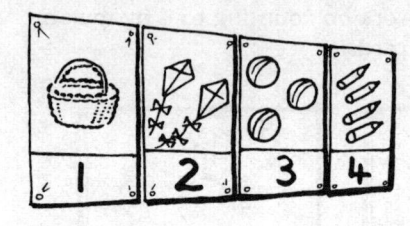

1 Wall chart

The teacher should continue to extend the wall chart that was started when counting to 3.

2 Oral work

Continued emphasis should be placed on this as outlined in 'Oral work involving counting to 4'.

3 Flashcards for numbers 1 to 4

The teacher should make several sets of these flashcards, [1] [2] [3] [4] These have various uses.

(a) Pick one card, e.g. [3] and put out the appropriate set.

(b) Make picture cards using commercially obtained gummed cut outs, e.g.

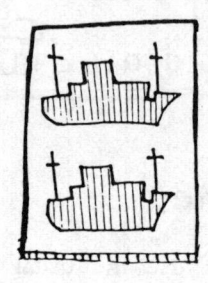

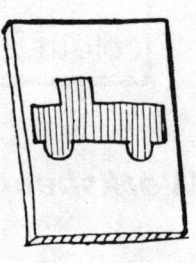

The children should pick a card and match the appropriate flashcard to it.

Teacher's Materials Pack, Card 1 provides an appropriate set of picture cards for this activity.

(c) *Snap game* This game is suitable for 2 children. One child has the set of picture cards. The other child has the set of flashcards. The game is played in the usual manner.

(d) *Pairs game* This game is suitable for 2 to 4 children. Place the flashcards and picture cards face down on the table. (It may be best, at first, to limit the number of cards to one set of flashcards, [1] [2] [3] [4] and one set of matching picture cards.)

One child picks one of each. If it is a pair e.g. [°°] and [2] then the pair is kept. If it is not a pair, e.g. [🍎] and [3] then these 2 cards are turned face down again and the next child picks two other cards to try to get a pair. The winner is the person with most pairs at the end of the game.

For less able children, the game could be played with a set of flashcards of one and two alone, e.g. [1] [1] [2] [2] and a set of matching picture cards (or sets of flashcards with three and four alone and matching picture cards).

Workbook 2: Counting to 4

4 Dice games with numbers 1 to 4

Using a cube, each of the numbers 1, 2, 3, 4 could be written on a face, leaving two faces blank.

A cube could be made out of cardboard thus:

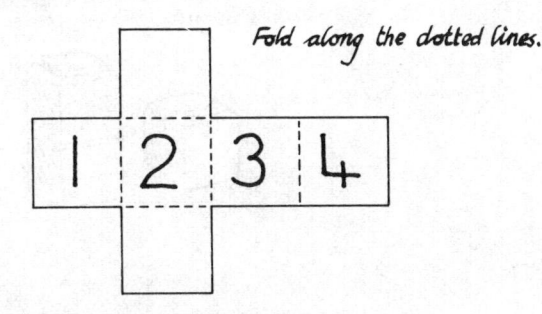

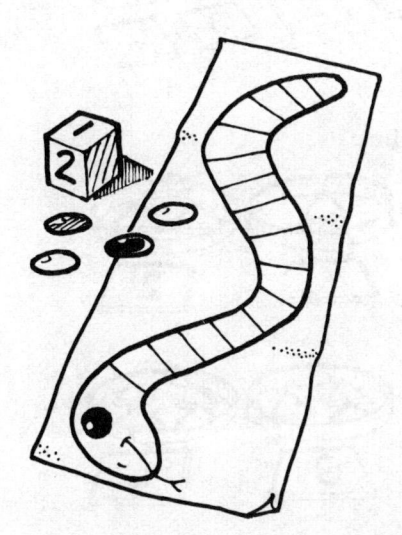

Fold along the dotted lines.

This die can have various uses, e.g.
(a) Throw the die, and put out the appropriate set.
(b) Throw the die and say the number; or pick up the appropriate flashcard.
(c) *Snake game for 2 children* Make a track game using a snake.

Each child throws the die in turn and moves a counter forward by that number of spaces. If a blank is thrown, then the child throws the die again. The winner is the first person to reach the head of the snake.

Cards 2 and 3 of the *Teacher's Materials Pack* contain a track for a Snake Game like this.

5 Counting to 4 game

This Bingo-type game is supplied in Cards 4 and 5 of the *Teacher's Materials Pack*

In this game each child has a player's card with pictures of 1, 2, 3 and 4 objects on it. There is also a pile of numeral cards with 1, 2, 3, 4 on them, placed face down. Each child picks a numeral card in turn and places it on top of the appropriate picture on his player's card. The winner is the first player to cover all his pictures with the appropriate numeral cards.

Teaching suggestions for Pages 14 and 15

The last two pages of this Workbook continue counting to 4 but they emphasize in particular the sequence of the numbers 1, 2, 3, and 4. This work may be suitable for only some of the children. A great deal of oral work with practical material will be needed to reinforce this idea.

Workbook 2: Counting to 4

Sequence of numbers 1, 2, 3, 4

Here are some suggestions for practical work about the two sequences 1, 2, 3, 4 and 4, 3, 2, 1.

1 Use Unifix-type cubes to build towers.
  Put out

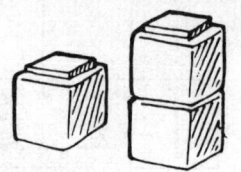

and then get the children to complete the sequence, putting flash cards underneath.

2 Put sets of shapes out on a table thus:

and complete the sequence.

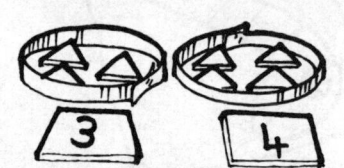

3 Put out sets thus:

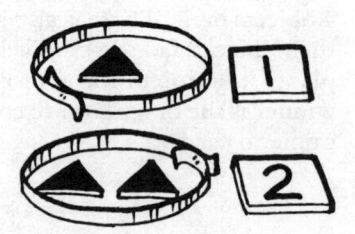

and complete the sequence.

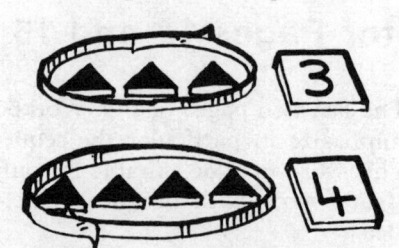

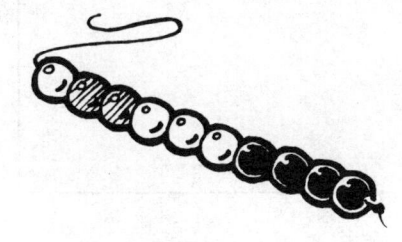

Workbook 2: Counting to 4   **45**

4   Thread beads of different colours on a string.

5   Put flash cards in order, both forwards and in reverse.

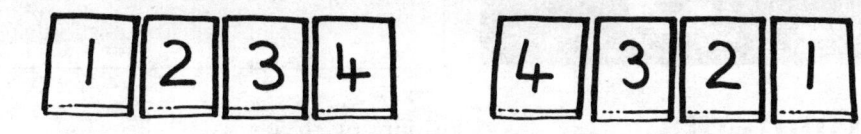

|1| |2| |3| |4| |4| |3| |2| |1|

6   Find the missing flashcard.

|1| |2| | | |4|

7   In all of this work, emphasis is placed on
    'What is the number after?'
    'What is the number before?'

    Put out |3|. The child then puts out the number which comes after: |3| |4| and/or the number before: |2| |3| |4| and so on.

Page 14   **How many?**   Counting to 4

Materials   None.

The top half of the page emphasizes the sequence 1, 2, 3, 4 illustrated 'horizontally', while the bottom half of the page illustrates the sequence of numbers 'vertically' in a pyramid-type illustration.

Page 15   **Write 1, 2, 3, or 4**   Counting to 4

Materials   None.

Pictures of sets of objects are given in the top half of the page to help the children complete the sequence 1, 2, 3, 4 or 4, 3, 2, 1.

The bottom half of the page asks children to fill in the missing numbers without pictures being given. Careful teaching is required before this bottom half can be attempted.

Workbook 3

Counting to 8

Contents

Counting to 5	Pages 1 to 3
Counting to 6	Pages 4 to 7
Counting: miscellaneous examples	Page 8
Counting to 7	Pages 9 and 10
Counting to 8	Pages 11 to 13
Counting: miscellaneous examples	Pages 14 and 15

Materials

A selection from the following is required:
    counters, beads, buttons, small toys, building bricks, straws, crayons, coloured pencils, wooden blocks, pegs, interlocking beads, interlocking plastic cubes.

The following items would also be useful:
    sorting box, pegboard, dowelling, dice.

The following wallchart would be useful:

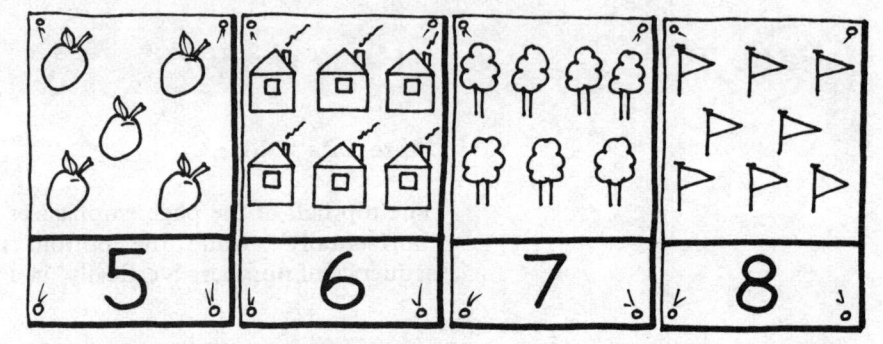

The following flashcards would be useful:

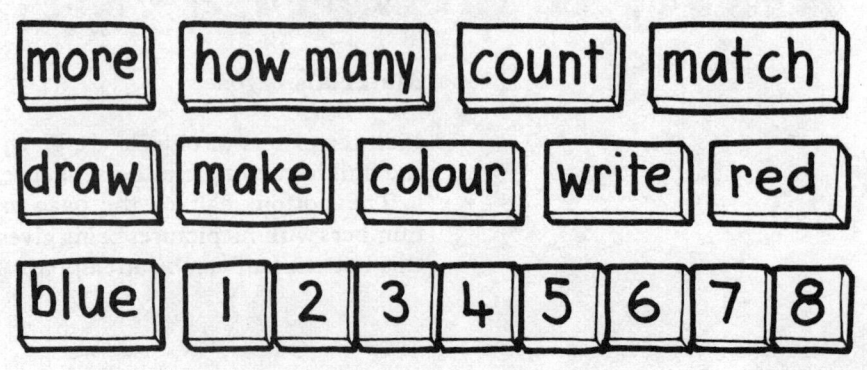

more | how many | count | match
draw | make | colour | write | red
blue | 1 | 2 | 3 | 4 | 5 | 6 | 7 | 8

The following cards from the *Teacher's Materials Pack* for the **First Stage** are appropriate to this Workbook:
    Snake game (Cards 2 and 3)
    Counting to 8 cards (Cards 6 and 7)

Counting to 8 (Pages 1 to 15)

Development

In **Workbook 2**, the process of counting was introduced and this involved the numbers 1, 2, 3, and 4. The activities of this Workbook extend counting up to 8.

The work provided is aimed at helping the children to learn
(a) to recite the number names to 'eight' in their correct sequence;
(b) to recognize and write the numerals 1 to 8;
(c) to count sets of up to 8 objects and to associate the correct numeral with each set.

The first part of **Workbook 4** continues the process of counting to include the numbers 9 and 10.

Practical activities and teaching

Sequence of number names

Popular rhymes and jingles help to familiarize the children with the number names and these are often presented in correct sequence. The names 'nine' and 'ten' may also be included here in readiness for the work of **Workbook 4**.

Some rhymes are included in Appendix 2 of the **Teacher's Notes**, and those especially appropriate for this section of the work are Rhymes 13 to 17 and Rhymes 21 to 40.

Once the number names are known, each one, in turn, has to be associated with its corresponding numeral. Children need much practice in drawing or writing the numerals and there is some provision for this in the Workbook pages.

Introducing counting to 5

Usually children first hear 'five' as the word following 'four' in a number-name sequence (nursery rhymes). Now the children have to learn the meaning of five as a number (five hats, five dolls, etc.) and must learn how to write the numeral 5.

Some suggestions for teaching activities are given below. There are many other ways in which teachers could introduce this work.

1. The first step is to add one more object to a set of four objects and then call the new set 'five'. Children count out four objects, add one more, and then say 'five'.

   The numeral $\boxed{5}$ can be placed beside the new set. This simple activity should be carried out using a variety of classroom material, e.g. counters, beads, building bricks, the children themselves, etc.

Workbook 3: Counting to 8

2 The children can now count out sets of five objects for themselves or count objects already laid out by the teacher. Instructions such as 'Put out five pencils'; 'Count out five beads'; 'Count the chickens in the picture'; or 'How many dolls?' are now appropriate.

3 The children can now be asked to draw pictures of sets of five objects. Each time an object is drawn, the child will often stop and count, and then draw another object, until five is reached.

Conservation of 5

It is, of course, only necessary to count a set of objects once. Also with small numbers like five, it is possible instantly to recognize the 'fiveness', especially if the objects are arranged in certain patterns. At this stage, however, it is still necessary to practise counting when the objects are arranged differently.

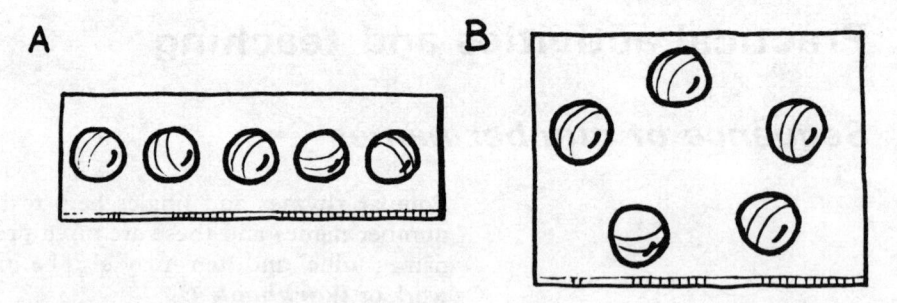

A

B

In arrangement B, the children might need to 'tick' or 'mark' each ball as they count. In A, the children are trained to count from left to right along the row.

Also, with a configuration such as that shown in B above, the balls might be counted more than once, by choosing a different starting ball each time.

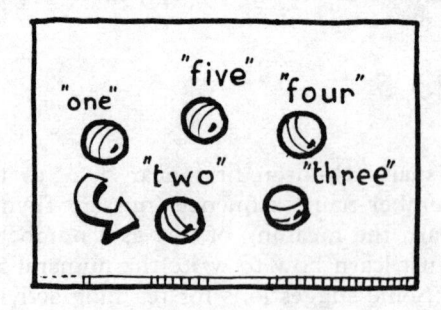

Matching

Matching objects to other objects also helps to establish the concept of 'fiveness'. For example, a child can be asked to 'put out' or 'count out' 5 cups and then be asked, 'Find a saucer for each cup'.

The teacher can now ask, 'How many saucers did you need?' It should not be necessary for the child to count the saucers.

Workbook 3: Counting to 8   49

Formation of the numeral 5

Although the word 'five' was introduced to the children at the start of this work, the shape of the numeral 5 has to be made, drawn, and written by the children when using the Workbook. Frequent practice will be needed before and after they start on the Workbook pages.

Often a large numeral is easier to deal with at the start, but gradually its size has to be reduced for normal writing.

Some ways to practise the formation of numerals include:
(a) drawing 'in the air';
(b) feeling the outline on sandpaper;
(c) making the numeral with string or plasticine;
(d) finger painting;
(e) following or writing over a dotted outline;

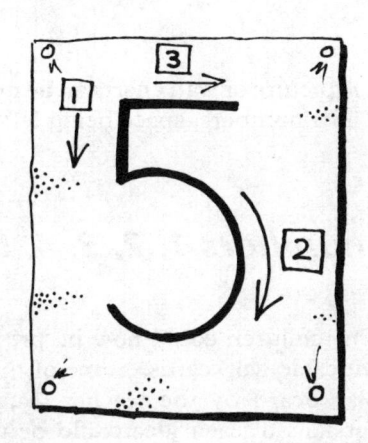

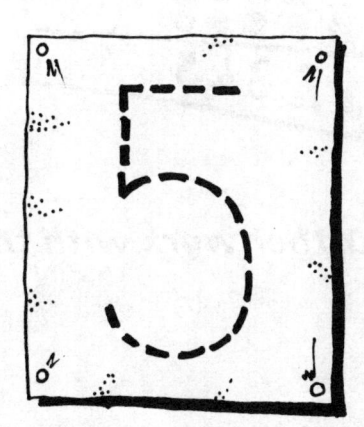

(f) tracing over a numeral. A 'wipeable' card, covered in clear plastic, or a card placed inside a clear plastic folder, is very useful in giving children controlled practice of tracing, following an outline, and copying.

Teaching suggestions

The numbers 1, 2, 3, 4, 5

The previous work was concerned largely with the new number 5 but it is now necessary to present activities which will involve 1, 2, 3, and 4 also.

For example, a representation of all five numbers using materials shows the comparison of one number to another and also displays the fact that each successive number represents one more. This can be done in different ways.

1. Interlocking plastic cubes are useful since the columns tend to be fairly rigid.
2. Interlocking plastic beads can also be used and laid out horizontally.

50   Workbook 3: Counting to 8

3   Beads slipped on to spikes is another method. The spikes can be made from dowelling rod cut to size, or might even be made from knitting needles.

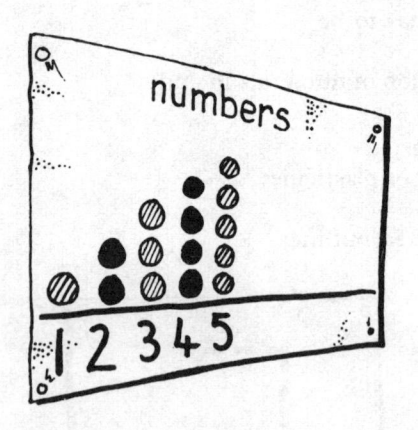

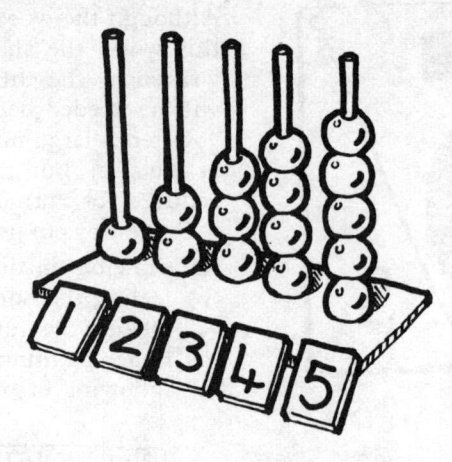

4   A picture or wall chart can be prepared for a more permanent display of the numbers, space being left for the numbers 6, 7, 8, 9, and 10.

Further work with the numbers 1, 2, 3, 4, 5

The children could now be presented with activities on worksheets or wipeable workcards. Some of these might also be demonstrated on the blackboard by the teacher. Suggestions are given below and several versions of each idea could be used.

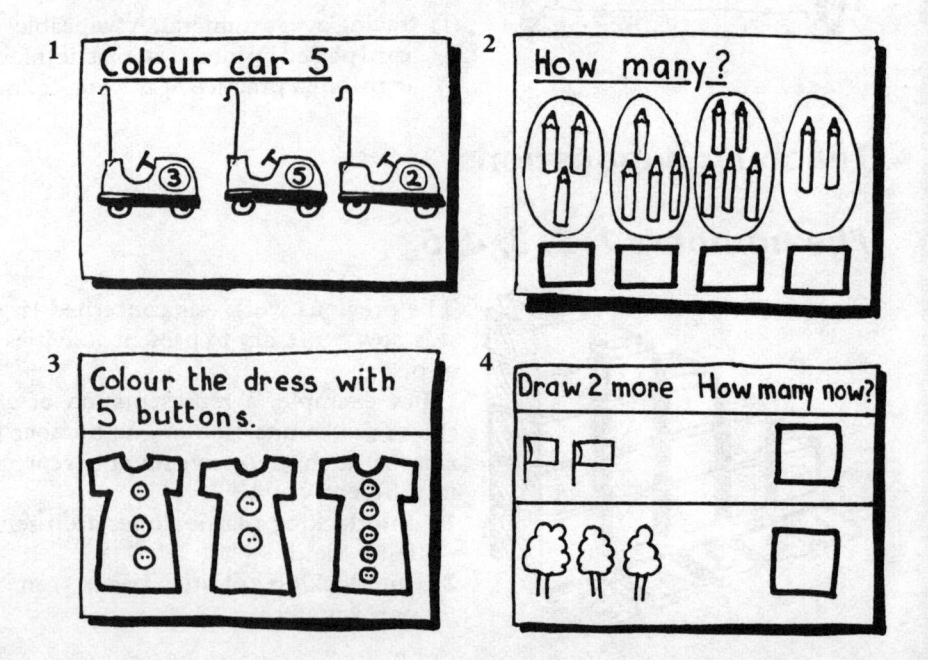

1   Colour car 5

2   How many?

3   Colour the dress with 5 buttons.

4   Draw 2 more   How many now?

Workbook 3: Counting to 8

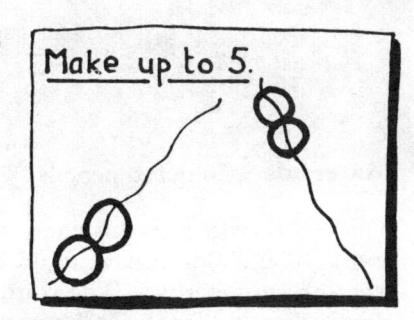

> 5
> Make up to 5.

This idea is particularly different and would require to be carefully taught (see note for **Page 3**).

The children can now be asked to do some of the pages in the Workbook. These follow on from the work outlined above.

Page 1 — 5 — Counting to 5

Materials Coloured pencils.

A space is provided at the top of the page for 'numeral' practice, although the size of numeral at this stage is reasonably large.

The children are now asked to add one more object to sets of one, two, three, and four. Each time they count the new total and write the answer. It may help some children to count the total number if they also colour the objects but this tends to be time-consuming.

This approach highlights the pattern and the structure of these numbers as well as revising previous work with numbers up to 4.

The fourth total is, of course, 5 and the two sets of objects at the foot of the page also each contain 5 objects. These objects are not in rows, however, and it may be necessary for the child to 'tick' or 'mark' each object as it is counted.

Page 2 — 5 — Counting to 5

Materials Coloured pencils.

The children are presented with eight sets of objects to count and each time the answer has to be written. The totals are not always 5 and this requires the children to be careful in their counting. It also provides revision in counting totals less than 5.

As for Page 1, ticking, marking, or even colouring may help the children to account for each object as they count. The teacher might even demonstrate on the blackboard one way of counting before the children begin the work on the page.

52 Workbook 3: Counting to 8

| Page 3 | 5 | Counting to 5 |

Materials Coloured pencils.

The two activities on this page are more difficult than those on Pages 1 and 2. The children have to draw the objects for themselves and stop when the number is 5. The word for each object is printed alongside a simple drawing for the children to copy, e.g.

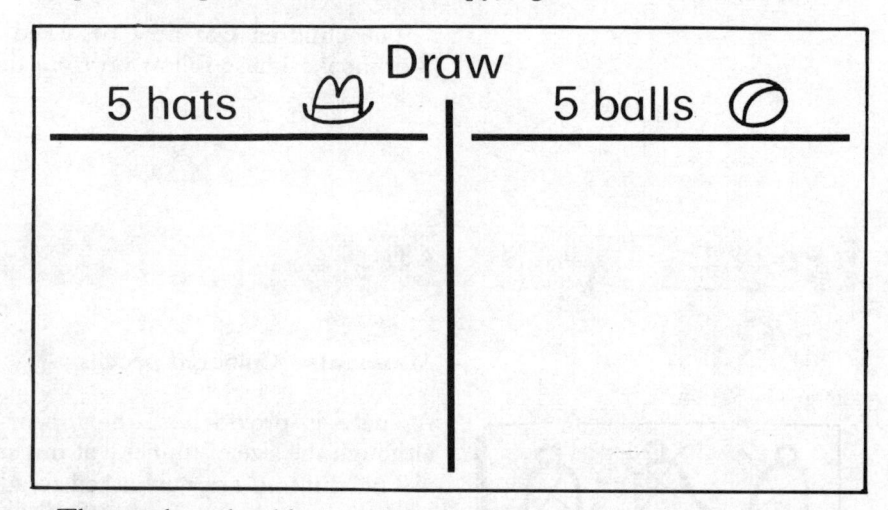

The teacher should encourage the children sometimes to 'scatter' their objects if the tendency is always towards a 'left to right' row.

The second type of activity on the page consists of making sets of objects up to 5 in number. Practice in doing this by laying out counters or cubes would be a worthwhile preliminary activity. A demonstration on the blackboard would also help. As each counter is added or drawn it is counted until the child says 'five'. This is not meant to be addition or subtraction and the children should *not* be asked, 'Three cubes and what make 5?' before or after the task.

Additional activities on counting to 5

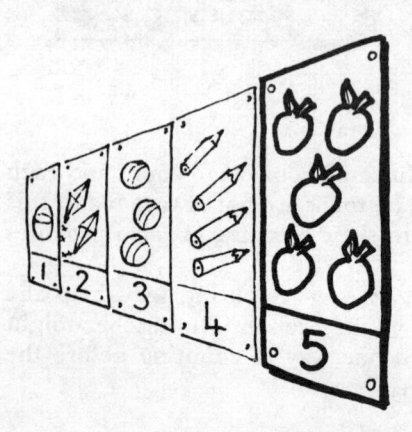

1 The picture for 5 could be added to the wall chart mentioned in the teaching notes for **Workbook 2**.
2 Simple games could be played by the children. These might include:
   (a) clapping hands 5 times (and 4 times, and 3 times, etc.);
   (b) saying the number names 'one, two, three, four, five' round the class;
   (c) nodding heads 5 times, hopping 5 times, stepping 5 times;
   (d) holding up 5 fingers (first right hand, then left hand).

Workbook 3: Counting to 8   53

3   A 'Book of 5' might be compiled by a group of children.

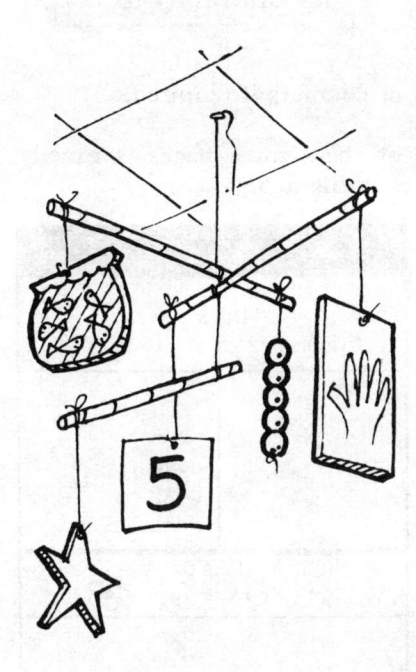

4   A mobile for 5 could also be made.

5   *Sorting box activities*   Counters could be placed in the box to correspond to the numeral flashcards.

Teaching suggestions

Introducing counting to 6, 7, and 8

Before the remaining pages are tackled, each of these numbers should be introduced, in turn, by a procedure similar to that previously outlined for 'Introducing 'counting to 5'.

One more object is placed with a set of 5, producing the new set 6. The numeral 6 is introduced by the teacher, and practice in drawing and writing the numeral should follow. The children would now engage in a variety of practical activities to consolidate the ability to count up to 6. Conservation work would be included, as would a demonstration of all six numbers in comparison with each other.

The appropriate pages in the Workbook could now be attempted and would be accompanied by teacher demonstrations, oral work, and supplementary additional activities.

54 Workbook 3: Counting to 8

Pages 4 to 6 | 6 | Counting to 6

Materials Coloured pencils; cubes or counters if required.

As seen below, the work sequence of these three pages is exactly similar to the work of Pages 1 to 3 on counting to 5.

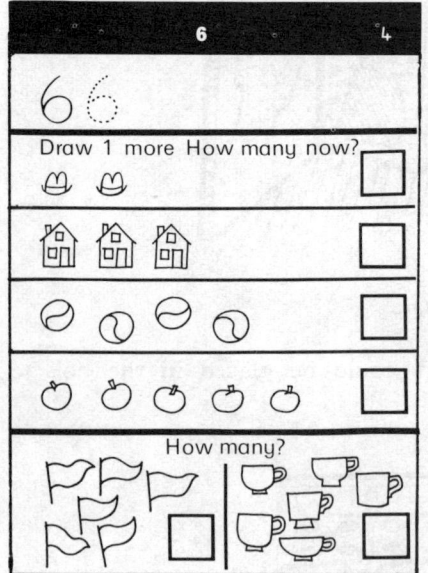

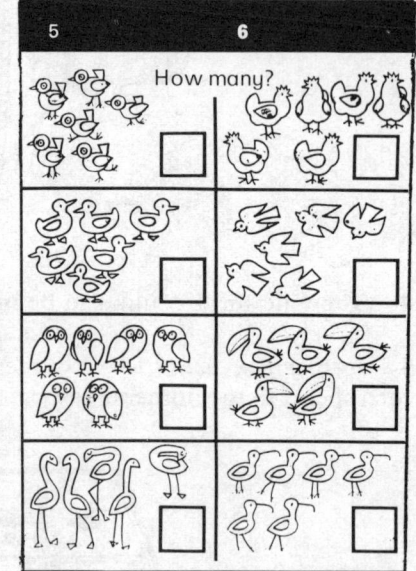

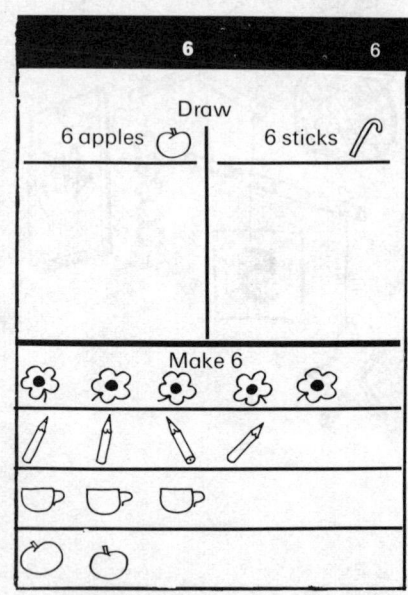

Extra work, including worksheets and workcards, on counting to 6 could be given along the lines suggested for counting to 5.

Page 7 | 5 or 6 | Counting to 6

Materials Coloured pencils.

This page consolidates the previous work dealing with 5 and 6. The children have to colour either 5 or 6 objects contained in groups of more than 5 or 6. This will have to be explained carefully to the children. Some similar work done on the blackboard would be helpful.
 More counting exercises up to 5 and up to 6 are also provided.

Page 8 | Match | Counting to 6

Materials None.

As well as counting sets of objects and recognizing numerals, the children are asked to match. Preliminary work on matching would be most helpful before the children are asked to tackle the page.

Workbook 3: Counting to 8   55

Matching cards might be useful for this:

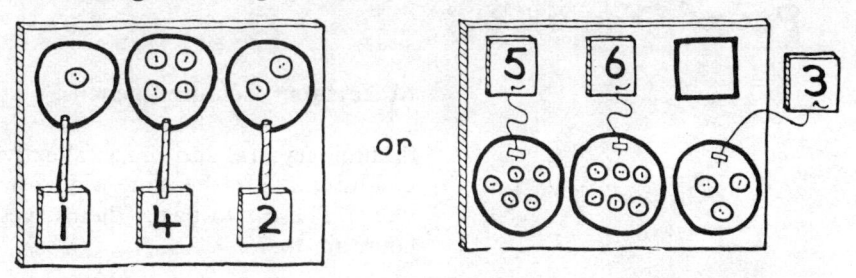

Groups of objects are placed in the circles and the children should place the appropriate numeral card on the square. A length of string could be attached to each numeral card so that 'matching' could actually be done.

Children could also be asked to draw matching lines on the blackboard to join numerals to sets which have been drawn by the teacher.

On this page, the children are asked to match each of the numerals 1 to 6 with the appropriate set of objects. Each set is counted, after which a line is drawn to the corresponding numeral.

| Pages 9 and 10 | 7 | Counting to 7 |

Materials   Coloured pencils; cubes or counters if required.

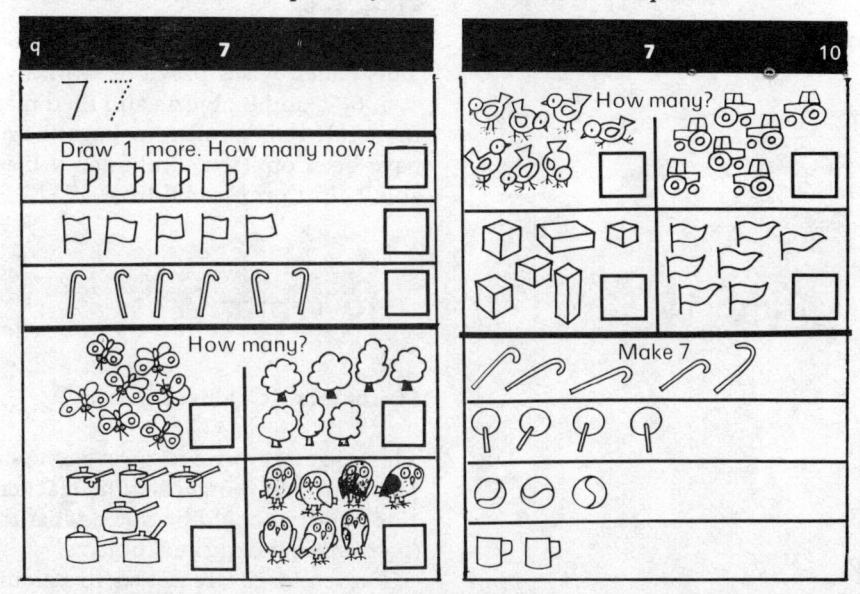

As with Pages 5 and 6, many practical activities which involve putting out, counting, drawing, and making sets of 7 would precede the completion of these pages. Numeral formation practice, oral work, wall charts, and simple games would also follow.

On Page 9, a set of 7 objects is obtained by adding one more to a set of 6. Sets of 5 and 6 are also produced and this serves as consolidation of previous work and again shows up the comparison between these three successive numbers. On both pages there are counting exercises, mostly up to 7, and the more difficult activity of making a set up to 7.

56 Workbook 3: Counting to 8

Pages 11 and 12 — 8 — Counting to 8

Materials Coloured pencils.

Preliminary oral and practical activities should precede these pages on counting to 8 in the same way as has already been suggested for earlier work. These two pages themselves follow the pattern established for counting to 7.

Page 13 — 7 or 8 — Counting to 8

Materials Coloured pencils; cubes or counters if required.

This page is similar in layout to Page 7 which dealt with 5 and 6.

Page 14 — Match — Counting to 8

Materials None.

This page revises previous work by asking children to count sets of 3, 4, 5, 6, 7, and 8 objects and then match each of these to the appropriate numeral. It is similar to Page 8 except that this time sets of 1 and 2 have been omitted. Preliminary blackboard work would provide valuable help to most children.

Page 15 — How many? — Counting to 8

Materials Coloured pencils.

This page also provides revision, since the picture contains groups of 4, 5, 6, 7, and 8 objects. The teacher would begin by using the picture. The children could be asked what they see in the picture or even asked to point to the various objects.

The children are asked to colour and count each of these sets. It would be worthwhile using different colours for different sets which are close to each other.

Workbook 3: Counting to 8   57

Additional activities

Suggestions for additional activities in counting to 5 appeared earlier in the teaching notes for this Workbook (page 52). These activities would also be appropriate for all the numbers up to 8. Some further suggestions are given below.

1. Children might colour and count from other pictures similar to the one on Page 15. If the pictures are to be used more than once then they should not be coloured.
2. The children might draw their own pictures with groups of up to 8 objects included. Several cards like the one shown could be used.

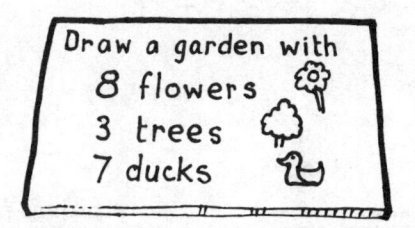

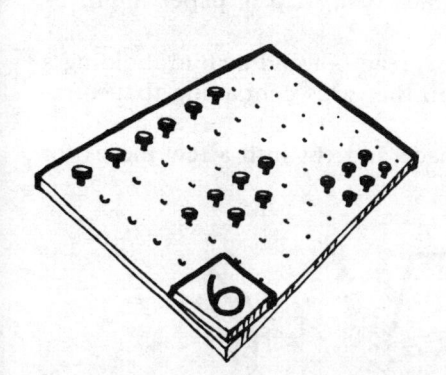

3. The pictures of the 'Counting to 8 cards' from the **Teacher's Materials Pack** (Cards 6 and 7) are also suitable for counting practice up to 8. They can be used along with numeral cards and, once the picture is counted, the numeral is placed alongside.
   The cards can also be sorted into those which have the same number.
4. The children might make different arrangements of the same number on a pegboard using the coloured pegs.
5. **The Snake game** This game is fully described in the Teaching Notes for **Workbook 2** (counting to 4). It could be played again, but this time the dice or flashcards would be marked 3, 4, 5, 6, 7, 8.
   The game will finish more quickly, of course, since bigger 'moves' are being made.

Additional worksheets for the teacher to make

The suggestions given here could each be used to make several such sheets. Also, each idea could be repeated for the other numbers up to 8.

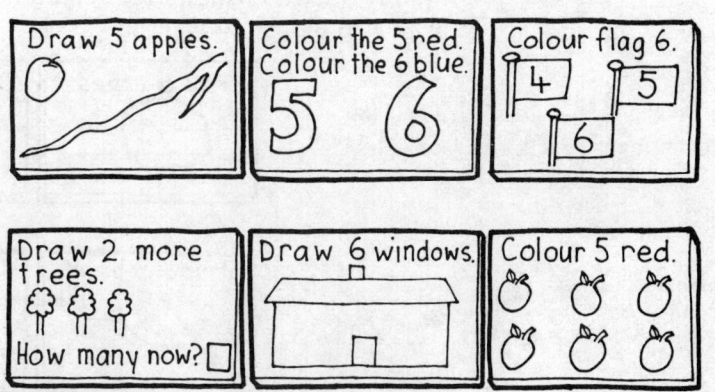

58   Workbook 3: Counting to 8

Additional workcards for the teacher to make

1. Further cards similar to **Teacher's Materials Pack**, Cards 6 and 7, could be made showing sets of objects for counting practice. These should mainly show 5, 6, 7, or 8 objects.

For recording purposes, objects might be copied or traced and the total written at the side. Alternatively, a numeral card might be placed beside it. The card might be 'wipeable', or a strip of paper might be clipped to it.

A group of picture cards could be spread out and a child, holding a particular numeral, might pick out all the cards containing that number of objects.

2. Large numeral cards could be made and cut into a few pieces for assembly by the children.

3. Cards with simple instructions for the children can be quickly made.

Each of these ideas could be varied and repeated for the numbers 5 to 8.

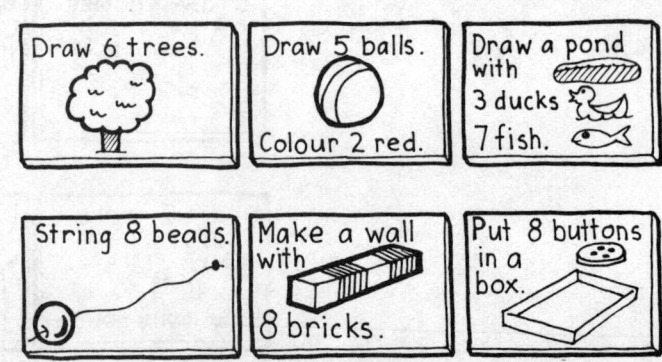

Workbook 4

Counting to 10
Concept of addition

Cards 1 to 14 | Counting to 10

Contents

Counting to 9	Pages 1 and 2
Counting to 10	Pages 3 to 5
Counting: Miscellaneous examples	Pages 6 and 7
Counting: 1p coins	Page 8
Counting: Number sequences	Page 9
Counting: Miscellaneous examples	Page 10

Counting to 10	Cards 1 to 14

Concept of addition	Pages 11 to 14
Adding 1	Page 15

Materials

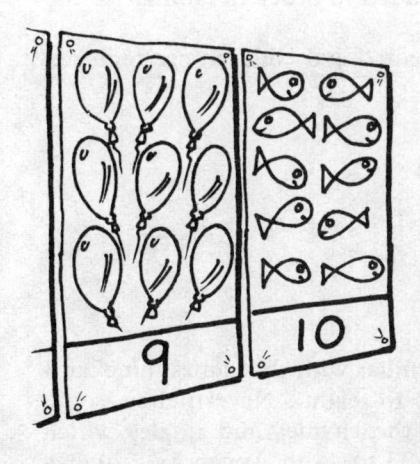

A selection from the following is required:
  counters, beads, buttons, small toys, building bricks, straws, crayons, coloured pencils, wooden blocks, pegs, interlocking beads, interlocking plastic cubes, 1p coins.
The following would also be useful:
  pegboard, sorting box, dice, dowelling, a wall chart to include 9 and 10.
The following flashcards would be useful:
  Numeral cards 1 to 10

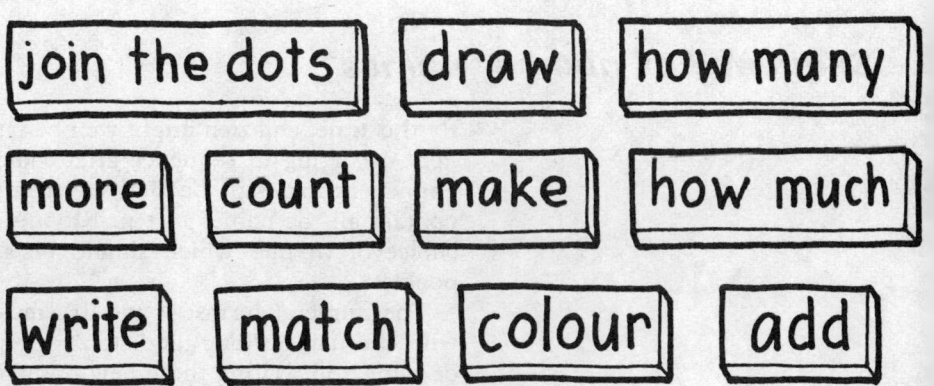

join the dots · draw · how many
more · count · make · how much
write · match · colour · add

Workbook 4: Counting to 10; Concept of addition

The following cards from the *Teacher's Materials Pack* for the **First Stage** are appropriate to this Workbook:
Counting to 4 cards (Card 1)
Counting to 8 cards (Cards 6 and 7)
Shopping cards (Card 8)
Buy-the-man game (Card 9)
1 to 10 train (Card 10)

Counting to 10
(Pages 1 to 10 and Cards 1 to 14)

Development

In **Workbook 2**, the process of counting was introduced and used to deal particularly with the numbers 1, 2, 3, and 4. The process of counting was continued in **Workbook 3** when the numbers 5, 6, 7, and 8 were introduced.

Pages 1 to 10 of this Workbook provide further counting activities and include the numbers 9 and 10. Cards 1 to 14 contain further examples for counting practice.

The sequence of number names is now completed, as are the first ten numerals. Sets with up to 10 objects are counted.

1p coins are used for the first time as objects which can be counted, and simple shopping activities are included in order to familiarize the children with coins and their uses.

Sequences of numerals are also presented and children are required to insert the missing numerals.

Practical activities and teaching

Sequence of number names

By this time, children might well be familiar with the names 'nine' and 'ten' occurring in sequence after 'one' to 'eight'. Nevertheless, some enjoyment can still be derived from the rhymes and jingles which contain all the names to ten. Rhymes 33 to 44 in Appendix 2 offer a choice of rhymes which should be appropriate to the work of this booklet.

The numeral forms, 9 and 10, must be introduced and associated with the names 'nine' and 'ten'. Frequent practice must be given in drawing and writing these new numerals. There is some provision for doing this in the Workbook pages.

Workbook 4: Counting to 10; Concept of addition 61

Introducing counting to 9 and 10

Each of these two numbers might be introduced, in turn, using the same practical approach as that suggested in the teaching notes for **Workbook 3** (Counting to 8).

1 To a set of 8 objects one more is added and the new set is called 'nine'. Children count out 8 objects, add one more, and then say 'nine'. |one| |two| ·· |eight| |nine|

The numeral |9| can be placed alongside the new set

2 The children should now undertake a variety of practical activities in relation to 9. These have been described for numbers up to 8 in previous Workbook notes, and include counting up to 9 objects, making sets up to 9 objects, and drawing and colouring up to 9 objects.

In counting larger groups of objects on paper, the children will, as before, need to mark each object with a tick or cross as they count.

3 The numeral 9 has now to be made, drawn, and written by the children. The activities which help to determine its shape are those suggested for 'shaping' the other numerals as outlined in the Teaching Notes for **Workbook 3**.

Later, when the numeral 10 is introduced and its shape drawn it is the '0' part which is new for the children.

4 Following the usual development, 9 has now to be seen in relation to the numbers 1 to 8. Models, pictures, or wall charts can now incorporate the new number.

Activities which involve all the numbers including 9 should now be carried out.
(a) Several sets of objects can be counted, to include totals of 9.
(b) Sets of objects can be made up to certain numbers, including 9.
(c) More objects can be added to a set and then the new set counted. For example, 'Draw 2 more. How many now?'

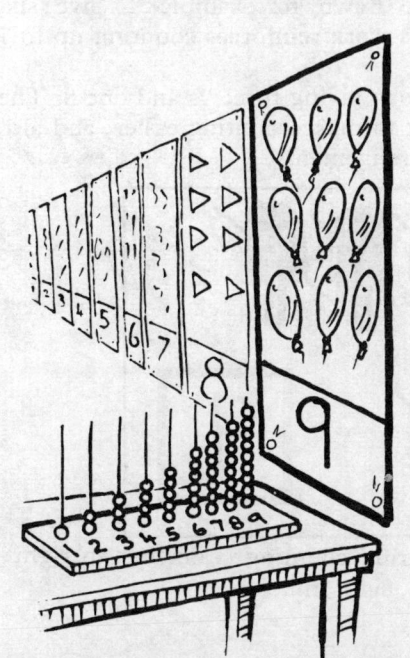

62 Workbook 4: Counting to 10; Concept of addition

(d) Sorting boxes can be used and their compartments filled with up to 9 objects.

Pages 1 to 7

After activities similar to those described above have been carried out for the numbers up to 9, Pages 1 and 2 of the Workbook can be used for further practice.

After a similar development for introducing 10, Pages 3 to 7 of the Workbook will provide follow-up written activities.

Page 1   9   Counting to 9

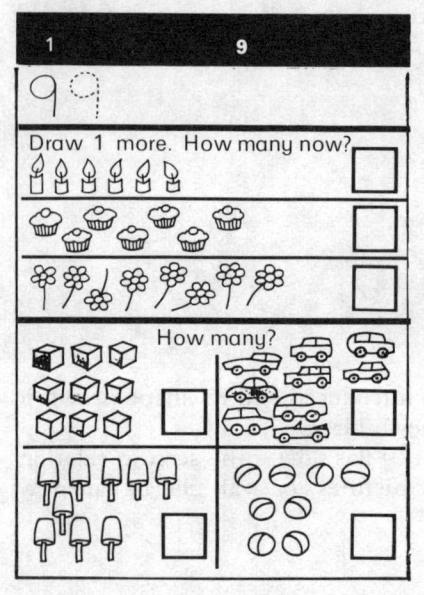

Materials Coloured pencils.

By means of blackboard illustration and discussion of the pictures of objects on the page, a careful explanation of what the children have to do will be needed before this page is begun.

A space is provided at the top of the page for practice in making the numeral.

The children are now asked to add one more object to sets of 6, 7, and 8, and, each time, they count the new total and write the answer. The last total is, of course, the new number 9. The children may also count 'orally' once each row is complete and pause before saying the name of the object which they have drawn, for example ... 'five, six, seven, eight———nine'. As always this work reinforces counting up to 7 and 8.

Four counting exercises then follow, giving three 9s and one 8. The objects are arranged to some extent to make counting easier, and also to present certain familiar visual arrangements.

Each object is ticked or crossed during counting (from left to right) 'one, two, three, four, five, six, seven, eight, nine'.

Workbook 4: Counting to 10; Concept of addition   **63**

Page 2 — 9 — Counting to 9

Materials   Coloured pencils.

On the top half of the page pictures of objects to be counted are presented and each time, after counting, the answer is written. The objects are arranged in such a way that crossing, marking, or ticking each one is necessary during counting.

The lower half of the page deals with the more difficult task of 'making up to 9'. Preliminary oral and practical work would be helpful before doing these exercises. For each row of objects on the page, the children draw one more object, count it, and then continue drawing and counting until 9 is reached. It is not advisable that questions like 'Six and what makes nine?' be asked before the activity, which is essentially about counting-on, is carried out.

Pages 3 and 4 — 10 — Counting to 10

Materials   Coloured pencils.

These two pages present the same activities for 10 as Pages 1 and 2 did for the number 9. They should, of course, follow a considerable experience in practical activities involving 10.

Page 5 — 9 or 10 — Counting to 10

Materials   Coloured pencils.

This page combines work on 9 and 10 and thus consolidates the work of the previous four pages. Children are asked to count or colour either 9 or 10 objects from groups which contain more than 9 or 10 objects.

Four counting pictures complete the work, the totals being 10, 9, 10, and 9.

64　**Workbook 4:** Counting to 10; Concept of addition

Page 6

Match

Counting to 10

Materials None.

On this page the children are expected to count the objects and match the sets to the numerals by drawing a line from each set to the corresponding numeral.

Blackboard demonstrations would be very helpful before the children do this page. Matching actual objects to numeral cards would also be a useful preliminary activity.

Page 7

How many?

Counting to 10

Materials Coloured pencils

The picture contains sets of objects which are coloured and then counted. The picture could be the basis of valuable language work which would help the children to identify certain objects. Similar pictures might be discussed and used as a preliminary activity to the work of this page.

If there is time available, the children could take pleasure in colouring in the whole picture and, in fact, might be asked to count any other sets of objects which are there, for example, the house, 4 windows, etc.

Workbook 4: Counting to 10; Concept of addition 65

Additional activities

Additional activities concerning counting are described in detail in the Teaching Notes for **Workbook 3** for the numbers 5, 6, 7, and 8. These are also appropriate for 9 and 10.

Introductory activities for Page 8

Counting 1p coins

Workbook Page 8 is concerned with counting collections of 1p coins. However, a preliminary start is needed to make children familiar with some of the different aspects of money work. These activities will be a useful basis for activities in money which come in later booklets.

The children should be introduced to the 1p coin and then, using real or token coins, they should carry out activities which might include the following.

1 Coins are laid out to represent values such as 2p, 5p, 10p, etc. 1p coins are used and the instructions may be oral or written in the form of a flashcard, for example ⎣3p⎦ . The letter 'p' has to be explained. After laying out collections of coins, the children can write in the values. The new instruction, 'How much?' is appropriate here.

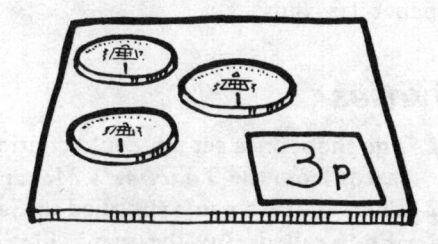

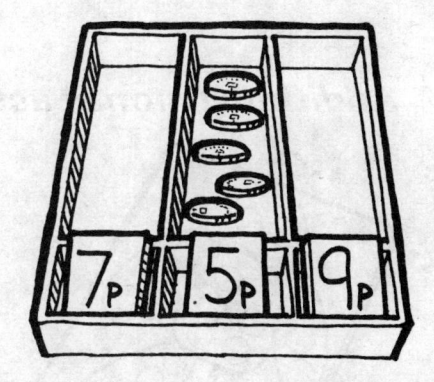

2 Flashcards can be used as price tags and sorting boxes with price tags could be provided for group or individual work. The children put the correct amount of money in the box according to the price on the tag. Conversely, a number of coins could be put into the compartments and the correct price tag selected.

3 The teacher might put out coins and the children could then be asked to say or write how much has been put out. Using a money stamp (1p), simple cards entitled 'How much?' can be made up for the children to do.

4 The teacher might arrange for 'selling' to take place. Using 1p coins, the children could come out and buy, for example, a straw costing 4p or a pencil costing 6p.

66   Workbook 4: Counting to 10; Concept of addition

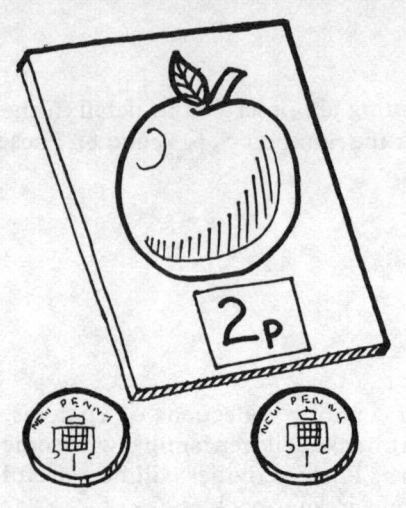

5   The teacher could help the children to set up a class shop. Articles collected by the children could be priced with a price tag at anything up to 10p. The children might choose the type of shop, e.g. sweet shop, book shop, toy shop. Articles might even be made using paper, card, boxes, or plasticine. Further suggestions about 'shop play' are given in Appendix 1 (page 227).

   Each child could be given ten 1p coins, say, and asked to buy something from the shop. The shopkeeper must check that the correct money is handed over.

6   Shopping cards are supplied in the *Teacher's Materials Pack* (Card 8), each showing a picture of an article and its price. Each child should select a card and put out the appropriate money.

| Page 8 | How much? | Counting to 10 |

Materials   1p coins.

Collections of coins have to be counted and the total value written in each time. Coins can be placed on top of the pictures or the coin pictures themselves can be counted. The 'p' is a dotted outline and the children are expected to go over this outline to form the letter. Extra workcards could be made using the rubber 1p coin stamp or stick-on paper 1p coins.

Additional money activities

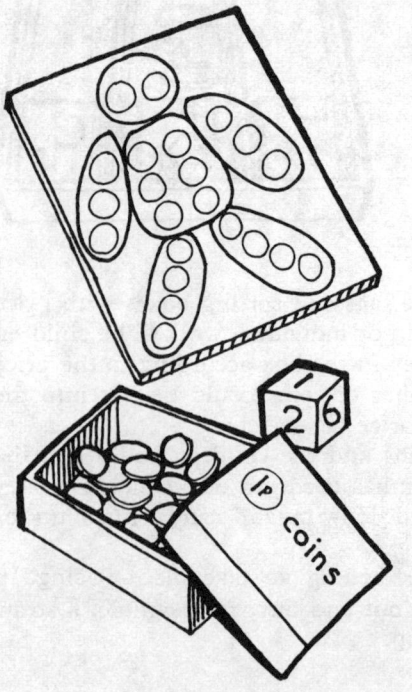

1   The shop, once set up, could continue to be used, as can the shopping cards from the *Teacher's Materials Pack*, Card 8.
2   There is also a game supplied in Card 9 of the *Teacher's Materials Pack* called 'Buy-the-man'. This game is for 2 children. A box of 1p coins and a dice with numbers 1 to 6 are required. Each child has a card which shows a picture of a 'man'. There are two ways to play.
   (a)   The children throw the dice in turn. A '1' is required for a player to start. During play if, for example, a '3' is thrown, three 1p coins are then placed to 'cover' one arm. If a '4' is thrown, then a leg is covered. The winner is the child who completes the covering of the man and so 'buys the man'.
   (b)   Play starts on the first throw of the dice. If, for example, a '5' is thrown, then 5 coins are picked from the box and any part of the man can be covered, e.g. 2 coins on the eyes and 3 coins on the arm. As before, the winner is the first child to 'buy the man'.

Workbook 4: Counting to 10; Concept of addition   67

Teaching suggestions for Page 9

Numeral sequences

Page 9 gives practice with written numeral sequences. It is worthwhile to practise simple oral recitation of the number names (including the use of number rhymes) before starting the page.

As well as saying 'one, two, three, ..., ten', parts of sequences can be given. For example,
(a) 'four, five, six, seven, eight'
(b) 'two, three, four, ..., ..., ...'
(c) 'one, two, ..., ..., ...'
Numeral cards can be laid out to correspond to the spoken sequences.

| Page 9 | 1 to 10 | Counting to 10 |

Materials   None.

Three numeral sequences are presented and the missing numerals are inserted. The teacher might carry out similar activities as demonstrations on the blackboard before the children do the page.

The children should recite the names from left to right before writing the missing numerals. All the outlines are dotted and the children should go over these for more practice in forming numerals.

In the dot pictures, the children join up the dots (numbers) in their correct counting sequence, thereby completing the picture. Again, extra pictures could be drawn by joining dots on the blackboard.

Additional activities on sequences

1 Numeral cards can be shuffled and then replaced in the correct order.

2 The teacher can place some cards face down and the child has to name the correct number before turning it over.

3 'Which number is in the wrong place?' 'What should it be?'

68 Workbook 4: Counting to 10; Concept of addition

4 Start with ⟨5⟩ and complete the sequence in both directions.
5 **Teacher's Materials Pack**, Card 10, is a train jigsaw, which a child can reassemble by placing the numerals in their correct sequence.

6 Dot-to-dot activities are fairly common in children's puzzle books and could be used for extra practice.

| Page 10 | How many? | Counting to 10 |

Materials Coloured pencils.

This page provides revision practice in counting totals from 4 to 10. The picture could be used as a basis for worthwhile language work which would help the children to identify the objects.

The picture is of a shop interior and groups of objects are to be counted by the children. The picture may, subsequently, be entirely coloured by the children.

| Cards 1 to 14 | Counting to 10 |

These cards provide further revision and practice in counting sets of up to 10 objects and, to some extent, consolidate the work of **Workbooks 2, 3,** and **4**. They are suitable for all children.

The odd-numbered cards provide pictures of sets of objects to count. The even-numbered cards ask children to draw given numbers of objects.

Workbook 4: Counting to 10; Concept of addition   **69**

Cards 1, 3, 5, 7, 9, 11, 13

How many?

Materials   Numeral cards [4] to [10] if required.

Each card contains four pictures with objects to count. The numbers are mainly in the range 6 to 10, but sometimes a smaller number is given.

The children may give the answer orally or perhaps lay the numeral cards beside the appropriate section of the card. Some children may write their own answers.

The reverse side of each of these cards instructs the children to draw sets of objects so that, on choosing a card, the child counts on one side and then carries out the drawing instruction on the other.

Cards 2, 4, 6, 8, 10, 12, 14

Draw

Materials   Coloured pencils.

The first three cards instruct the children to draw their own sets containing up to and including 10 objects similar to the ones shown on the cards. The outline drawings are intended to be simple enough to be easily copied, although the quality of the child's drawing is not important.

Cards 8, 10, 12, and 14 are more difficult in that they have to draw objects against a 'background'—windows on a house, spots on a snake, beads on a string, flowers in a garden. The outline of the house (Card 8) and the snakes (Card 10) might be traced. However, accurate drawing is less important than having the correct number of objects in each drawing.

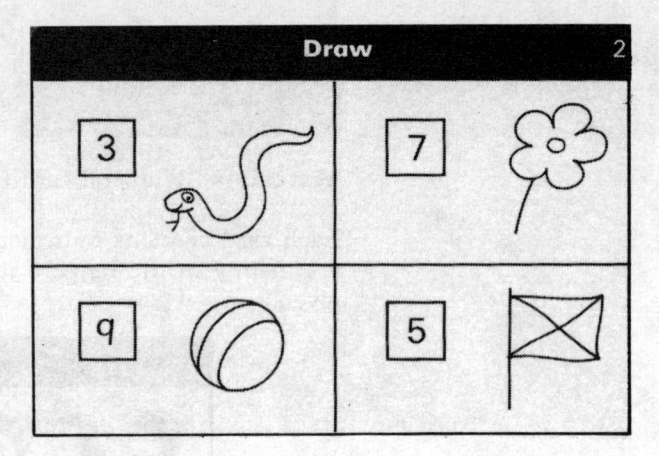

70 Workbook 4: Counting to 10; Concept of addition

Additional worksheets and cards for the teacher to make

Worksheets and cards modelled on Cards 1 to 14 can be made by the teacher if more practice is needed. A few suggestions are given below.

1 Cards

2 Worksheets

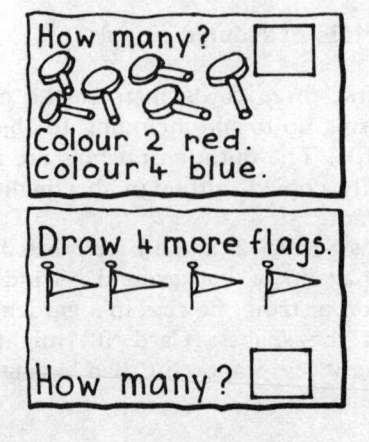

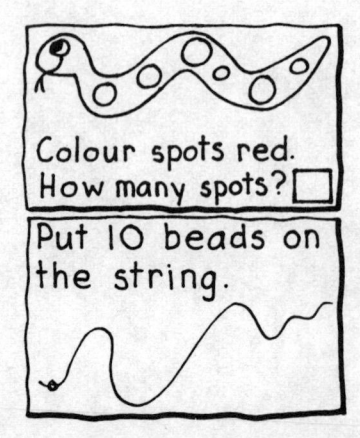

Workbook 4: Counting to 10; Concept of addition 71

Concept of addition (Pages 11 to 15)

Development

This part of the Workbook provides practice in counting and recording the number of objects in each part of a set, and the total number of objects in the set. Totals are not greater than 10.

Addition of 1p coins is also included. The last page deals with adding 1. The addition facts are presented in random order. Systematization comes later in **Workbooks 5, 7,** and **8.**

Practical activities and teaching

Introductory addition activities

Children require considerable practice and experience of starting with 2 sets of objects, counting the number in each set, physically bringing the 2 sets together, and counting the grand total.

Some suggestions for oral and practical work are given below.

1. The teacher might use the children themselves as counting 'objects' and ask, 'How many boys do we have in this set? How many boys do we have in that set?' The boys could then be asked to stand closer together, and the following asked, 'How many boys are there altogether?'

2. The child might put 4 red beads on a string and then 2 yellow beads. The beads could then be counted and the correct numeral card placed beside the string.

72   Workbook 4: Counting to 10; Concept of addition

3. The teacher might put 3 counters and 2 counters on the child's table, separated by a pencil or straw.
   The child is asked to match each set with a numeral card.

   The child then counts how many there are altogether and puts the appropriate numeral card on the right of the collection.

   The teacher should continually repeat the appropriate language, e.g. 'How many in this set? How many in this other set? How many *altogether?*'

4. Another variation of this kind of activity is to give the child labelled containers such as margarine tubs. The child puts cubes into each tub according to the numeral on the side, places the tubs side by side, counts how many cubes there are altogether, and places the corresponding numeral card alongside.

5. Sorting boxes are also suitable for introducing addition. The child is asked to put, say, 3 objects in one compartment, 3 in another, and then place the appropriate numeral cards as shown.

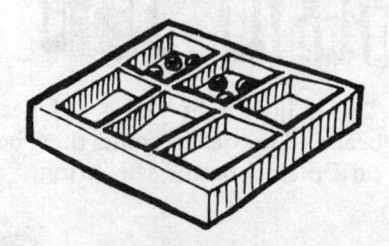

6. *Money*   As well as counters, cubes, etc., children should be given 1p coins to count and add. In this, as in all other activities, the teacher should use, and encourage the children to use, appropriate language, e.g. 'How many pennies in this set? How many in this other set? How many pennies have we altogether?

Workbook 4: Counting to 10; Concept of addition 73

7 Large cards like the one shown, with an arrow to indicate the total number of objects, may be used over and over again.

The child places counters, or similar objects, and the appropriate numeral cards, as shown. The teacher should take care that totals do not exceed 10 at this stage.

This will prepare the child for the work on Page 11 which looks just like this.

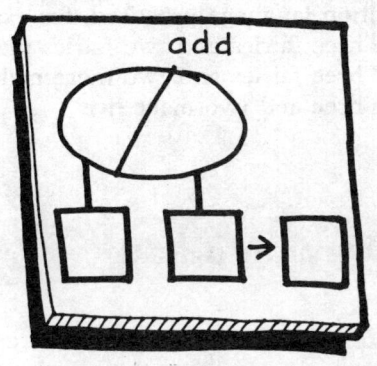

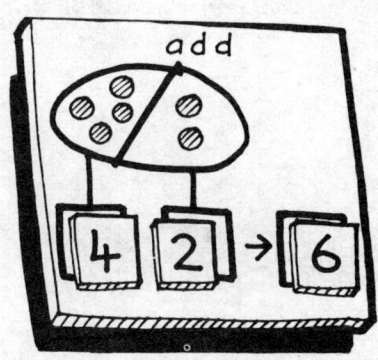

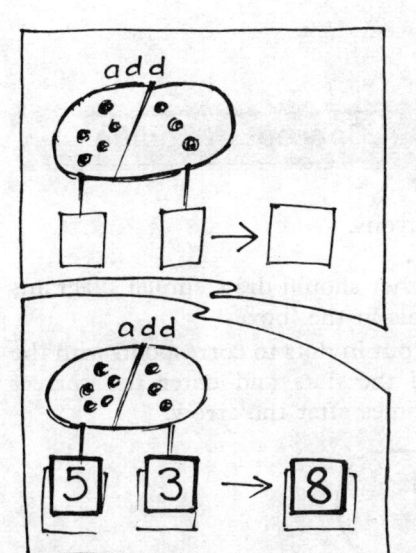

8 *Blackboard work* The teacher could also draw partitioned sets on the blackboard, similar to those found on Page 11. Dots could be added and children invited to write the corresponding numerals. The meaning of the arrow must also be explained to the children.

Suitable language should accompany all activities of this kind: 'Five dots and three dots make eight dots altogether'. 'Five dots and three *more* dots make eight dots'. 'Five and three make eight'.

It is important that children experience plenty of activities, such as those outlined above, before they are asked to do the Workbook Pages 11 to 14.

| Pages 11 and 12 | Add | Concept of addition |

Materials Counters, beads, buttons, cubes, etc.

These pages provide practice in counting the number of objects in each part of the partitioned set, and then the total number of objects in the whole set. The children write the corresponding numerals in the boxes provided. The teacher should make sure that the children understand what is involved and that the arrow points to the 'How many altogether?' box.

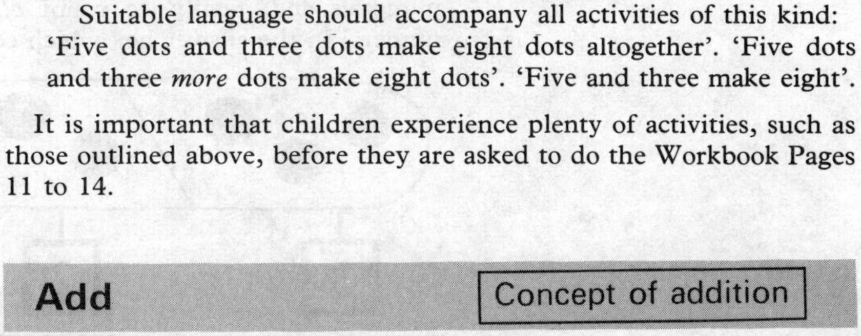

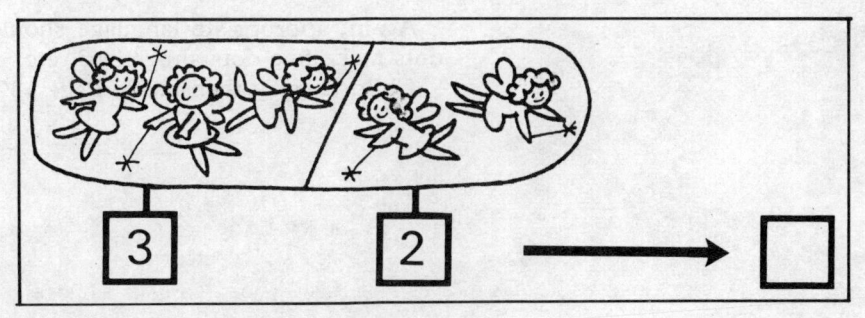

74 Workbook 4: Counting to 10; Concept of addition

Less able children may benefit from covering each drawn object by a button, cube, counter, etc., before they count.

To begin with, children will probably count the grand total from the beginning, 'one, two, ..., five'. The teacher should, however, encourage 'counting on' from *three*, when it is felt that a child is ready for this.

After the page has been completed, oral work could take place and addition language practised, for example,

'Three fairies and two fairies make five fairies altogether'.
'Three fairies and two more make five'.
'Three and two make five'.

Page 13 — Draw and add — Concept of addition

Materials Coloured pencils or crayons.

Before children do this page the teacher should draw similar diagrams on the blackboard and write numerals in the 'boxes'.

Children might then be invited to put in dots to correspond with the numerals and, finally, to count *all* the dots and enter the correct numeral in the answer box which comes after the arrow.

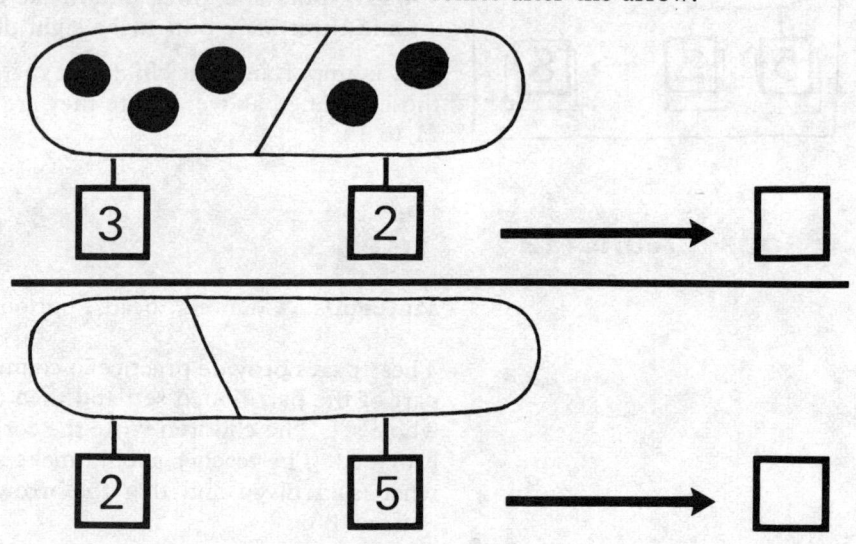

Again, appropriate language should be used: 'Three dots and two dots make five dots altogether', etc.

Children may then tackle Page 13.

Workbook 4: Counting to 10; Concept of addition 75

Page 14

Add

Concept of addition

Materials 1p coins.

Before children attempt this page they should have had practice with coins. The large cards referred to on page 73 are useful for this purpose.

Coins (not more than ten) are laid out as shown, and matched with numeral cards. After counting the total the child places the correct numeral card in the 'answer' box.

Sometimes the teacher may place numeral cards in the two left-hand 'boxes'. The child then puts the correct number of coins above each numeral and finally the answer numeral card in the extreme right-hand 'box'.

Children may then do Page 14. Some children may benefit from being allowed to place coins over the coin illustrations on Page 14 before counting, totalling, and writing the numerals in the appropriate 'boxes'. The teacher should also see that the children write over the dotted letter 'p' each time. Language should be encouraged: 'Three pennies and five pennies make eight pennies altogether'. 'Three pence and five pence make eight pence', etc.

Teaching suggestions

Adding on 1

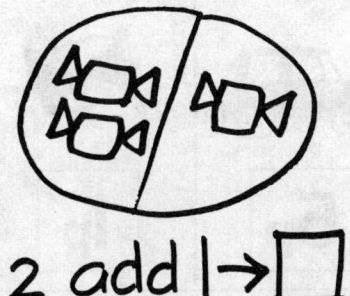

Early work in number led children to see that 4 is 1 more than 3, 5 is 1 more than 4, and so on. In this connection, wall charts which help promote this idea were mentioned.

Also, ideas of counting up in ones, 1 more, adding on 1, are contained in Number Rhymes 26 to 40 in Appendix 2.

Pages 1 and 3 of this Workbook have presented further experience of 'one more than'. For instance, the child starts with 8 balls (Page 3) and is asked to draw 1 more and say how many there are now.

This work is very closely related to that in which the child is being asked to add 1 onto 8. The easiest additions involve adding 1 to another number, because of the connection with the counting sequence. The child should be given activities where one of the sets of objects consists of only *one* member.

A few children may come to see that if they have counted 6 objects, say, in one set and there is *one* object in the other set, then there there are 7 objects altogether, *without* starting to count all over again from 1 to arrive at a total of 7.

In order to prepare children for the work on Page 15, teachers might give children practice by using blackboard illustrations similar to those on Page 15.

The use of a flash card add 1 might also be helpful.

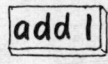

76 **Workbook 4:** Counting to 10; Concept of addition

Page 15

Add 1

Concept of addition

Materials None.

After some preliminary teaching such as that described above, children could be asked to do this page.

The work gives children experience of an addition statement, for example

$$3 \text{ add } 1 \rightarrow 4$$

This is a step towards later recording which occurs in **Workbook 5**, such as

$$3 + 1 = 4$$

Some children will continue to count the sweets in order to arrive at the total. Some of the more able children may arrive at the answer without counting the sweets.

Additional activities

The Counting to 4 cards and the Counting to 8 cards from the **Teacher's Materials Pack** (Cards 1, 6, and 7) could be used to provide sets for children to add as long as the objects on the cards were chosen to be of the same kind.

The Shopping cards (**Teacher's Materials Pack**, Card 8) could also be used for adding to totals up to 10p.

Workbook 4: Counting to 10; Concept of addition

Cards and worksheets for the teacher to make

1. Children could record their answer on paper clipped to the card, or, in the case of the 'Draw' card, underneath their drawing.

Find 3	Draw 5	Put out 6
Find 2 more	Draw 3 more	Add 1
How many altogether?	How many altogether?	How many altogether?

2. Teachers may wish to make extra worksheets, or 'wipeable' workcards:

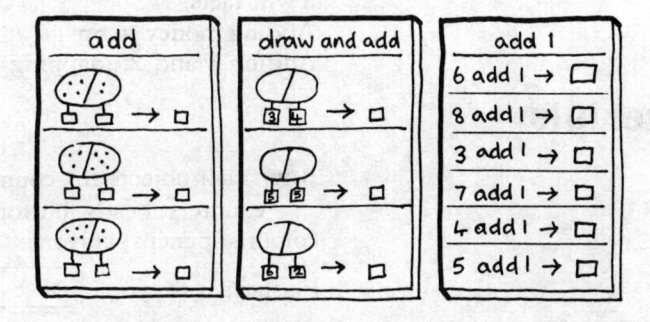

add	draw and add	add 1
		6 add 1 → ☐
		8 add 1 → ☐
		3 add 1 → ☐
		7 add 1 → ☐
		4 add 1 → ☐
		5 add 1 → ☐

'Wipeable' cards can be made by covering a card with clear plastic, or a stretched polythene bag, so that the child may write on the plastic surface with a chinagraph pencil or felt pens filled with water-soluble ink.

Workbook 5

Addition to 6

Contents

Revision and introduction of + and =	Page 1
Totals to 4	Pages 2 and 3
Totals to 5	Pages 4 to 7
Totals to 6	Pages 8 to 10
'Stories' of 3, 4, 5, and 6	Page 11
Twin facts	Page 12
Adding money to 6p	Pages 13 and 14
Adding 1 and 2: mapping diagrams	Page 15

Materials

Any small objects for counting such as:
　　counters, beads, buttons, bricks; Unifix and other cubes; 1p coins; coloured pencils, crayons.

Flashcards of type 3+2   1+4

Numeral cards 1 2 3 4 5 6

Flashcards of important words:

add   draw   stories   buy

make   more

　　The following items from the *Teacher's Materials Pack* for **Infant Mathematics, First Stage**, will be a useful supplement to this Workbook:
　　Animal jigsaws (Cards 11 and 12)
　　Fishing game (Card 13)
　　Window card (Card 14)
　　Fair game (Cards 15 and 16)

Addition to 6 (Pages 1 to 15)

Development

Before children start to learn addition facts in a systematic way, they must have a clear idea of what is involved in adding two numbers. The notes for **Workbook 4** referred to the kind of experiences which help to promote this concept of addition.

The work of this Workbook relates to the learning of early addition facts with totals to 6. The symbols + and = are introduced for the first time. Systematic additive composition of each of the numbers 2 to 6 is dealt with. Emphasis is given to the commutative property of addition. Addition of money (1p coins) is dealt with, and also the mapping diagram method of recording for adding on 1 and 2.

Practical activities which should precede and supplement the work of the booklet are referred to in detail in the teaching notes which follow.

The work covered in this Workbook is developed further by the practical activities and written work of **Workbooks 7** and **8**.

Practical activities and teaching

Addition activities

Children should be given plenty of oral and practical work involving the use of concrete material before Workbook pages are attempted. The concrete material may comprise small objects such as cubes, counters, buttons, beads, toy cars, toy animals, and also the children themselves. Crosses and dots may be drawn on the blackboard and totals found. Language associated with addition should be constantly practised, for example 'How many cows altogether?'

80 Workbook 5: Addition to 5

Here are some other suggestions for activities.

1. Children could make addition 'stories' using small objects which are placed on 'adding boards' made of stiff cardboard. They record by placing numeral cards on the blank 'boxes'.

"blank"

"stories of 4"

The teacher should encourage language, such as, 'Three and one make four'; 'Two and two make four'.

Since the symbols + and = are used for the first time in **Workbook 5**, children should be taught to recognize and write these symbols. They must also learn what words to say when they see these symbols. This recording may be verbalized as

$$\boxed{3} + \boxed{1} = \boxed{4}$$

'Three and one make four' at this stage.

There are many arguments about the respective merits of the symbols → and =. The writers have decided to introduce the symbol = at this point. Children do tend to find it easier to write than →.

2. A child may be asked to put out 2 cars and 1 car and find how many there are altogether, using numeral and symbol cards to record, like this:

$$\boxed{2} + \boxed{1} = \boxed{3}$$

Again the teacher should encourage language, such as, 'Two and one make three'.

Alternatively the teacher might set the cards down for the child, who then matches the numbers to be added and finds the total:

$$\boxed{3} + \boxed{2} = \boxed{} \qquad \boxed{3} + \boxed{2} = \boxed{5}$$

Workbook 5: Addition to 5   **81**

3   The teacher draws objects on the blackboard and invites the children to come and write the appropriate numerals in the blank 'boxes':

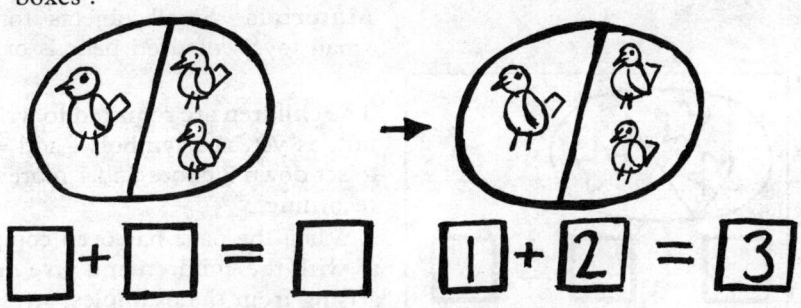

☐ + ☐ = ☐   1 + 2 = 3

4   The child strings beads, e.g. 2 red and 3 blue beads, and then records how many there are altogether:

2 + 3 = 5

5   The child is given, say, 4 objects and asked to make up adding stories:

2 + 2 = 4   3 + 1 = 4

6   Counting cards such as **Teacher's Materials Pack**, Card 1, may be used to provide groups of objects of the same kind.

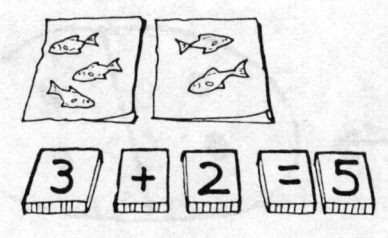

3 + 2 = 5

In all of the foregoing activities the teacher should make sure that the children understand the meaning and the use of the symbols ' + ' and ' = '.

The teacher will use discretion to decide when the children have had sufficient of these addition activities and are ready to proceed to the Workbook pages.

Rather than do a lot of this work and the associated recording *before* allowing children to begin the Workbook, it is better that some practical activity should be done, followed by a related page, or pages.

For example, some activities relating to the story of 4 should be followed by the work on Pages 2 and 3. Again, activities relating to the story of 5 should be done, and followed by the work on Pages 4, 5, 6, and 7, and so on.

The teacher should decide when a child is ready to attempt a Workbook page. At this early stage in the learning process it is important that children are not pushed on too quickly to the Workbook before having had sufficient concrete experience. This is particularly the case with the less able child.

82 Workbook 5: Addition to 5

Pages 1 and 2 | Add | Totals of 2, 3, and 4

Materials Small objects for counting—counters, buttons, cubes, small toys; coloured pencils or crayons.

The children are required to write the correct numerals in the boxes and not, as yet, the symbols + and =. Some children may find it beneficial to set down 2 cubes and 1 more cube before proceeding to complete the recording.

When the page has been completed, the teacher might 'talk through it' with the children and give oral practice in the language of addition arising from the examples, stressing again the meaning and use of '+' and '='.

The teacher may wish to give the children extra worksheets of similar work for consolidation. 'Wipeable' workcards may be considered for this purpose. These consist of workcards covered with transparent plastic. The child writes in the answer 'boxes' using a special water-soluble pen, or even a felt pen. By this means the same card may be used over and over again.

Page 3 | Draw and add | Totals to 4

Materials Coloured pencils or crayons.

The teacher can prepare the children for this work by imitating it on the blackboard. The child is asked to draw in the dots and then write the total in the 'box' provided.

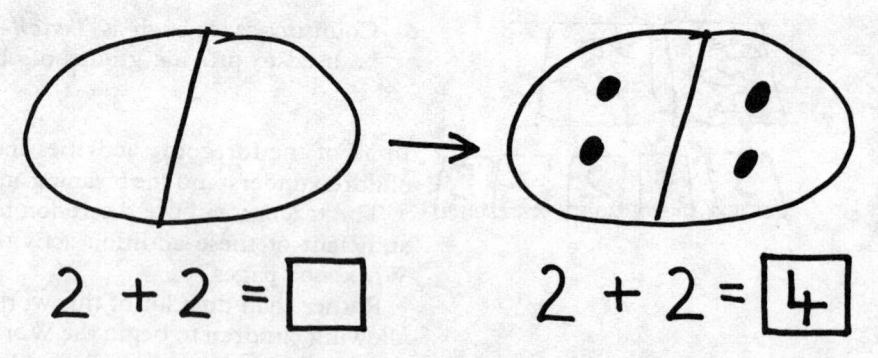

$2 + 2 = \square$ $2 + 2 = \boxed{4}$

In the examples on the bottom half of the page the child is also required to write the '=' sign. It will be necessary for the teacher to give some prior practice and also to remind the children when they are about to start the bottom half of the page.

The teacher may wish to provide extra worksheets or cards with similar work for further practice and consolidation.

Again, the completed page may be 'talked through' and children encouraged to verbalize the recordings:

$3 + 1 = \boxed{4}$ 'Three and one makes four'.

Workbook 5: Addition to 5   **83**

Page 4 — Add — Totals of 5

Materials As for Pages 1 and 2.

This page is intended to follow oral and practical work with concrete material, giving children plenty of practice in adding to make 5.

The work of the page is similar to that of Pages 1 and 2, but the children are also required to write the '=' sign. They will require to be reminded about this.

All the number pairs which add to 5 are covered. Some of the facts appear twice.

The teacher may wish to provide further written work.

Oral 'mental arithmetic' should also take place frequently and the children should be encouraged to memorize the facts by these means.

The teacher must guard against putting too much pressure on children to memorize. There are always some children who are slower to progress in this direction. For them, concrete material, pictures of objects, and patience on the part of the teacher, is the answer!

Page 5 — Draw and add — Totals to 5

Materials Coloured pencils or crayons.

The work here is similar to that on Page 3. Children draw dots to correspond with the given numerals and write the numeral corresponding to the total number of dots in the 'box'.

They also have to write the '=' sign each time. They will probably need to be reminded about this.

More able children may be capable of writing the total in the box without drawing dots.

Again, the teacher should provide extra work if this is felt to be necessary. Oral work should continue as before.

Practice in writing 'adding stories'

Page 6 (and also Page 8) require children to write 'adding stories' complete with numerals and the symbols '+' and '='. It is advisable, therefore, to let children practise this before they proceed to Page 6.

The teacher might provide 'adding story' cards for the children as shown. A paper strip may be clipped to the bottom part of the card. The child then writes the story on the strip. 'Wipeable' cards are also a possibility.

The teacher might also draw partitioned sets of objects on the blackboard (dots would do) and invite children to come and write the adding story. When the teacher considers that the children are 'ready' she can direct them to Page 6.

84 Workbook 5: Addition to 5

Page 6 | Add | Totals to 5

Materials As for Pages 1 and 2.

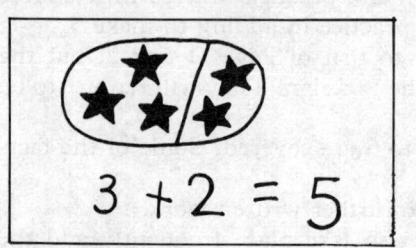

The totals on this page are mostly 5 but three of the examples have a total of 4 so that children have to be careful when adding.

There are no boxes provided and the child has to write the whole story as shown, including the '+' and '=' signs.

After completion, the page may be used as the basis for oral work. The stories may be read aloud first of all. The children are then asked to close their books. The teacher asks questions such as, 'What does four and one make?', and the children say the answer.

Stories without pictures

So far, the pages have all contained pictures or dots so that children may count to find the answer.

Pages 7, 10, 13, 14, and 15 do *not* contain pictures of objects which are countable in this way, and the aim is to get the children to recall the facts without having to resort to counting pictures of objects.

Children should be allowed, however, to use cubes or other small objects when in difficulty with a 'sum'. This will apply particularly to the slower learner.

Again, completed pages may be used as the basis for oral work.

Addition flashcards may also be used at regular intervals to help consolidate memorization of the facts. The teacher holds the card up so that the children see the 'front'. The 'back' of the card may be shown as and when necessary.

Page 7 | Add | Totals to 5

Materials As for Pages 1 and 2.

This is a page of miscellaneous examples giving further practice in additions which the children have already met with totals ranging from 2 to 5. Concrete material should be available for any children who need it.

Workbook 5: Addition to 5

Additional cards for the teacher to make

Teachers may wish to provide further practice cards at this point covering all the pair bonds already met.
Here are two such cards.

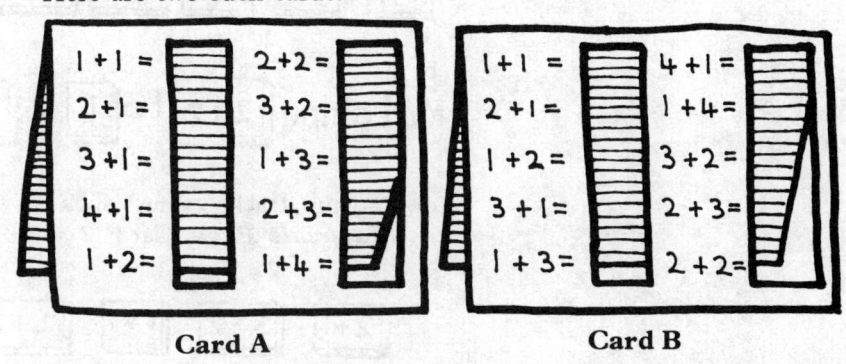

$$
\begin{array}{ll}
1+1= & 2+2= \\
2+1= & 3+2= \\
3+1= & 1+3= \\
4+1= & 2+3= \\
1+2= & 1+4=
\end{array}
$$

Card A

$$
\begin{array}{ll}
1+1= & 4+1= \\
2+1= & 1+4= \\
1+2= & 3+2= \\
3+1= & 2+3= \\
1+3= & 2+2=
\end{array}
$$

Card B

These cards could be designed like *Teacher's Materials Pack* Card 14, or otherwise, as the teacher prefers.

The advantage of the *Teacher's Materials Pack* design is that the teacher simply inserts a sheet of paper between the cardboard covers. The paper is then held securely by the pressure of the child's hand while he writes the answers in the 'window'.

Card A gives all the pair bonds (zero facts omitted) already met. The sums progress from adding 1 to adding 2, then 3, then 4.

Card B lists the sums as 'twins', reading from top to bottom, i.e. $2+1$ is followed by $1+2$; $3+1$ by $1+3$, and so on.

Consolidation of addition to 5

Here are some other ideas for consolidation of addition to 5 which might be used at this point:
(a) Questions of the type 'What does 3 and 2 make?';
(b) Flashcards, e.g.

(c) 'Three pencils in this box; two pencils in that box. How many pencils altogether?'
(d) *Stories of 4* 'Give me two numbers which add to make 4.'
  'Give me another two which add to make 4.' etc.
(e) 'There are 2 cows in a field. Two *more* come along. How many cows are there now?'

86 Workbook 5: Addition to 5

Additional activities

(a) Sorting cards into stories of 3 and 4, or 4 and 5, or 3, 4, and 5.

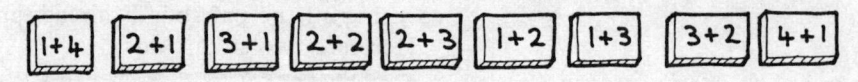

[1+4] [2+1] [3+1] [2+2] [2+3] [1+2] [1+3] [3+2] [4+1]

(b) Matching [2+2] to [4] ; [4+1] to [5] and so on.

(c) Playing track games such as the Snake Game (*Teacher's Materials Pack*, Cards 2 and 3) using cards instead of dice.

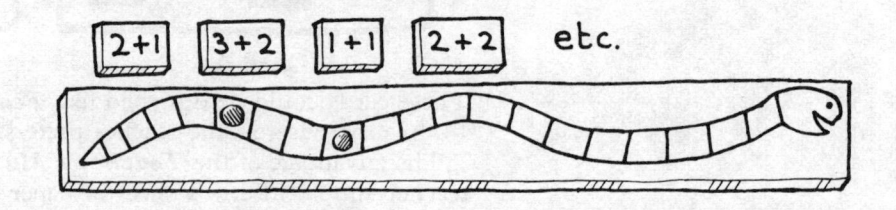

[2+1] [3+2] [1+1] [2+2] etc.

| Page 8 | Add | Totals of 6 |

Materials As for Pages 1 and 2.

This page should be preceded by plenty of practical and oral work using counters, cubes, etc., which involves additions with totals of 6.

The page contains all the addition 'stories' of 6, each of which occurs twice.

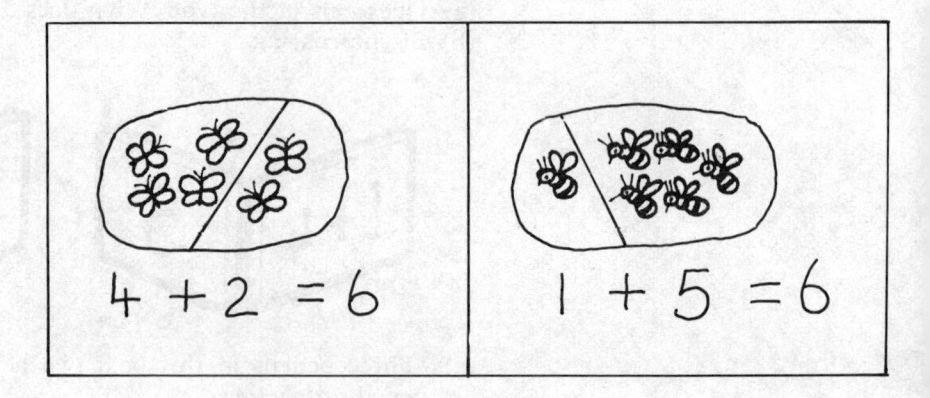

4 + 2 = 6   1 + 5 = 6

The child has to write the whole 'story' underneath the drawing as was done on Page 6. The teacher may wish to provide additional work of a similar kind.

Workbook 5: Addition to 5   **87**

Page 9

Teacher draws.

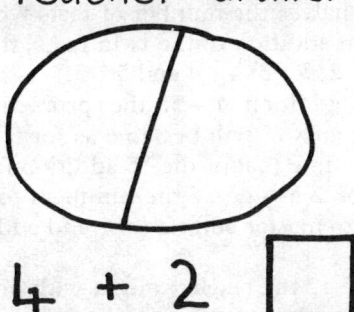

4 + 2 ☐

Draw and add | Totals to 6 |

Materials Coloured pencils or crayons.

The teacher should prepare children for this page by doing blackboard work.

The child is asked to draw in the dots and write the total.

The work on this page is like that on Page 5 but with totals to 6. As well as drawing in the dots and writing the total in the 'box', the child has to write the '=' sign. Children may need reminding about this.

Page 10

Add | Totals to 6 |

Materials As for Pages 1 and 2.

This page is similar to Page 7, but with totals to 6. The page is divided into two halves, each of which provides a manageable amount of work for some children. The completed page may be used as a basis for oral practice aimed at memorization of the facts.

Page 11

Stories | Totals to 6 |

Materials As for Pages 1 and 2.

This page gathers together, in a systematic way, all the addition stories for 3, 4, 5, and 6.

The teacher could discuss the 'stories' with the children *before* they complete the page. After the page has been completed further discussion might take place:

Teacher: 'How many giraffes are there?'
Children: 'Four.'
Teacher: 'Give me a story of four.'
Children: 'Three and one make four.'
Teacher: 'Give me *another* story of four.'
Children: 'Two and two make four.'
        and so on.

The teacher should continue with consolidation work on addition to totals of 6 (see suggestions in the notes for Page 7).

88 Workbook 5: Addition to 5

Twin facts—the commutative property

It is clearly important that children should appreciate as soon as possible that 3 + 2 gives the same answer as 2 + 3. In a sense, the understanding of this concept almost halves the number of facts which the child must commit to memory. (In addition to the twin facts, there are, of course, the 'doubles': 1 + 1; 2 + 2; 3 + 3; 4 + 4 and 5 + 5.)

When a child is faced with the addition 1 + 5, the problem is diminished by the realization that the answer will be same as for 5 + 1.

It may be interesting for teachers to note that of the 15 addition facts with totals to 6, 14 of these have 1 or 2 as one of the numbers to be added, so it is important for children to master adding on 1 and adding on 2 as soon as possible.

Before children are asked to do Page 12 the teacher might with profit spend some time discussing this idea with them

1 For example, if 5 boys are asked to stand like this:

the following discussion might take place:

    Teacher: 'How many boys have we here?'
    Children: 'Three.'
    Teacher: 'And how many here?'
    Children: 'Two.'
    Teacher: 'How many altogether?'
    Children: 'Five.'
    Teacher and children: 'Three and two more make five.'

After physically re-arranging the boys like this:

similar questions and responses could follow. In this case the first question would be:

    Teacher: 'How many boys have we here?'
    Children: 'Two.'
    Teacher and children: 'Two and three more makes five.'

Workbook 5: Addition to 5   **89**

2   The number 'stories' could be written on the blackboard:

$$3+2=5 \qquad 2+3=5$$

The dialogue above could then be repeated with six girls standing like this:

This time the children need not be physically re-arranged half way through the discussion.

3   The teacher might also demonstrate the principle by having, say, four cubes in one hand and two in the other.

Discussion similar to that outlined above could take place, the teacher emphasizing by use of her hands which number is mentioned *first* in the addition.

Interlocking cubes of two different colours might also be used.

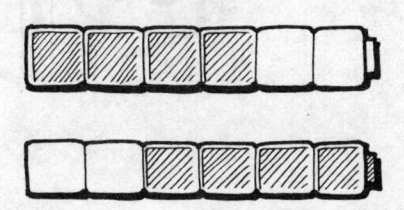

Page 12 — Add — Twin facts

Materials   As for Pages 1 and 2.

The teacher should discuss this page with the children before they begin.

For instance, the children could be asked to count the cats (four). They could then be asked to separate the cats with their pencil in different ways:

and then be asked to say the corresponding 'stories' of four:

'One and three (makes four).' 'Two and two.' 'Three and one'.

After the page has been completed it may be used as a basis for further discussion and questions aimed at emphasizing the 'twins' principle.

Flash cards could also be used for this purpose. For example:

Shopping activities

The class shop is mentioned in Appendix 1 on Free play (page 227). The shop and the activities associated with it form an important part of the 5 year-old child's education in the use of money.

1   A basic activity consists of the child 'buying' articles with 1 penny coins. The prices should be stated by the teacher-'shopkeeper', or child-'shopkeeper,' or should be displayed on price tickets, and the child-'shopper' then allowed to purchase *two* articles of known price. No price ticket should be for more than 5p.

Workbook 5: Addition to 5

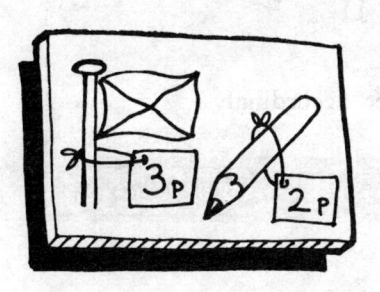

The child-'shopper' counts out pennies to the value of the articles and says what the *total* price is. Alternatively the prices may be added mentally, and 4 pennies counted out in payment.

If 'concrete' articles are not available, cardboard imitations will do.

2 Another activity which relates to the work on Page 14, involves 'pricing up' articles.

The child-'shopkeeper' is given the job of putting up all prices by 2p. For example, for an article which is priced at 4p, the new price must be worked out and the price ticket altered accordingly.

This may be done by setting down four 1p coins, adding 2 more, and finding the total, or the new price of 6p may be arrived at by recall of addition fact

$$4 + 2 = 6$$

Activity of this kind is highly desirable to ensure that children have a good understanding of simple addition problems involving money, so that they are well prepared for exercises such as those appearing on Pages 13 and 14.

3 Practice with flashcards would also be worthwhile.

| buy | new | prices | make | each | more |

4 The teacher might also prepare children for Pages 13 and 14 by doing blackboard work which imitates the work of the pages:

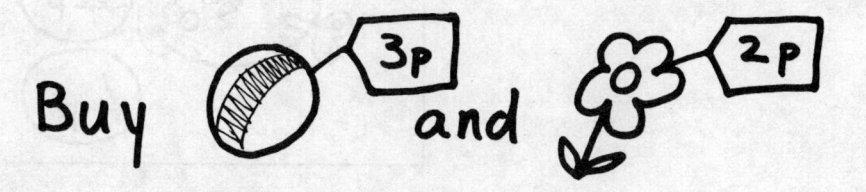

Teacher: 'How much would you need altogether?'

92 Workbook 5: Addition to 5

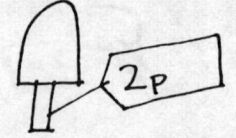

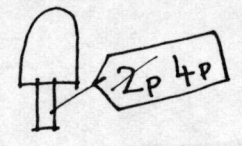

or, 'Make the price 2p more.'
and the child alters the 'price ticket' accordingly.

| **Page 13** | **Shopping** | Totals to 6p |

Materials   1p coins; coloured pencils or crayons.

This page requires children to use their knowledge of addition facts with totals to 6p. Some children may need to use coins in order to arrive at the total cost.

Children should also be reminded to write over the dotted 'p' which comes after each 'box' and shows that the answer is an amount of money and not just a number.

| **Page 14** | **New prices** | Totals to 6p |

Materials   As for Page 13.

In doing this page, children are required to use their knowledge of addition facts with totals to 6 and, in particular, the facts involving adding on 1 and adding on 2. They should cross out the old price and write the new price in the 'blank' price ticket.

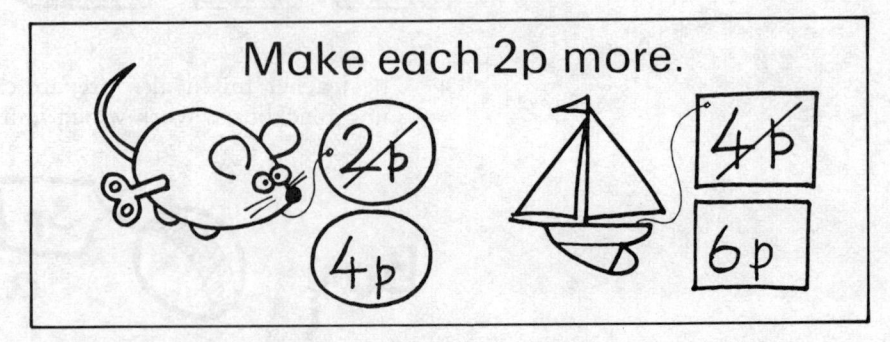

Some children may still need the security of having coins to help them arrive at the answer.

Workbook 5: Addition to 5   93

Mapping diagrams

Some teaching is necessary to explain this form of recording to children. This can be done effectively by blackboard diagrams.
 Initially, examples with *one* arrow only should be practised. Examples with *two* arrows may be dealt with subsequently.

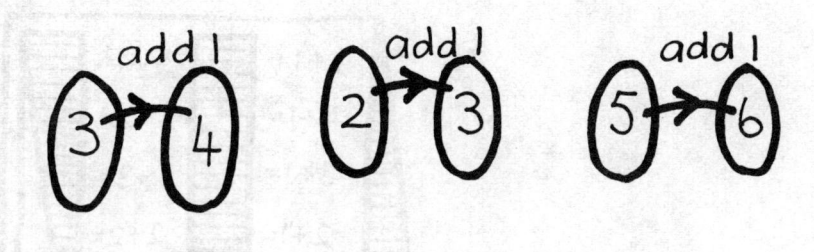

Children have to be taught that, for any given example, the arrows in the diagram all mean *the same* although each arrow does not have the words 'add 1', say, written above it.

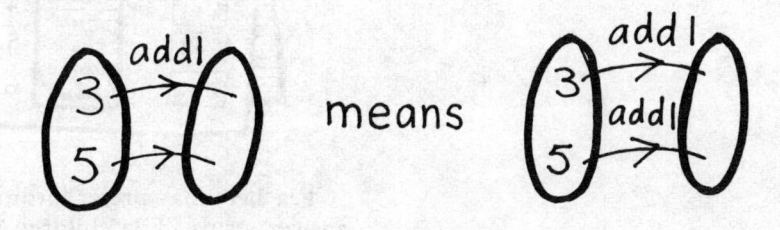

Once the teacher is satisfied that children understand this kind of recording, they can be asked to attempt Page 15.

| Page 15 | **Add** | Totals to 6 |

Materials   Counters, cubes, etc.

This page gives practice with mapping diagrams as referred to in the preceding notes.

Workbook 5: Addition to 5

Additional activities

Some children will continue to need concrete material to help them with the addition facts.

All children will require further practice in doing additions with totals to 6. Here are a few further suggestions.

1 *'Window' cards* like the one supplied in **Teacher's Materials Pack**, Card 14, are useful.

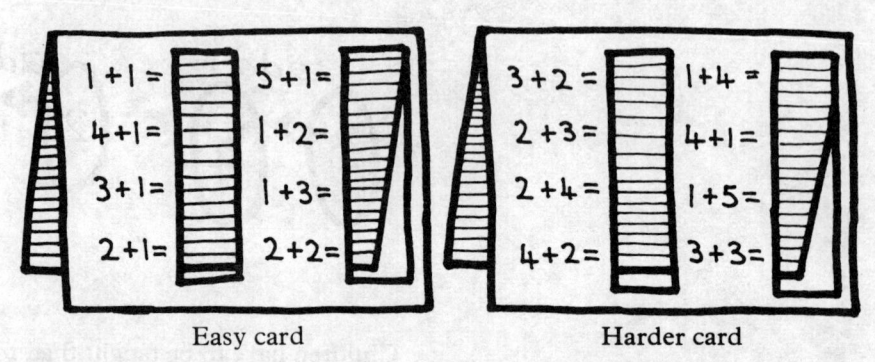

Easy card   Harder card

2 *'Window'* or plastic-covered *'wipeable'* matching cards are also useful.

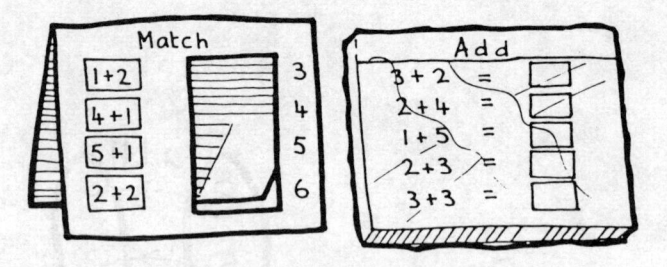

Teachers may prefer 'ordinary' workcards to which they can clip answer strips. The children then write matching lines or answers on the strips.

3 *Flashcards* are useful for giving frequent oral practice in the addition facts. Children may also be given, say, 5 flashcards to arrange in order, as an individual exercise. The ordered cards might look like this:

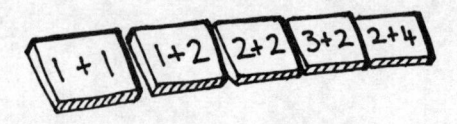

This kind of exercise may be self-checking if the total is written on the reverse side of each card.

4 *Snake game* This is a simple track game. Each child has a counter and progresses by turning up a card from a 'face-down' pile, e.g. $\boxed{3+2}$ would entitle him to move forward 5 squares.

A game like this is provided on Cards 2 and 3 of the **Teacher's Materials Pack**.

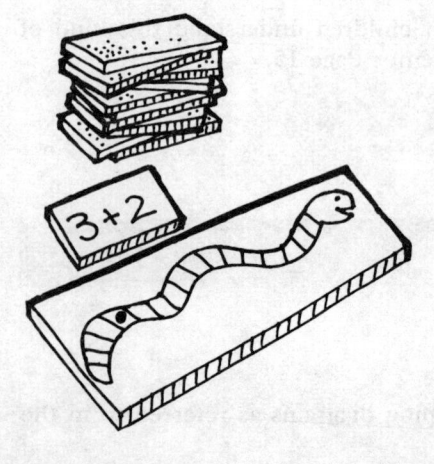

Workbook 5: Addition to 5   95

5 *Animal jigsaws* The child proceeds by matching the 'total' pieces to the corresponding part of the 'board'. Cards 11 and 12 of the **Teacher's Materials Pack** contain jigsaws like these.

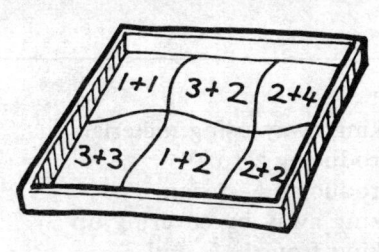

6 *Fishing game* (similar to that on Card 13 of **Teacher's Materials Pack**). The child 'fishes' for numbered fish, two at a time. The numbers on the two fish are added and this score is compared with the opponents' scores.

The fish may have paper-clip 'noses' and be fished for with magnet fishing lines, or they may simply be 'face-down' cards which are turned up two at a time.

Workbook 6

Subtraction within 6

Contents

Taking away using materials	Pages 1 to 3
Introducing zero '0'	Page 4
Introducing '−' sign	Page 5
Taking away by covering up	Pages 6 and 7
Taking from 1, 2, and 3	Page 8
Taking from 4	Page 9
Taking from 5	Page 10
Taking from 6	Page 11
Miscellaneous examples and problems	Page 12
Subtraction of money within 6p	Pages 13 and 14
Mapping diagrams for subtraction	Page 15

Materials

Counters, buttons, conkers, pebbles, toys, cubes, 1p coins, interlocking plastic Unifix-type cubes, etc.

The following cards from the **Teacher's Materials Pack** should be useful for some of the work in this Workbook:

    Counting to 8 cards (Cards 6 and 7)
    Window card (Card 14)
    Fair game (Cards 15 and 16)

It would be worth making flashcards to cover new words and phrases used in the booklet, for example:

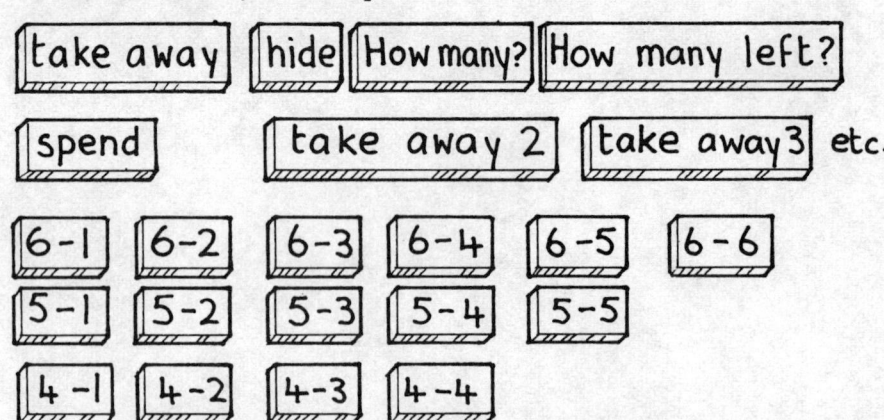

| take away | hide | How many? | How many left? |

| spend | | take away 2 | take away 3 | etc.

6−1	6−2	6−3	6−4	6−5	6−6
5−1	5−2	5−3	5−4	5−5
4−1	4−2	4−3	4−4

Some teachers may prefer to make these cards with space for an answer:

| 6−4=☐ |

Workbook 6: Subtraction within 6   97

Subtraction within 6 (Pages 1 to 15)

Development

In the first part of the Workbook the concept of subtraction is introduced through the physical removal of objects from a set. Zero is introduced to record the answer when all the objects are removed and the ' − ' sign is used to replace 'take away'. The facts are dealt with in a random fashion at this stage.

In the second part of the Workbook the facts are systematized to aid memorization and some money and mapping ideas are included. Subtraction is further developed in **Workbook 9**.

Practical activities and teaching

Concept of subtraction

The idea of 'taking away' is the most important at this stage. Many concrete materials are available that are suitable for this work; some are listed above. The language of subtraction has to be developed, and this is best done orally. Much practical work should be done before children progress to the written work. Here are some activities which help to establish the idea of physical removal.

1   **Children on the floor**
    Ask 5 children to come forward. Send two back, or outside the door, and ask, 'How many are left?'

2   **Milk bottle activities**
    Put out 6 milk bottles.
    Let 3 children take their milk.
    Then ask, 'How many left?'

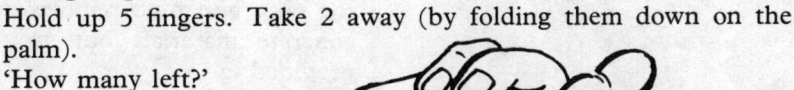

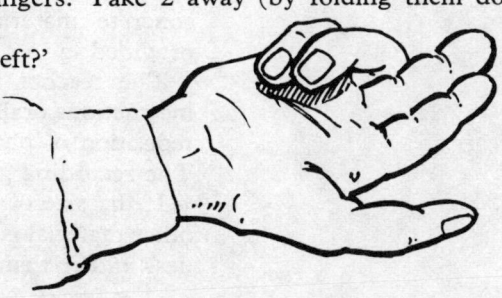

3   **Using fingers**
    Hold up 5 fingers. Take 2 away (by folding them down on the palm).
    'How many left?'

Workbook 6: Subtraction within 6

4 Dots on blackboard
Make dots or shapes on the blackboard. Ask a child to count them, and then to rub out say 2, 'How many are left?'

5 Putting out objects

"Take away 1 sweet."

"four sweets"

"three sweets left"

6 Using a sorting box
Articles could be put in some compartments and children have to carry out the instruction [take away 2] or [take away 3].

Flashcards may be used for this.

These are a sample of activities which could be done orally. The children would not be expected to read the instructions.

Another technique used in the Workbook involves covering or hiding objects. Children may use a hand or a piece of card to do the covering. Again, examples involving this idea should be done prior to the Workbook pages.

| Page 1 | **Use counters** | Concept of subtraction |

Materials Counters.

Children are expected to lay out counters on top of all the circles on the page and then remove some. They are continuing to work with concrete materials but are recording their answers in the boxes provided.

The teacher should demonstrate what is required and give the instructions orally. Many children will find the words difficult, but the repetition of phrases should help as they progress through the book. The recording gives further practice in making the number symbols.

If the size of counter available does not suit the circles, or if some other material is used, the counting aids may have to be put out on the desk rather than on the page itself.

Workbook 6: Subtraction within 6

Page 2

Use 1p coins — Concept of subtraction

Materials 1p coins.

The work on this page could be done either by putting out a matching set of 1p coins, or by placing 1p coins on top of the pictures of coins and then taking away the appropriate number of coins. The teacher would have to ensure that the children knew what to do by giving the instructions orally.

The work is similar to that on Page 1 in layout and language. The coins are used as counters and a number is required for the answer, not a value. Later the question 'How much is left?' is used, and at that stage an answer will be recorded as '2p'.

Page 3

Use buttons — Concept of subtraction

Materials Buttons (or perhaps counters or cubes).

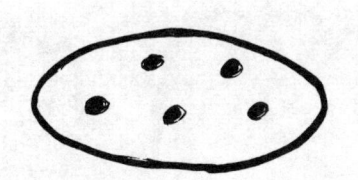

The '=' sign is used for the first time in this Workbook as is the new compact setting '6 take away 3'. Both of these will need careful explanation. The use of flashcards and blackboard work would help.

The use of the 'equals' sign is similar to its use in **Workbook 5**. There are many ways in which children may read it at this stage, namely, 'makes', 'gives', 'leaves', etc., and the choice of word is left to the teacher.

Since it may be difficult to find sufficient buttons to suit the drawings, children might have to put out a matching set on the desk instead of over the drawings. It may even be necessary to use some other material such as counters or cubes.

Page 4

Take away — Introducing 0

Materials Cubes, etc. (if necessary).

Before attempting this page there should be much practical work using materials and the children themselves. This is the first time they meet the symbol '0', so they will have to practise writing it. **Here are some activities to help children understand what is meant by zero.**

1. Bring out 3 children. Send 3 away. 'How many left?' Write '0' on the blackboard or use a flashcard.
2. Put out a set of objects, say 6 cars. Physically remove all 6 cars. 'How many are left?'
3. Draw sets on the blackboard. For example, draw 3 ducks, then a child rubs out 3. 'How many are left?'

It is important that the children put into words what they are doing. 'Four take away four'. 'How many are left?' 'None'; or 'Leaves none'; or 'What is left?' 'Nothing'; or 'No cubes left'; and so on.

Cubes or other suitable material should be used by children attempting this page. There are two examples which do not give the answer '0'. These are included to ensure that the children think about what they are doing for each example and do not just fill the page with zeros.

100 **Workbook 6:** Subtraction within 6

Page 5 — Take away — Introducing the − sign

Materials Cubes, etc. (if required).

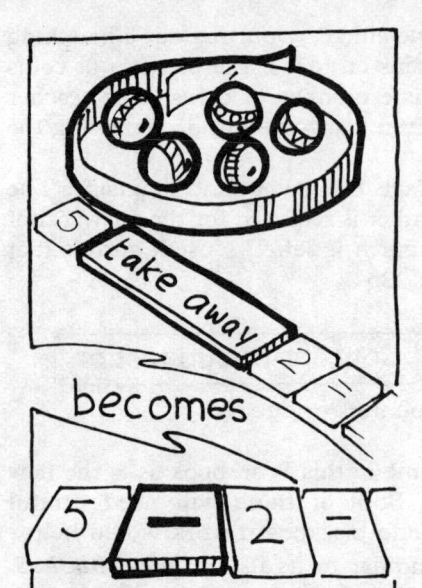

This page introduces the '−' sign for the first time. Activities, such as those described for Page 3, could be repeated and a flashcard of the sign '−' used to replace the 'take away' card, e.g. −

Blackboard explanations are also helpful.
The '−' sign should be read as 'take away' at this stage, rather than as 'minus' or 'subtract'.

Cubes or other suitable objects should be used by children attempting the work on this page.

Pages 6 and 7 — Hide — Concept of subtraction

Materials None.

These pages contain a new idea and some preliminary work should be done before tackling the pages. The children could put out some objects; then cover some with a hand or piece of card, and see how many are left. Drawings of birds, flowers, etc., on the blackboard could be covered in a similar way and again the appropriate language and questions should be used. A flashcard with the word hide might be helpful to introduce the new word.

On the Workbook pages the children have to make use of the pictures. They first count the objects and enter the answer in the upper box. They then 'hide' the appropriate number and count how many are left. The answer is recorded in the second box. The covering can be done with fingers, but some children may prefer to use a piece of card.

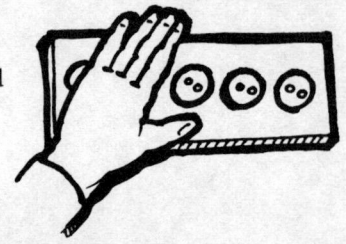

Workbook 6: Subtraction within 6

Memorizing facts

The preliminary activities and those outlined on Pages 1 to 7 are concerned with developing the child's understanding of the concept of subtraction. The facts are presented in a random order and children are not expected to have memorized all these subtraction facts at this stage.

Pages 8 to 11 present subtraction stories in a systematic way and the children should now be encouraged to memorize the facts. This is a long process which will be helped by constant oral practice. Children should be encouraged to recall the facts without the use of concrete materials. Less able pupils may still require to use materials or some visual aid.

Here are a few suggestions for oral and practical work. There are many other ways in which this could be done.

1. Large picture cards could be used.

   These could be removed and replaced to build up the stories for '4':

   $4 - 1 = 3$
   $4 - 2 = 2$ and so on.

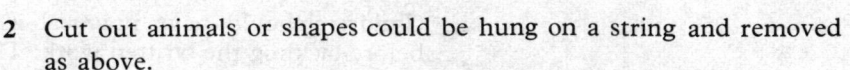

2. Cut out animals or shapes could be hung on a string and removed as above.

3. The children themselves could be used. Line up 5, say, and then 'take away':

   $5 - 1 = 4$
   $5 - 2 = 3$ and so on.

4. Use beads on a string or a simple abacus. The 'take away' this time is really putting to one side.

   In each case the beads have to be replaced before the next subtraction (always starting with 5 in this case).

   Interlocking cubes could be used in a similar way.

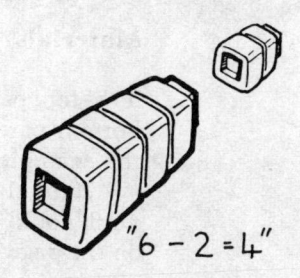

   "$6 - 2 = 4$"

Workbook 6: Subtraction within 6

5   A 'covering up' type of display card could be constructed. This is best used lying flat on the desk by a few children. If used in a vertical position it is necessary to devise some means of sticking the flaps in the 'up' position.

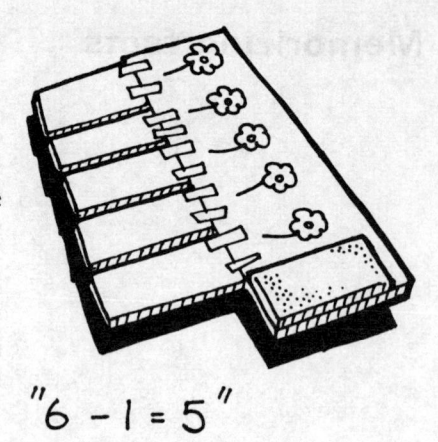

"6 − 1 = 5"

6   Some of the Number Rhymes and Songs (see Appendix 2, page 231) deal with subtraction ideas such as counting back 6, 5, 4, 3, 2, 1; jumping back in twos; etc. A song like '10 green bottles' is particularly suitable to illustrate taking away 1.

Page 8   Stories   Taking from 1, 2, and 3

Materials   Counters, cubes, etc. (if required).

Children should have practical experiences like those listed above before tackling the written work. They may wish to cover the pictures as an aid to finding the answers. The teacher could show children who find the work too difficult, or too abstract, how to use materials (counters, cubes, etc.) to find the answers.

The top part of the page gives the subtraction stories for 1, 2, and 3, but 'take away nothing' is not included. The bottom part of the page covers the facts again in a random way with repetitions for all but the two facts $1 - 1 = \square$ and $3 - 3 = \square$.

Children should use known 'memorized' facts to do the bottom part of the page if at all possible, otherwise they should use counters, cubes, etc., to do the subtractions.

Page 9   Stories   Taking from 4

Materials   Counters, cubes, etc. (if required).

The top part of the page gives the subtraction 'stories' for 4. The bottom part repeats these in random order, together with revision of the examples on Page 8.

Again, children who have difficulty with the abstract nature of the work could be shown how to use either actual objects, or the pictures on the page and a covering technique.

Workbook 6: Subtraction within 6

Page 10 | Stories | Taking from 5

Materials   Counters, cubes, etc. (if required).

The top part of the page covers the subtraction stories of 5. The bottom part gives a mixture of 'taking away' from 4 and 5.
   The well-known rhyme about 5 little ducks (Appendix 2) might be used here.
   Again, children who have difficulty with the abstract nature of the work could be shown how to use either actual objects, or the pictures on the page and a covering technique.

Page 11 | Stories | Taking from 6

Materials   Counters, cubes, etc. (if required).

The top part of the page gives the subtraction stories of 6. The bottom part contains a mixture of 'taking away' from 5 and 6.
   These higher order subtraction facts are more likely to cause difficulties, and using either concrete materials, or the pictures on the page and 'hiding', should help most children to find the answers.

Page 12 | Take away | Subtraction within 6

Materials   Counters, cubes, etc. (if required).

The top part of the page gives miscellaneous subtraction from 3, 4, 5, and 6. The bottom part of the page contains two word problems which may cause reading difficulties. Every effort should be made to help children read these problems and then carry out the instruction. For example, read

              'How many apples?'

The children then count the apples on the tree and record the answer in the box. Then read

              '2 fall off. How many left?'

This type of problem is used fairly often and it is hoped that children will soon recognize the words in the questions. Pictures are given to help the children. It is important that children meet this type of problem on the blackboard before attempting the page.

Cards for the teacher to make

At this stage teachers may wish to make practice cards to show other ways of systematizing the facts. For example, 'Take away 1'; 'Take away 2'; 'Take away 3'; etc.

Workbook 6: Subtraction within 6

Card 1:
1-1 =
2-1 =
3-1 =
4-1 =
5-1 =
6-1 =

Card 2:
2-2 =
3-2 =
4-2 =
5-2 =
6-2 =

Card 3:
3-3 =
4-3 =
5-3 =
6-3 =

Card 4:
4-4 =
5-4 =
6-4 =
5-5 =
6-5 =

These same subtraction facts could also be put on cards to give miscellaneous sets of examples, e.g.

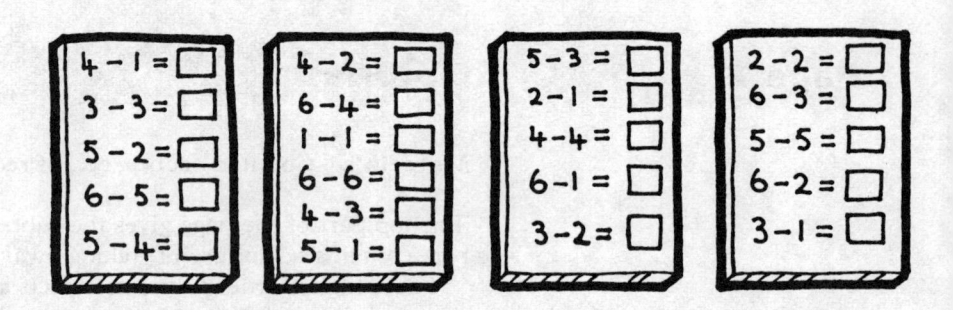

Card A:
4-1 =
3-3 =
5-2 =
6-5 =
5-4 =

Card B:
4-2 =
6-4 =
1-1 =
6-6 =
4-3 =
5-1 =

Card C:
5-3 =
2-1 =
4-4 =
6-1 =
3-2 =

Card D:
2-2 =
6-3 =
5-5 =
6-2 =
3-1 =

Another possibility for the 'Take away 1', 'Take away 2', cards would be to present these facts in random order.

Able pupils could copy everything from the card but less able children would be helped by clipping a blank strip of paper to the card. Only the answer would need to be filled in, and this strip would then be presented for correction.

Some cards could include the picture problem type, especially if the clip-on strip of paper is used for recording answers. Another possibility is to produce worksheets similar to Page 12.

Class shop (see Appendix 1, Free play)

Worksheet:
I have 4p
I spend ☐ p
I have ☐ p left
I have 5p ○

I have 5p
I spend ☐ p
I have ☐ p left
I have 6p

It is recommended that the shop is set up with articles priced up to and including 6p. This number restriction may make it impossible to have realistic prices on all articles.

The shop should be used prior to and in conjunction with Pages 13 and 14. The type of activity envisaged involves a child taking five 1p coins to the shop, spending 3p, and then counting how much is left. This practical work is very important.

It would be worthwhile preparing worksheets for the shop activities on which the children could record their purchases. The worksheets might be as shown on the left.

A flashcard with the word [spend] would be helpful when introducing the word.

Workbook 6: Subtraction within 6

Page 13 | Spending | Subtraction within 6p

Materials 1p coins (if necessary).

Practical activities, like those suggested above using the class shop, should be done before attempting the page. The whole page is about spending and purses and piggy-banks are used in the drawings. The subtraction is from 4p, 5p, and 6p and at no time does the child spend all the money. This is because of the difficulty in writing '0p' for an answer.

The teacher should explain, particularly to the poor readers, exactly what they have to do. This oral explanation together with the repeated phrases should help these children to cope with the work.

Page 14 | A sale | Subtraction within 6p

Materials 1p coins (if necessary).

Changing the prices in the class shop is a suitable activity to introduce this page. Some discussion about a sale and sales in general would be worthwhile. 'Why do your parents go to sales?'

The top part of the page deals with '2p off'; the bottom part with '3p off'. Children should cross out the given price and write the new price in the box. It is important to stress that in the top half 2p must be *taken off* each price.

Children would benefit from further work of this kind. Extra worksheets similar to Page 14 could be made, especially if duplicating facilities were available.

Extra work could be given on cards like these, provided the children had to write only the new price. This might be done by clipping a piece of paper to the card for the answer to be written on.

In **Workbook 5** on addition, children were asked to do a similar exercise about increasing prices.

Page 15 | Take away | Subtraction within 6

Materials 1p coins, cubes, counters, etc. (if required).

This page uses the mapping diagram method of recording. Children met this in **Workbook 5** but it will be worth reminding them that the one instruction applies to both numbers in the set. Similar examples can be demonstrated on the blackboard to ensure that the children know what they are expected to do in the Workbook. Zero facts are included when dealing with numbers, but are not included in the money examples.

106 Workbook 6: Subtraction within 6

Cards for the teacher to make

1 These miscellaneous example cards could be made using **Teacher's Materials Pack**, Card 14, as a template. This would allow the answers to be filled in without copying everything, and should help the less able pupils.

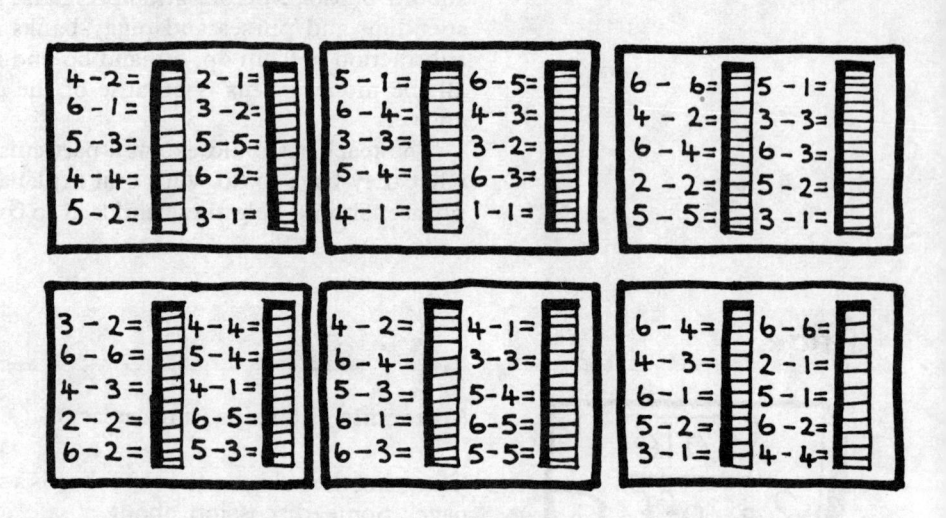

Card 1	Card 2	Card 3	Card 4	Card 5	Card 6
4−2= 2−1= 6−1= 3−2= 5−3= 5−5= 4−4= 6−2= 5−2= 3−1=	5−1= 6−5= 6−4= 4−3= 3−3= 3−2= 5−4= 6−3= 4−1= 1−1=	6−6= 5−1= 4−2= 3−3= 6−4= 6−3= 2−2= 5−2= 5−5= 3−1=	3−2= 4−4= 6−6= 5−4= 4−3= 4−1= 2−2= 6−5= 6−2= 5−3=	4−2= 4−1= 6−4= 3−3= 5−3= 5−4= 6−1= 6−5= 6−3= 5−5=	6−4= 6−6= 4−3= 2−1= 6−1= 5−1= 5−2= 6−2= 3−1= 4−4=

2 *Flashcards* As suggested in the materials list, it would be worth making flashcards of the subtraction facts. These could be of two types—one large set to be used with the class or group and a small set about playing-card size (16 to an A4 card). These small cards can be used by individual children or small groups to play games. Some possible games are suggested later.

The facts to cover at this stage are:

1−1=☐   2−2=☐   3−3=☐   4−4=☐   5−5=☐   6−6=☐
2−1=☐   3−2=☐   4−3=☐   5−4=☐   6−5=☐
3−1=☐   4−2=☐   5−3=☐   6−4=☐
4−1=☐   5−2=☐   6−3=☐
5−1=☐   6−2=☐
6−1=☐

Where a game would require equal numbers of cards giving each answer from, 0 to 5, possible additional cards would be:

6−1=☐   6−1=☐   6−1=☐   6−1=☐   6−1=☐
5−1=☐   6−2=☐   5−1=☐   6−2=☐
4−1=☐   5−2=☐   6−3=☐
5−3=☐   6−4=☐
6−5=☐

Workbook 6: Subtraction within 6

Additional activities

1. **Teacher's Materials Pack** Cards 6 and 7, 'Counting to 8 cards', could be used for subtraction activities. First select pictures with not more than 6 objects. These cards are ideal for the 'Hide' problems. An instruction such as 'Hide 3' could be written on the back. Children could record their answers as

$$5 - 3 = 2$$

2. Another possibility with these counting cards would be a single instruction for several cards. For example, 'Take away 1'; 'Take away 2'; etc. The recording would be $4 - 1 = 3$; $3 - 1 = 2$; and so on.

3. **Teacher's Materials Pack** Card 8 (Shopping cards) could be used in a similar way. The cards selected would have to have articles costing 6p or less. The sale technique could be used. 'Take 2p off'. 1p coins could be used by less able pupils. The recording in this case might be restricted to the answer only, since the 'p' should be shown.

"Take off 2p."

Record answer 3p

Games

The flashcards mentioned earlier can be used in several ways.

1. When the extra cards are included to give equal numbers of each answer, the flashcards can be used for 'snap'. Two or three children can play the game. Cards would be turned over in the same way as for 'ordinary snap', but 'snap' would be called when two cards gave the same answer.

   Snap could also be played with cards such as $\boxed{6 - 1 = \square}$ and $\boxed{5}$ giving a 'snap'.

2. The flashcards can be used as a method of progressing in a board game. The cards would be placed face down. The child who starts selects a card, works out the answer, and puts the card down 'face up'. If the answer is correct, the child can move the appropriate number of squares. If it is wrong no move is made. The next player then has a turn.

   Teacher's Materials Pack, Cards 15 and 16, provide a Fair Game that could be played in this way.

3. *Bingo* Here the flashcards could be used as caller cards.

   It is necessary to make up 'Players' cards for this game, but since the answers are all less than 6 a simple card with 4 numbers on it would be sufficient. Here are some possibilities.

108   Workbook 6: Subtraction within 6

Two or more children could play this game. Each player has a Player's card. The flashcards are used to produce the numbers. Each player in turn takes a card from the pile and answers it. If the answer is correct and that number is on that player's card, the number is covered with a counter. If it is wrong a counter is taken off, if one is on the card. If there are no counters, or if the number does not suit the card, the next player takes a turn.

This game is slightly different from ordinary bingo but it gives everyone a chance of working out the subtraction facts. When the pile of cards is used the discard pile is turned over and the game continues until a card is completed.

4   Individual children could match the flashcard to numerals or dot patterns, in a number recognition activity.
5   This game requires a die marked from 0 to 5. A flashcard is selected and the die thrown. If the answer to the card agrees with the die the player keeps the card. This game could be played by several children and the one to collect most cards wins.

6   *Counter game for two or more children*   Each child should lay out their counters in rows as shown. A die is thrown and the appropriate number of counters is removed. A six would have to be thrown to remove the row of 6 counters, but the child could instead choose to remove rows which total to 6, say 5 and 1; 4 and 2; or 3, 2, and 1. This gives some element of choice, within the restriction that whole rows must be removed each time. If a '3' is thrown counters can be taken from the '3 row' or the '1' and '2' rows', but not from any of the others. The first person to lose all his counters is the winner.

This game brings in addition as well as the removal of objects.

Workbook 6: Subtraction within 6

7 *Ring-a-Roses* This is an action game for 6 children in a ring. They go round singing (with the teacher's help):
    Ring-a-ring-a roses,
    A pocketful of posies,
    Atishoo! Atishoo!
    And two fall down. [Teacher touches two children on head.]
    How many left standing?
The rhyme is then repeated.

Workbook 7

Addition to 8

Contents

Revision of addition to 6	Pages 1 and 2
Addition involving 0	Page 3
'Twin' facts and 'doubles'	Page 4
Miscellaneous practice in addition to 6	Page 5
Totals to 7	Pages 6 to 8
Totals to 8	Pages 9 to 11
'Twin' facts; totals to 8	Page 12
Addition of money to 8p	Pages 13 and 14
Problems	Page 15

Materials

Small objects for counting such as:
  counters, beads, buttons, bricks, Unifix-type and other cubes, 1p coins, coloured pencils, crayons
Flashcards:

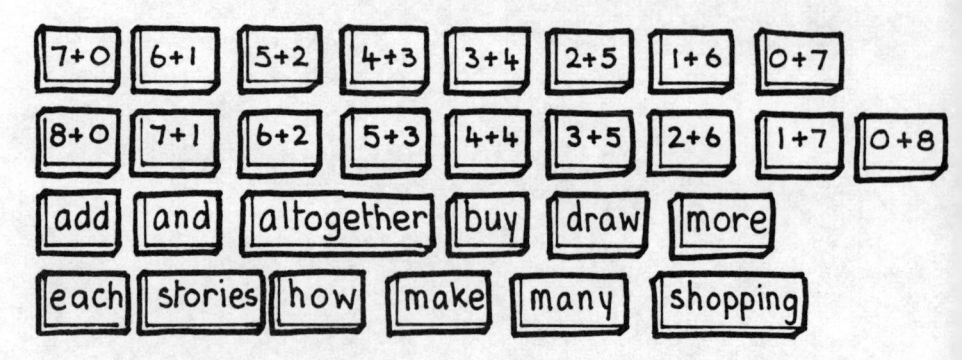

7+0 6+1 5+2 4+3 3+4 2+5 1+6 0+7
8+0 7+1 6+2 5+3 4+4 3+5 2+6 1+7 0+8

add and altogether buy draw more
each stories how make many shopping

The following cards from the ***Teacher's Materials Pack*** could be useful for addition with totals to 8:
Counting to 4 cards (Card 1)
Snake game (Cards 2 and 3)
Counting to 4 game (Cards 4 and 5)
Counting to 8 cards (Cards 6 and 7)
Shopping cards (Card 8)
Animal jigsaws (Card 11 and 12)
Fishing game (Card 13)
Window card (Card 14)
Fair game (Cards 15 and 16)

Workbook 7: Addition to 8

Addition to 8 (Pages 1 to 15)

Development

In **Workbook 5**, addition to 6 was dealt with, including addition of 1p coins to totals of 6p.

Workbook 7 deals with revision of addition to 6 and goes on to deal with the addition facts to totals of 7 and then to totals of 8. Additions with zero are also introduced for the first time, the zero having been first introduced in **Workbook 6** in the context of subtraction. 'Doubles' are also included.

The work of this book is continued in **Workbook 8** with addition to totals of 9 and 10.

Practical activities and teaching

Revision of addition to 6

Before the children are asked to attempt Pages 1 and 2, the teacher should involve them in some oral and practical work aimed at revising the addition facts with totals to 6.

Here are a few suggestions:

1 Using children themselves to illustrate the 'stories', for example

"3 + 2 = 5"

2 Children make up and record the addition stories using, say, Unifix-type cubes or similar materials.

(3 + 1 = 4)

(2 + 2 = 4)

Workbook 7: Addition to 8

3 Cardboard figures which may be moved along a 'washing line'.

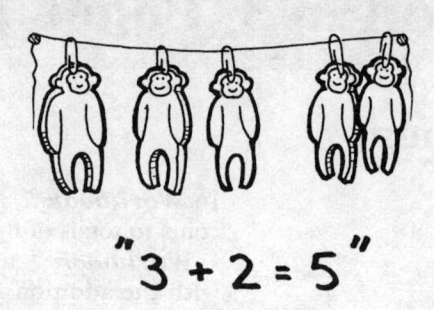

"3 + 2 = 5"

4 Flashcard work

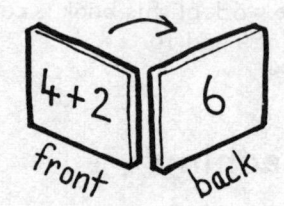

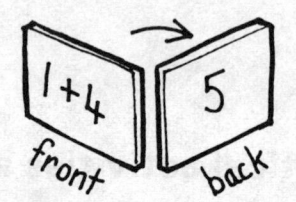

4 + 2 | 6
front | back

1 + 4 | 5
front | back

5 Practice with 'window' or other workcards.

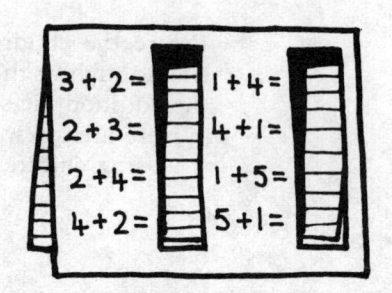

3 + 2 =
2 + 3 =
2 + 4 =
4 + 2 =

1 + 4 =
4 + 1 =
1 + 5 =
5 + 1 =

Pages 1 and 2 — Stories of 3, 4, 5, and 6 [Revision]

"3 + 1 = 4"

Materials Counters, beads, cubes, etc. (to be available if required); flashcards: [stories] [and]

After some oral and practical work such as that outlined in the preceding notes, children may proceed to Pages 1 and 2.
  There are two types of example on each page:
(a) Examples in which there are countable objects, such as three balloons of one colour and one balloon of a different colour

(b) Examples which require the recall of known facts, e.g.

2 + 2 = ☐

Workbook 7: Addition to 8

The teacher may wish to provide further similar work for the children after they have completed Pages 1 and 2. This could take the form of worksheets, 'wipeable' or other workcards, oral work with flashcards, and so on.

Addition with zero

We saw in the notes for **Workbook 6** that zero was introduced as the result of starting with, say, a set of 5 objects and taking away all 5 so that nothing remained. This was then recorded as

$$5 - 5 = 0.$$

Children have now to learn to deal with 0 in the context of addition. The following note describes a good preliminary activity for helping children to understand addition with zero.

The teacher puts 3 beads in the child's right hand, say. Then the following dialogue might take place.

Teacher: 'How many beads in that hand?'
Child: 'Three'
Teacher: 'How many beads in this other hand?'
Child: 'None'
Teacher: 'Now bring both your hands close together. How many beads have you *altogether*?'
Child: 'Three'
Teacher: 'We say "three and nothing makes three". We write it down like this'

$$3 + 0 = 3$$

This should be repeated many times with different children. Later, the same kind of activity should take place, the teacher pointing this time to the *empty hand first* and then to the hand containing the beads, cubes, etc.

This leads to the verbalization

'Nothing and three makes three'

and to the recording

$$0 + 3 = 3$$

After this kind of activity and discussion, children could be asked to attempt Page 3 of the Workbook.

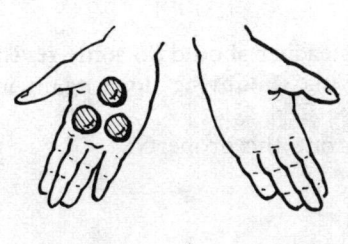

114   Workbook 7: Addition to 8

Page 3 — Stories with 0 — Addition with 0

Materials Counters, beads, cubes, etc., should be available if required; flashcard `stories`

This page provides practice in adding 0 to a number and in adding a number to 0. The page should only be attempted by children when the teacher is satisfied that they have had sufficient practical experience designed to establish the concept of adding nothing.

Further oral and written practice could be given by the teacher to reinforce the children's learning of these new addition facts.

Teaching suggestions

Twin facts—the commutative property

Before the children attempt Page 4 the teacher should do some revision of the 'twin' facts with totals to 6. This should be done again in a number of ways, for example:-

(a) Using children themselves to illustrate the property:

$2 + 3 = 5$

$3 + 2 = 5$

(b) Using cubes in the hands, and emphasizing by use of hand movement which number is taken first:

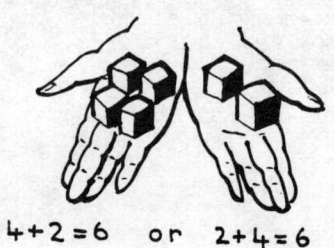

$4 + 2 = 6$ or $2 + 4 = 6$

(c) Use of interlocking cubes:

$5 + 1 = 6$

$1 + 5 = 6$

Doubles

The 'doubles' facts which appear on Page 4 should first be illustrated by concrete and visual means.

Verbalization and written recording should be practised.

'One and one make two' ⟶ $1 + 1 = 2$

'Two and two make four' ⟶ $2 + 2 = 4$
and so on.

"$1 + 1 = 2$"

"$2 + 2 = 4$"

'Three and three make six' ⟶ $3 + 3 = 6$
and so on.

$3 + 3 = 6$

The 'doubles' idea may also be illustrated on the blackboard:

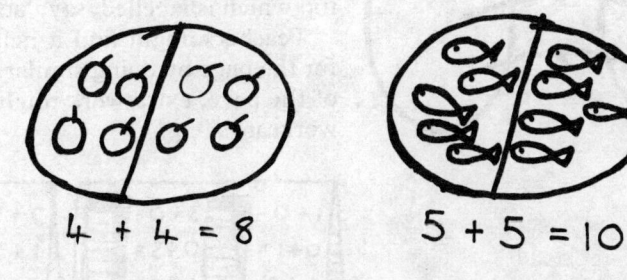

$4 + 4 = 8$

$5 + 5 = 10$

116 Workbook 7: Addition to 8

Page 4 — Add — Twin facts and doubles

Materials Counters, beads, buttons, cubes, etc., should be available in case they are needed; flashcard [add]

The top part of this page provides revision of the 'twin' facts with totals to 6. Children should be reminded to work *down* the page rather than across so that their attention is drawn to the 'twin' facts. When the top part of the page has been done the teacher should again take the opportunity to question orally on these facts since they are so important to the learning and memorization processes.

The bottom part of the page is devoted to the 'doubles' facts

$$1+1=2$$
$$2+2=4$$
$$3+3=6$$
$$4+4=8$$
$$5+5=10$$

The last fact is included since it goes naturally enough with the others listed. This is a minor departure from the main purpose of the workbook which is to concentrate on the addition facts with totals to 8. Further practice may be given by the teacher, both oral and written, according to the children's needs.

Page 5 — Add — Revision Totals to 6

add 2

4 →
3 →
2 →

Materials As for Page 4.

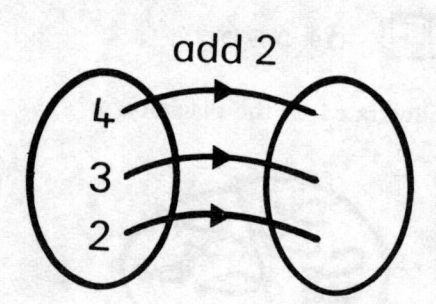

This page gives revision of addition facts with totals to 6. Some zero facts are included. The bottom half of the page provides further experience of recording additions using mapping diagrams. Teachers should remind children that *all* arrows in any one diagram mean the same as the one at the top which is labelled, say, 'add 2'.

Teachers might find it helpful to give some preliminary preparation for the page by doing similar work on the blackboard. After completion of the page, extra work might be given orally, or on worksheets, or on workcards, e.g.:

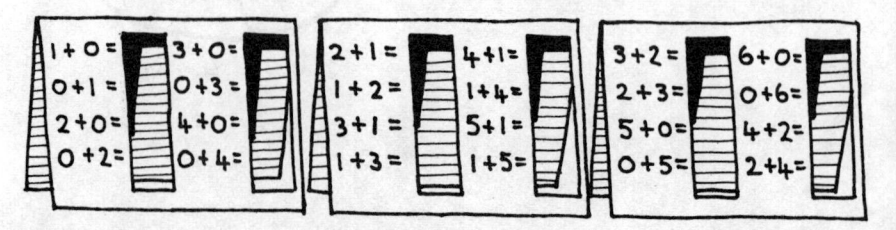

1+0=	3+0=	2+1=	4+1=	3+2=	6+0=
0+1=	0+3=	1+2=	1+4=	2+3=	0+6=
2+0=	4+0=	3+1=	5+1=	5+0=	4+2=
0+2=	0+4=	1+3=	1+5=	0+5=	2+4=

Other 'collections' of examples might be based on adding on 1; adding on 2; 'doubles'; etc.

Workbook 7: Addition to 8   117

| Page 6 | Stories of 7 | Totals of 7 |

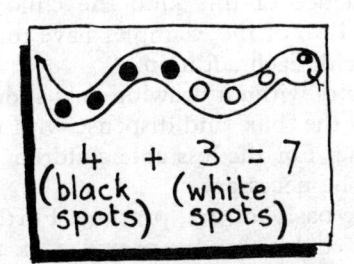

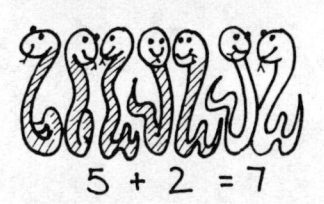

Materials   Flashcard: stories

Before children attempt this page the teacher should spend some time explaining, with blackboard illustrations, how the page is to be completed. The top part of the page should be dealt with first.

Children have to understand that the numbers are written underneath to correspond to the spots of one colour (4, in this case) and the spots of the other colour (3, in this case). They then get the total by counting all the spots. Children should be warned to leave enough room at the right for writing the answer 7.

In the examples on the bottom part of the page, they have to write numbers according to the number of whole snakes of *one* colour and the number of whole snakes of the *second* colour.

All the pair bonds for 7, or complements of 7, (except the zero facts) are illustrated in the six 'spotty snake' examples, i.e.

6+1, 5+2, 4+3, 3+4, 2+5 and 1+6

On the lower part of the page four of the pair bonds are represented again, this time with the complete snakes of contrasting colour

    i.e.   5+2, 4+3, 3+4 and 2+5

The teacher might use the completed page as the basis for oral practice on the stories of 7.

| Page 7 | Draw and add | Totals to 7 |

Materials   Coloured pens or crayons; flashcards: draw and add

Before children attempt this page the teacher should explain, with blackboard illustrations, what is to be done.

The following example might be used:

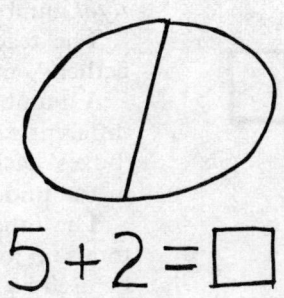

5 + 2 = ☐

118 Workbook 7: Addition to 8

A child is invited to draw five dots in the left-hand part and two dots in the right-hand part. The child then counts the total number of dots and writes the answer in the 'box':

This is repeated for other additions, different children being chosen to draw the dots and find the answer.

After they have had sufficient practice of this kind the children should be asked to attempt the page. Two of the examples have totals of 6, so the children must take care with each addition.

Children who are able to add correctly without drawing dots should be encouraged to write the answers in the 'box' and dispense with the drawing of dots if they find this boring. For the less able children, on the other hand, the dots are likely to be necessary.

The completed page might form the basis for oral practice. Further worksheets or 'wipeable' workcards could also be provided if the teacher felt this to be necessary.

Page 8 — Add — Totals to 7

Materials Counters, cubes, buttons, etc. (for those children who may need them); flashcards: add . How many altogether?

Before the children are asked to do this page, the teacher should explain, with the aid of blackboard illustrations, word and picture 'problems' of the type shown in the middle of the page. For example:

The teacher should discuss this with the children to make sure they understand that they write a number in each of the top two 'boxes' to correspond with the chicks to the left of the 'box', and that they write the *total* number of chicks in the bottom 'box'.

The teacher should also point to the question, 'How many altogether?', and say the words with the children.

A number of examples like this should be 'talked through' and different children asked to come out and write the numerals in the 'boxes' each time. The children should then be ready for the examples in the middle of the page.

The other examples on the page are miscellaneous additions with totals up to 7 requiring recall of known facts. Counters, cubes, etc., may be used by children when they are unsure of the answer.

Workbook 7: Addition to 8

Consolidation—cards for the teacher to make

Before going on to the work in the remaining part of the Workbook, teachers may wish to give children further oral and written practice in the addition facts covered so far. Here are some suggestions:

1. Below are 6 specimen cards which include all the addition facts for 5, 6, and 7, including zero facts. There are 17 totals of 7, 7 totals of 6, and 6 totals of 5 in these cards.

Add	Add	Add	Add	Add	Add
1 + 5 =	2 + 5 =	5 + 2 =	5 + 1 =	6 + 1 =	0 + 6 =
0 + 7 =	2 + 3 =	1 + 6 =	6 + 1 =	3 + 2 =	5 + 2 =
5 + 0 =	4 + 2 =	4 + 1 =	4 + 3 =	7 + 0 =	3 + 4 =
3 + 4 =	4 + 3 =	0 + 7 =	0 + 5 =	4 + 3 =	3 + 3 =
6 + 0 =	4 + 1 =	7 + 0 =	2 + 4 =	2 + 5 =	1 + 6 =

2. Cards which help to consolidate the 'twin' or commutative facts are also useful. For example,

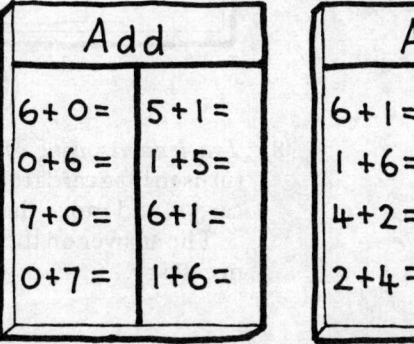

Add		Add	
6 + 0 =	5 + 1 =	6 + 1 =	5 + 2 =
0 + 6 =	1 + 5 =	1 + 6 =	2 + 5 =
7 + 0 =	6 + 1 =	4 + 2 =	4 + 3 =
0 + 7 =	1 + 6 =	2 + 4 =	3 + 4 =

3. Cards with examples involving adding on 1, adding on 2, etc., might also be provided to cover the following facts:

0 + 1	4 + 1	1 + 2	5 + 2	3 + 3	2 + 4	2 + 5	1 + 0	5 + 0
1 + 1	5 + 1	2 + 2	0 + 3	4 + 3	3 + 4	0 + 6	2 + 0	6 + 0
2 + 1	6 + 1	3 + 2	1 + 3	0 + 4	0 + 5	1 + 6	3 + 0	7 + 0
3 + 1	0 + 2	4 + 2	2 + 3	1 + 4	1 + 5	0 + 7	4 + 0	0 + 0

4. *Illustrated 'stories' of 5, 6, and 7* Children could be asked to make, say, the 'stories' of 7, using squared paper and crayons. Each story could be recorded alongside:

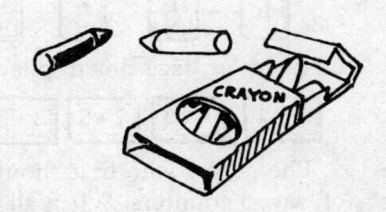

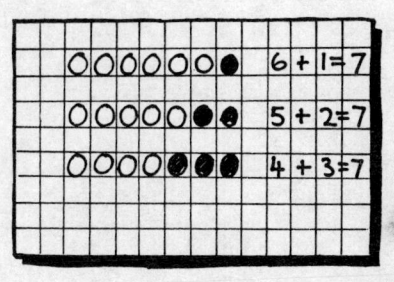

$6 + 1 = 7$
$5 + 2 = 7$
$4 + 3 = 7$

120 Workbook 7: Addition to 8

"stories of 6"

4+2
0+6
3+3

"stories of 7"

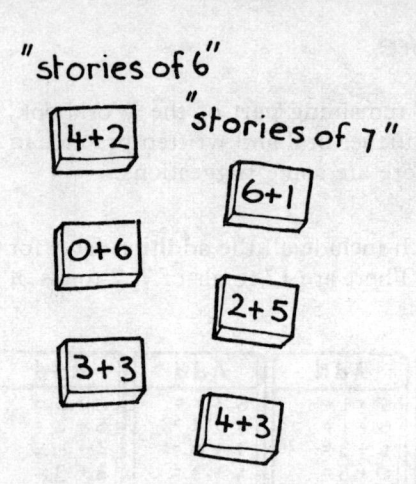

6+1
2+5
4+3

5 *Flashcard work* Sorting cards into sets, e.g. 'stories of 6' and 'stories of 7'.
6 Oral 'problems', e.g.:
   'Four birds sat on a tree. Two more came to sit beside them. How many birds were there altogether?'
7 Matching activities using workcards with a strip of paper clipped on, or plastic-covered 'wipeable' cards, e.g.

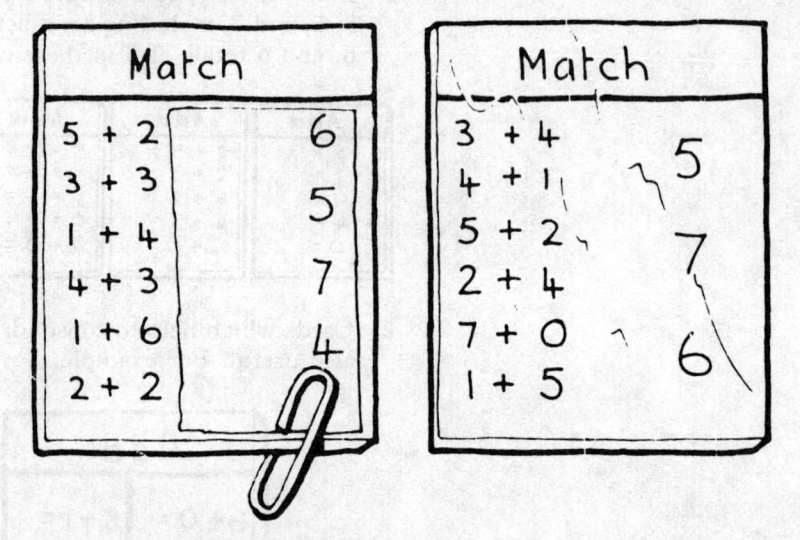

Match
5 + 2   6
3 + 3
1 + 4   5
4 + 3   7
1 + 6
2 + 2   4

Match
3 + 4   5
4 + 1
5 + 2   7
2 + 4
7 + 0   6
1 + 5

8 *Track games using cards instead of dice* Children play in pairs taking turns to lift a card from a 'face-up' pile. They say what the answer to the card is and move their counter accordingly.
   The answer on the reverse side of the cards may be used as a check if necessary.

4+3
1+3
3+2
2+2
0+5

9 *Game of 'Snap'* Two children play. One has set of cards in a 'face-down' pile, each card having one number on it,
   e.g. [4] [5] [5] [7], etc. The other child has a set of cards in *his* 'face-down' pile, each one of the type
   [3+2] [4+0] [2+5] [3+3], etc.
   The player who first shouts 'snap' takes a counter from a 'kitty' of, say, 5 counters. When all the counters have been taken the child who has more counters is the winner.

Workbook 7: Addition to 8   121

Stories of 8

Children should be given experience of the complements of 8 in various practical ways before they go on to try Page 9. This experience might include using:

(a) the children themselves to illustrate the 'stories';

$\rightarrow 5 + 3 = 8$

(b) the 'washing line' idea with cardboard figures which can be moved to form the different stories;

$\rightarrow 6 + 2 = 8$

(c) interlocking cubes;

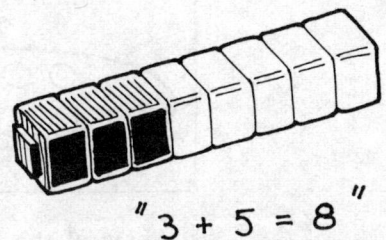

"$3 + 5 = 8$"

(d) pegs in peg board, arranged in rows of 8 pegs in two contrasting colours;
(e) squared paper and crayons of two contrasting colours to illustrate the different stories.

| **Page 9** | **Stories of 8** | Totals of 8 |

Materials None, except perhaps flashcard [stories]

Before children attempt this page the teacher should discuss what needs to be done with the help of blackboard illustrations. It must be explained that numbers have to be written to correspond to the eggs of one colour and to the eggs of the second colour.

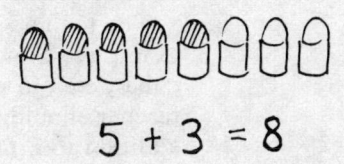

$5 + 3 = 8$

122 Workbook 7: Addition to 8

Children should be asked, in turn, to write the story under the blackboard 'picture'.

When the teacher is satisfied that children understand what is required they can be asked to do Page 9.

All the 'stories' of eight, except those with zero, are included. Four of the stories are repeated on the lower part of the page. After the page has been completed the teacher might use it as a basis for oral practice; the children read the 'stories' on the page and later try to say them without looking at the page.

Page 10 — Draw and add — Totals to 8

Materials Coloured pencils or crayons; flashcards [draw] [and] [add]

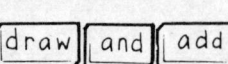

The work of this page is similar to that on Page 7. Again, the teacher should do some preparatory blackboard work as described in the note for Page 7. Thereafter, the children may proceed to do Page 10.

Two of the examples have totals of 7, not 8, so the children have to take care with each addition.

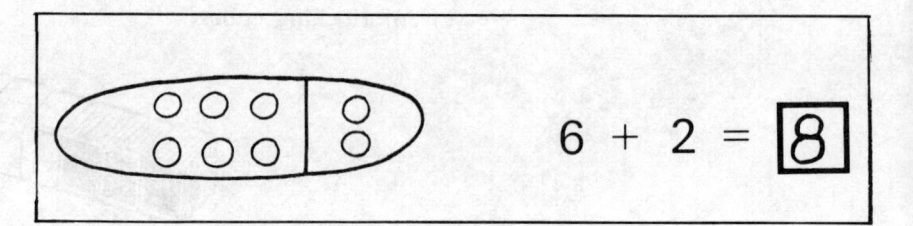

$$6 + 2 = \boxed{8}$$

Some of the children may manage the additions without drawing dots. The teacher need not insist that dots are drawn if a child finds this boring and unnecessary.

Further work of a similar nature could be given if the teacher felt it to be necessary.

Page 11 — Add — Totals to 8

Materials As for Pages 1 and 2; flashcards of important words [add] [How many altogether?]

This page is very similar to Page 8 and the notes for Page 8 are also apt for Page 11. Some blackboard illustration and discussion of the 'word and picture' type of problem would be beneficial to prepare children for the work on the page.

The top and bottom parts of the page provide miscellaneous practice examples. Slow learning children should have access to counters or cubes, etc., in case they have difficulty with any of the examples. The teacher should continue with further oral and written work relating to addition to 8 to help promote memorization of the facts.

Workbook 7: Addition to 8   123

| Page 12 | Add | Twin facts   Totals to 8 |

Materials   As for Pages 1 and 2; flashcard `add`

The top part of this page gathers together the important 'twin' facts for 7 and 8. The teacher should discuss the facts with the children before, and indeed after, they do the page, and again draw their attention to the fact that 4 + 3 gives the same total as 3 + 4; 6 + 2 the same as 2 + 6; and so on.

Although children often have these facts presented to them, as they are here, they do not always grasp this important concept unless the teacher takes every opportunity to emphasize it. Frequent use of actual objects and also the children themselves helps to make this commutative property more obvious—time spent in this way is not wasted.

The bottom part of the page gives further experience of recording additions by means of mapping diagrams.

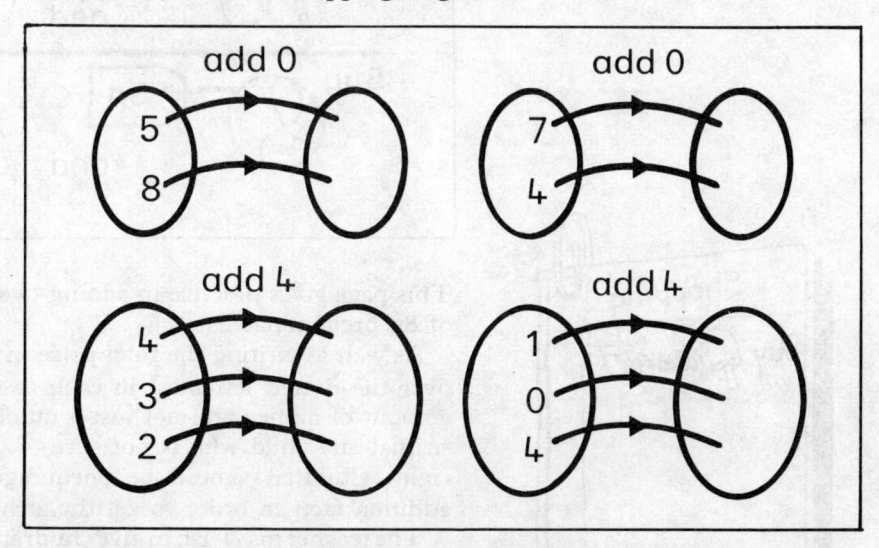

A little preliminary blackboard work would be helpful. Teachers should remind children that, for a given diagram, the arrows *all* have the same meaning as the arrow at the top.

124 Workbook 7: Addition to 8

Class shop activities

Before children attempt Pages 13 and 14, they should have the opportunity to 'buy' two priced articles and 'pay' the correct number of pennies to the 'shopkeeper'. They should also act out the 'marking up' of price tickets in preparation for the work of Page 14.

Teachers are referred to the notes on shopping activities for **Workbook 5** (page 90). The shopping cards (**Teacher's Materials Pack**, Card 8) could also be used for shopping activities, for example

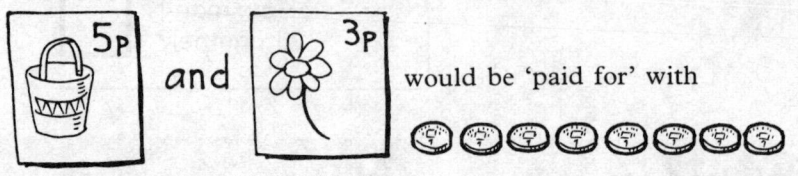

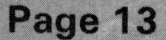

5p and 3p would be 'paid for' with ⊙⊙⊙⊙⊙⊙⊙⊙ .

Page 13 Shopping   Totals to 8p

Materials 1p coins; flashcards shopping   buy   and

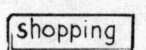

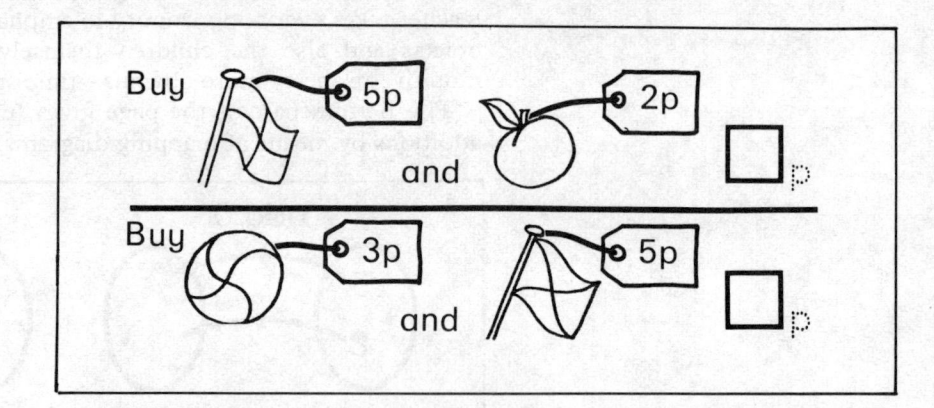

Buy — 5p   and   2p   ☐p
Buy — 3p   and   5p   ☐p

This page gives practice in adding two sums of money in pence. Totals of 8p predominate.

As well as writing the total price in the 'box', children have to write over the dotted letter 'p' in each case to show that the answer is an amount of money and not just a number. 1p coins should be available so that any child who is not sure of the total may be helped to get it right. Children should be encouraged, of course, to recall known addition facts in order to get the answer.

The teacher may wish to give children further work of the same kind and workcards would be quite suitable for this purpose. Paper strips on which the answers may be written could be clipped to the right-hand side of the card.

Workbook 7: Addition to 8   125

Page 14 — New prices — Totals to 8p

Materials 1p coins; flashcards

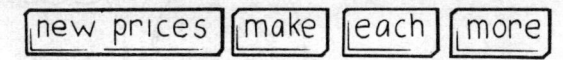

| new prices | make | each | more |

Prior to doing this page children should have had practical activities of the kind referred to in the preceding notes on class shop activities.

The teacher should make sure that the procedure of scoring out the old price and writing the new price on the blank 'ticket' is understood. It is important that children understand that all prices in the top half of the page must be increased by 2p and that all those in the bottom half of the page are to be increased by 3p. Children should also be reminded to write 'p' in each case. Again, coins should be available for those children who need them but all children should be encouraged to do without the coins if they can.

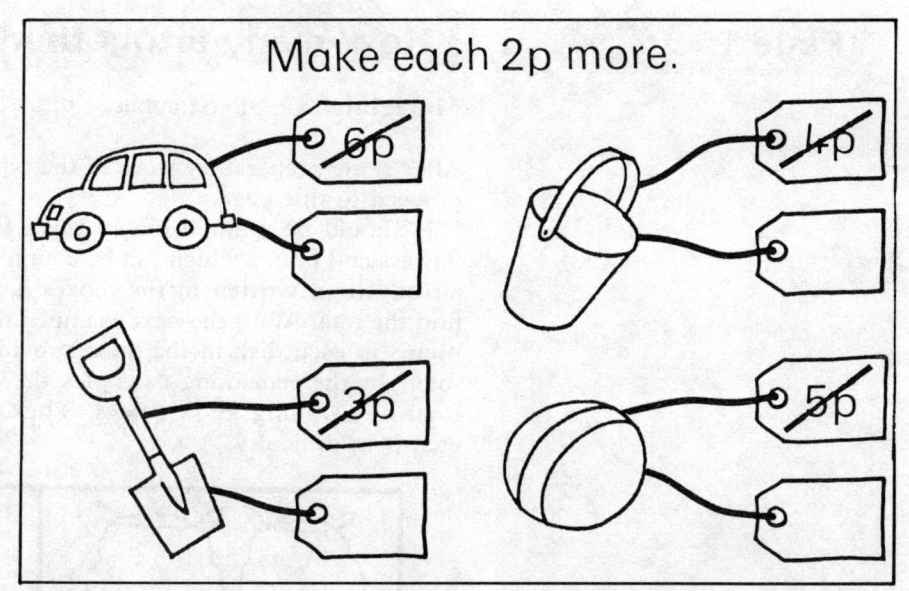

Make each 2p more.

(car — 6p crossed out; bucket — 4p crossed out; spade — 3p crossed out; ball — 5p crossed out)

The teacher may wish to provide further work of a similar nature. The 'wipeable' type of work card would be very suitable for the Page 14 format.

Word and picture problems

On Pages 8 and 11 there were word and picture problems composed of pictures of eggs, plums, etc., which could be counted individually. The top two examples on Page 15, which children have already met, are of this type. Nevertheless, the teacher should ensure, by blackboard demonstration, that children know what they have to do.

The remaining problems on Page 15 do *not* have pictures of 'countable' objects and the children are expected to recall known facts in order to get the answer.

126 Workbook 7: Addition to 8

It would be helpful if some preparatory work took place, with blackboard illustration, before children were asked to do Page 15.

[6 fish] [2 fish]   [3 sweets] [4 sweets]

How many altogether? ☐   How many altogether? ☐

The teacher could help the children with the words and give emphasis to the phrase, 'How many altogether?', which is used again and again on Page 15. Children could be asked, in turn, to come and write the answer in the 'box'.

Page 15 • How many altogether? | Problems |

Materials Counters, cubes, etc; flashcard | How many altogether? |

After some preparatory work of the type outlined above, children may proceed to this page.

It should be pointed out to them that the top two examples have flowers and plums which can be counted. The numbers of flowers have already been written in the 'boxes' and the children require only to find the total. With the next example, they have to write the number of plums in each dish in the 'box' provided, before going on to find the total. In the remaining examples the children should try to find the total by recalling known facts. They may resort to counters, cubes, etc., if in difficulty.

| 4 sweets, 3 sweets — How many altogether? ☐ | 4 pencils, 4 pencils — How many altogether? ☐ |
| 5 eggs, 2 eggs — How many altogether? ☐ | 3 fish, 5 fish — How many altogether? ☐ |

After completion of the page the teacher may wish to provide extra work of a similar kind for some, or all, of the children. The 'wipeable' type of workcard would be suitable for the Page 15 format.

Workbook 7: Addition to 8

Additional activities

Teachers may wish to give children further consolidation practice in addition to totals of 8. Here are some suggestions:

1 *Miscellaneous examples* These three workcards contain all the addition facts for 7 and 8.

Add	
7 + 0 =	6 + 2 =
4 + 4 =	6 + 1 =
2 + 6 =	5 + 2 =
3 + 5 =	5 + 3 =

Add	
4 + 4 =	7 + 1 =
3 + 4 =	6 + 2 =
0 + 7 =	2 + 6 =
1 + 6 =	2 + 5 =

Add	
2 + 5 =	3 + 4 =
0 + 8 =	4 + 3 =
5 + 3 =	8 + 0 =
1 + 7 =	3 + 5 =

2 Examples which highlight the 'twin' or commutative facts.

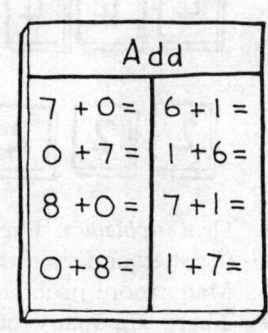

Add	
7 + 0 =	6 + 1 =
0 + 7 =	1 + 6 =
8 + 0 =	7 + 1 =
0 + 8 =	1 + 7 =

Add	
5 + 2 =	4 + 3 =
2 + 5 =	3 + 4 =
6 + 2 =	5 + 3 =
2 + 6 =	3 + 5 =

3 Examples involving addition of 1, addition of 2, addition of 3.

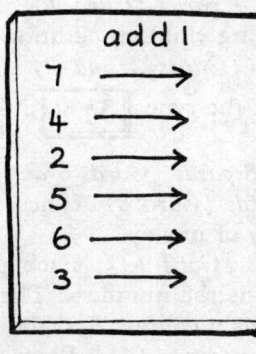

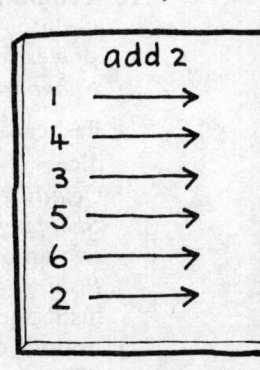

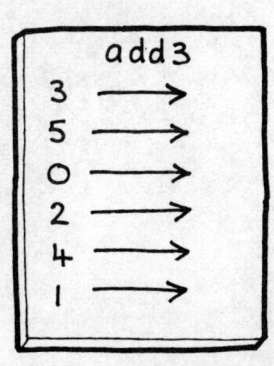

add 1
7 →
4 →
2 →
5 →
6 →
3 →

add 2
1 →
4 →
3 →
5 →
6 →
2 →

add 3
3 →
5 →
0 →
2 →
4 →
1 →

4 *Flashcards*

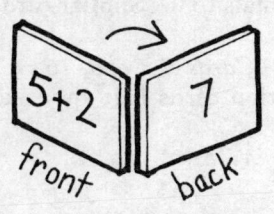

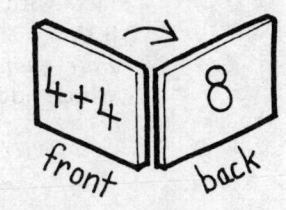

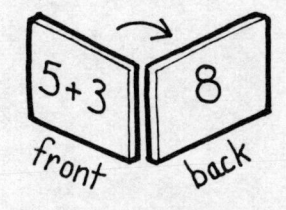

5+2 (front) | 7 (back)

4+4 (front) | 8 (back)

5+3 (front) | 8 (back)

128 Workbook 7: Addition to 8

5 Arranging flashcards in family groups.

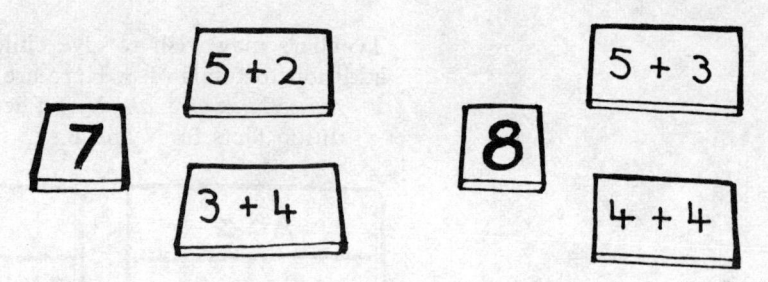

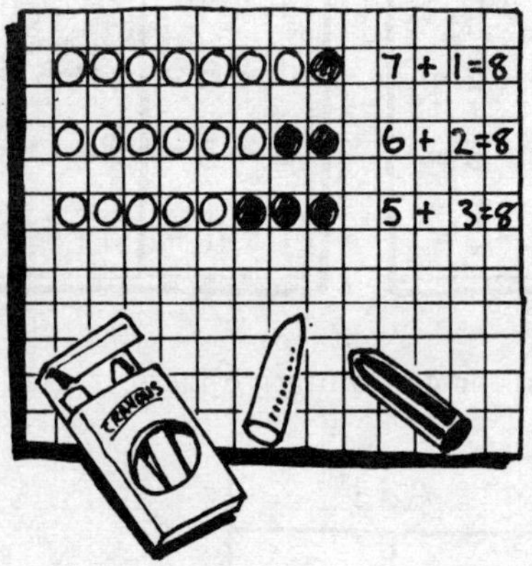

6 *Squared paper work* 'Stories of 8'.

7 *'Lucky Dip' game* Two or more children play. Each in turn picks two number cards out of a bag and adds the numbers. The child who has the smallest total in a 'round' of play is 'knocked out'. The game quickly produces a winner and then all 'come in' again and the game proceeds as before.

The cards used are:

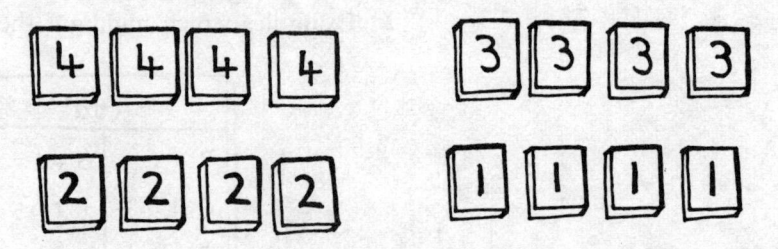

8 *Oral problems* The teacher says, for example, 'Five cows went into the shed and then three more. How many cows altogether went in?' Many more problems of the same kind should be used.

9 There are many other possible activities. See also the notes on 'Consolidation— cards for the teacher to make', on page 119.

10 **Teacher's Materials Pack**
Counting to 4 cards (Card 1) Selected pairs are useful to give slower learning children addition practice.
Snake game (Cards 2 and 3) This is a track game for which flashcards of the type 3 + 4 , 5 + 1 , etc., are used instead of dice.
Counting to 8 cards (Cards 6 and 7) See note for Card 1 above.
Shopping cards (Card 8) These are useful for practice in adding two amounts of money.
Fishing game (Card 13) Each player 'fishes' for two numbered 'fish' and adds the numbers. The child with highest score in each 'round' claims a counter and the game proceeds.
Window cards (Card 14) These are useful for revision of addition facts with totals to 6. (Similar cards may be made for totals to 7 and 8.)
Fair game (Cards 15 and 16) This is another track game for which addition cards may be used instead of dice.

Workbook 8

Addition to 10
Number Names

Cards 25 to 38 — Addition to 10

Contents

Totals of 9	Page 1
Totals to 9 and problems	Pages 2 and 3
Totals of 10	Page 4
Totals to 10 and problems	Pages 5 and 6
'Twin facts': totals to 10	Page 7
Addition of money to 10p	Page 8
Addition to 10	Cards 25 to 38
Addition of three numbers	Pages 9 to 11
Number names to five	Page 12
Number names to ten	Page 13
Number names and sequences	Page 14
Ordering: first, second, third	Page 15

Materials

Addition to 10

Small objects for counting such as:
 counters, beads, buttons, bricks, Unifix-type interlocking cubes, 1p coins, coloured pencils or crayons.

Flashcards of all the complements of 9 and 10 on the front and the answer (9 or 10) on the back:

Workbook 8: Addition to 10; Number names

Flashcards of key words and phrases might be useful:

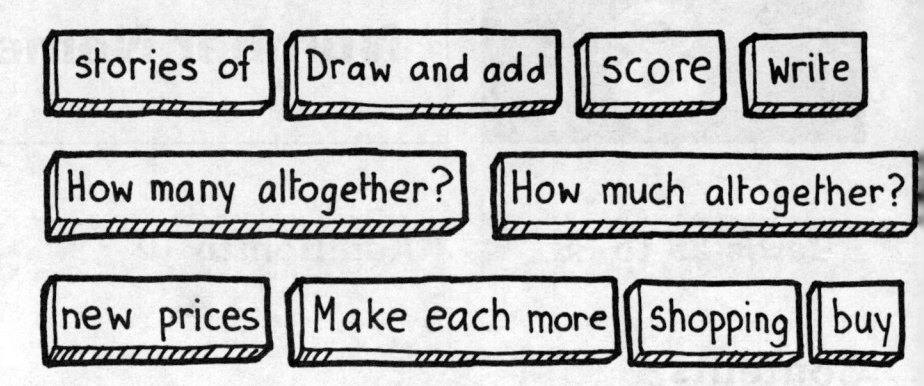

> stories of | Draw and add | score | Write
>
> How many altogether? | How much altogether?
>
> new prices | Make each more | shopping | buy

The following cards from the *Teacher's Materials Pack* should prove useful in relation to the work on addition in this Workbook.

Counting to 4 cards (Card 1)
Snake Game (Cards 2, 3)
Counting to 8 cards (Cards 6, 7)
Shopping cards (Card 8)
Fair Game (Cards 15, 16)
Animal Jigsaw 1 (Card 11)
Animal Jigsaw 2 (Card 12)
Fishing Game (Card 13)
Window Card (Card 14)
Make 7 and 8 cards (Card 17)
Make 9 and 10 cards (Card 18)
Make a Dinosaur (Card 19)

Number names

A selection from the following is required:
  counters, beads, toy-cars, interlocking Unifix-type cubes or pegs, sorting box.
The following would also be useful:
  coloured gummed outlines or shapes; cubes to make special dice.
The following flash cards would be useful:

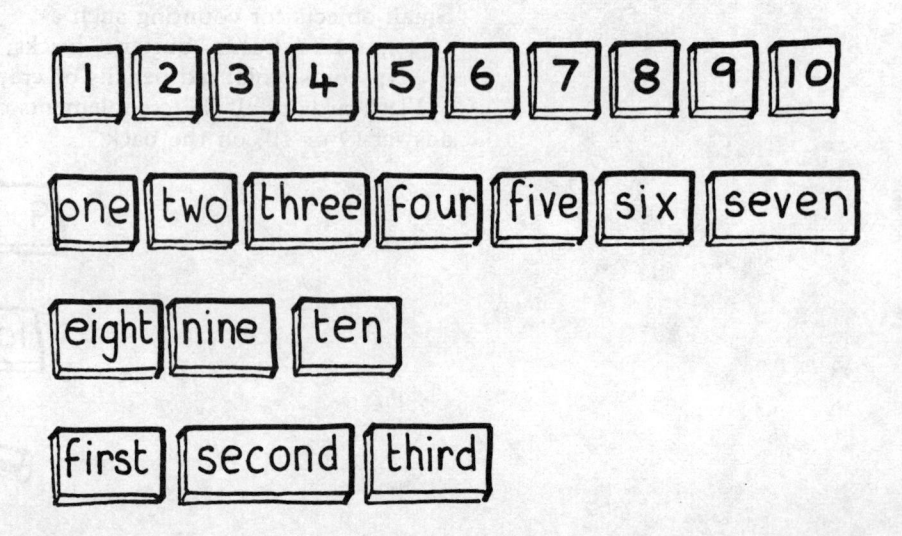

> 1 | 2 | 3 | 4 | 5 | 6 | 7 | 8 | 9 | 10
>
> one | two | three | four | five | six | seven
>
> eight | nine | ten
>
> first | second | third

Workbook 8: Addition to 10; Number names 131

A wall chart to show number names linked to sets of objects and numerals would be an additional aid.

The following cards from the *Teacher's Materials Pack* are appropriate:
Counting to 4 cards (Card 1)
Snake game (Cards 2 and 3)
Counting to 8 cards (Cards 6 and 7)
Fair game (Cards 15 and 16)
Horses 1 to 10 and Stables one to ten (Cards 20 and 21)

Addition to 10 (Pages 1 to 11 and Cards 25 to 38)

Development

In *Workbook* 7, the children's experience of addition was extended to the addition facts for 7 and 8. Addition facts with zero were included as well as 'word and picture problems' and work involving addition of money to totals of 8p.

This Workbook, together with Cards 25 to 38, extends the work to include addition facts for 9 and 10, further 'word and picture problem' work, and addition of money to 10p. There is also a section of work devoted to addition of *3* numbers with totals to 10 and addition of *3* sums of money, with totals to 10p.

132 Workbook 8: Addition to 10; Number names

Addition beyond totals of 10 is, of course, undertaken in *Infant Mathematics: Second Stage*.

The number names one to ten are introduced towards the end of this workbook. The concept of ordering into first, second and third completes the work of the booklet.

Practical activities and teaching

Revision of addition to 8

Before proceeding to activities involving addition to totals of 9 and 10, teachers should revise the addition facts with totals to 8. This work may be to a large extent oral, but should also include written work covering all the facts previously met.

Activities involving stories of 9

Before children start to do Page 1 of the Workbook, the teacher should involve them in a variety of activities aimed at exploring the 'stories', or complements, of 9. Here are a few suggested activities:

1 Arranging 9 children on the floor to illustrate the 'stories'.

"5 + 4 = 9"

2 Making the 'stories' with interlocking cubes (or counters of 2 colours).

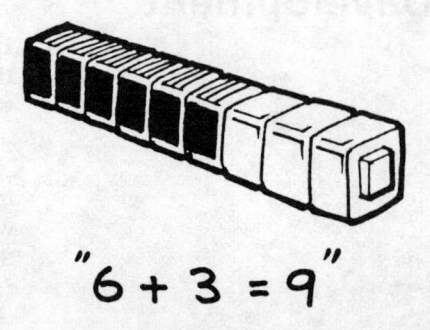

"6 + 3 = 9"

Workbook 8: Addition to 10; Number names 133

3 *'Washing line' activities*   Cardboard 'socks' are slid along the line to form different sub-sets of 9.

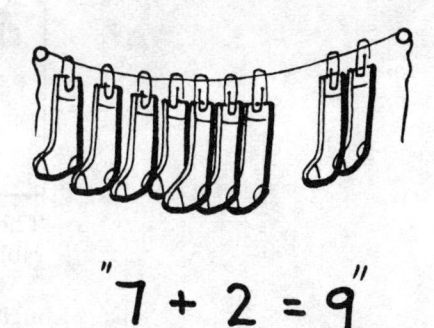

"7 + 2 = 9"

4 *The commutative property*   Two rows of cubes of two colours are arranged to illustrate 'twin' facts.

→ 7 + 2 = 9
→ 2 + 7 = 9

5 Squared paper work.

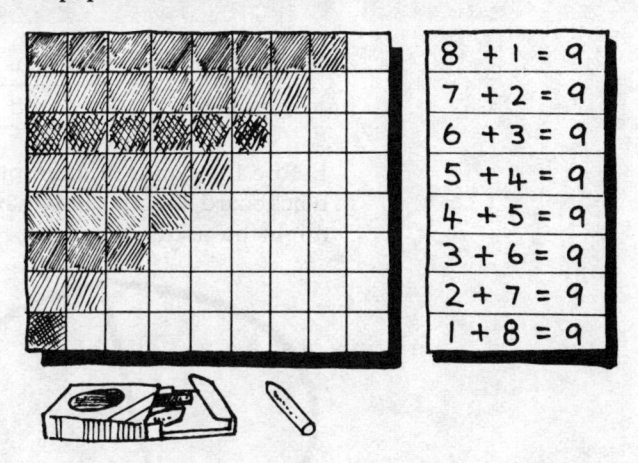

| 8 + 1 = 9 |
| 7 + 2 = 9 |
| 6 + 3 = 9 |
| 5 + 4 = 9 |
| 4 + 5 = 9 |
| 3 + 6 = 9 |
| 2 + 7 = 9 |
| 1 + 8 = 9 |

In all of this work the children should be encouraged to record the addition 'stories'. When the teacher feels that sufficient time has been spent on preparatory activities of this kind, the children can be asked to do Page 1 of the Workbook.

| **Page 1** | **Stories of 9** | Totals of 9 |

Materials   Flashcard stories of

The teacher should use blackboard illustrations to explain to the children what they have to do.

134 **Workbook 8:** Addition to 10; Number names

$$8 + 1 = 9$$

The numeral 8 in the first panel refers to the number of coloured rabbits, and the numeral 1 refers to the remaining white rabbit.

With the exception of the zero facts, all the complements of nine are included and two of them are repeated at the bottom of the page.

When the page has been completed, it can be used as the basis of discussion. The children 'say the stories' looking at the page, and later try to say them *without* looking.

The teacher may wish to give the children further written practice in writing all the stories.

| **Page 2** | **Draw and add** | Totals to 9 |

Materials Coloured pens or crayons for drawing dots (pencil would do); flashcard Draw and add.

Before the children attempt this page the teacher should explain, with blackboard illustrations, what they have to do. The following example might be used:

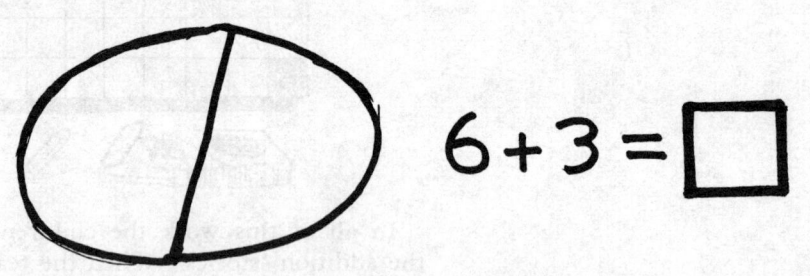

6 + 3 = ☐

A child is invited to draw 6 dots in the left-hand part and 3 dots in the right-hand part. The child then counts the total number of dots and writes the answer in the 'box'.

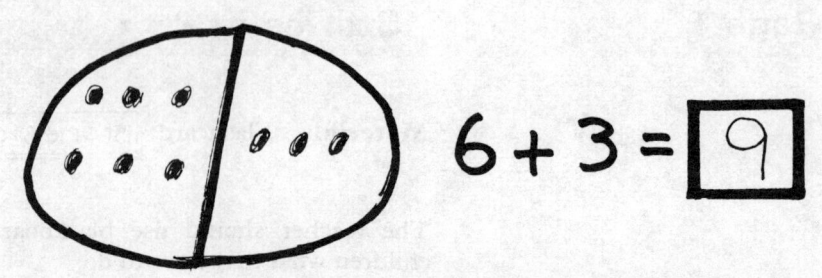

6 + 3 = 9

Workbook 8: Addition to 10; Number names 135

This should be repeated for other additions, with other children.

After they have had sufficient practice of this kind, the children should be asked to attempt the page. Two of the examples have totals of 8 so the children must take care with each addition.

Children who are able to add correctly without drawing dots should be encouraged to write the answers in the 'box' and dispense with drawing the dots if they find this boring.

For the less able children, on the other hand, the dots are likely to be necessary.

The completed page might form the basis for oral practice.

Further worksheets or 'wipeable' workcards could also be provided if the teacher felt this to be necessary.

Word and picture problems

On Pages 3 and 6 there are problems of the type shown below.

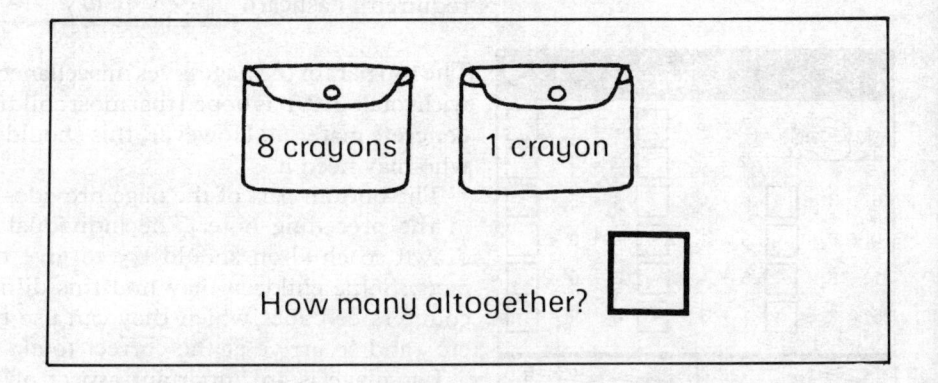

[8 crayons] [1 crayon]

How many altogether? □

A little time spent in related activities would be helpful in preparing children for the work of these pages.

For example, a child is given labelled margarine tubs containing beads. The child has to add 5 and 4 and match the tubs to the correct numeral card. If he is in doubt the beads can be emptied out and the answer checked by counting.

136 Workbook 8: Addition to 10; Number names

Again, the teacher might draw bags of sweets on the blackboard and a child then asked 'How many sweets are there altogether?' The child writes the answer '9' on the board. If there is doubt as to the answer, sweets can be drawn by the child and the total found.

Page 3 | Add | Totals to 9

Materials Counters, buttons, cubes, etc. (to be available if required); flashcard How many altogether?

The top part of the page gives miscellaneous examples of addition, mostly with totals of 9. It is hoped that most children will manage without the aid of concrete material. However, this should be available for the slower child who may need it.

The bottom part of the page provides problems of the type discussed in the preceding note. The individual pencils, crayons, etc., are not drawn so children should try to give the answer by recalling known facts. Some children may find this difficult and should have access to counters or cubes which they can use to represent the pencils, books, etc., and so arrive at the correct total.

Language is an important aspect of this work. The teacher should help the children to read the words and even the less able children should be encouraged to do the problems although they may require more help with the reading.

The teacher should give further oral and written practice in the complements of 9 and in addition with totals to 9. 'Window' workcards are useful for practice in additions with totals to 9.

Oral 'problems' are also valuable, e.g.

'Greedy Tom ate *6* cherries and then he ate *3 more*. How many did he eat *altogether*?'

Workbook 8: Addition to 10; Number names   **137**

Page 4   Stories of 10   Totals of 10

Materials   Flashcard `stories of`

This page is very similar to Page 1 and the advice given for that page is valid here also.

It should be noted that the complements of 10 are particularly important and teachers should take every opportunity to give oral practice aimed at helping children to memorize these facts.

Page 5   Draw and add   Totals to 10

Materials   Coloured pens or crayons for drawing dots (pencil would do); flashcard `Draw and add`

This page is very similar to Page 2 and the advice given for that page is valid here also.

138 Workbook 8: Addition to 10; Number names

| Page 6 | Add | Totals to 10 |

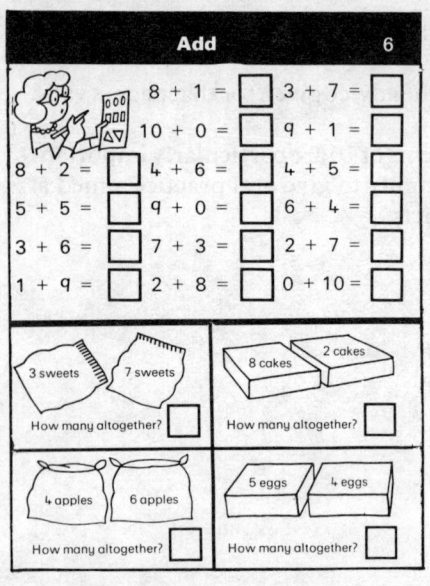

Add   6

8 + 1 =	3 + 7 =	
10 + 0 =	9 + 1 =	
8 + 2 =	4 + 6 =	4 + 5 =
5 + 5 =	9 + 0 =	6 + 4 =
3 + 6 =	7 + 3 =	2 + 7 =
1 + 9 =	2 + 8 =	0 + 10 =

3 sweets   7 sweets — How many altogether?

8 cakes   2 cakes — How many altogether?

4 apples   6 apples — How many altogether?

5 eggs   4 eggs — How many altogether?

Materials Counters, buttons, cubes, etc. (to be available if required); flashcard | How many altogether? |

This page is very like Page 3 and the advice given for page 3 is relevant for this page also.

Teaching suggestions

Twin facts—the commutative property

Before children go on to Page 7, a little time might well be spent once more on activities which emphasize the important commutative property of addition.

Here are a few suggested activities:

1. Using the children themselves as illustration with accompanying verbalization and recording.

"Six and four make ten" → 6 + 4 = 10

"Four and six make ten" → 4 + 6 = 10

Workbook 8: Addition to 10; Number names

2 Using counters in the hands, and emphasizing by hand movement which number is taken first.

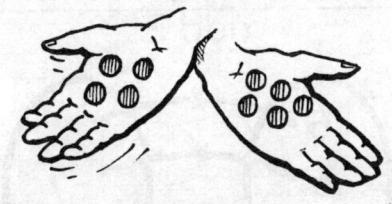

3 Use of interlocking cubes.

"Four and five make nine"
4 + 5 = 9

"Five and four make nine"
5 + 4 = 9

7 + 3 = 10

3 + 7 = 10

4 Marbles in tubs, adding from left to right.

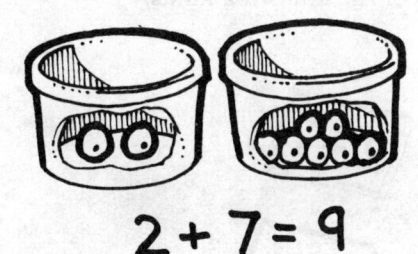

2 + 7 = 9   then   7 + 2 = 9

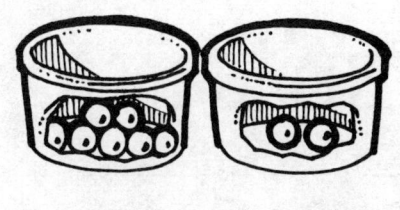

Interchange the positions of the tubs to emphasize the commutative property.

After activities of the kind described above, the children may proceed to Page 7.

Page 7 — Add — Twin facts Totals to 10

Materials Counters, buttons, cubes, etc. (to be available if required).

The top part of this page provides practice in the 'twin' facts with totals of 8, 9, and 10.

Teachers should use the completed additions as a focus for additional oral practice aimed at emphasizing once again the twin facts. Later, when children have to do an addition such as 2+8, they are helped by knowing that 8+2 will give the same answer, and 8+2 is probably easier to memorize, initially.

The bottom part of this page gives a little more practice with mapping diagrams. The teacher should once again make sure that children understand that, for any given diagram, *all* the arrows mean the same as the top-most arrow.

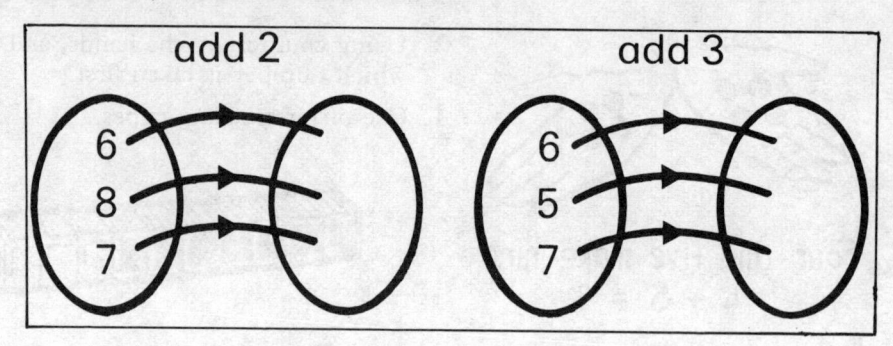

Workbook 8: Addition to 10; Number names

[add 2 mapping diagram: {6, 8, 7} → ; add 3 mapping diagram: {6, 5, 7} →]

Consolidation

Before tackling the remaining part of the Workbook, some consolidation of the addition facts covered is necessary. Oral and mental work is an important element in this.

The teacher might consider work of the following kinds.

1 Oral work with flashcards.

[flashcards: 7+3, 2+7, 9+0, 6+4]

[flashcard: 7+3 (front), 10 (back)]

2 Individual work with flashcards.
   The reverse side of each card could have the 'answer'; so that children could check their own efforts.
   Children might arrange cards in families, e.g.

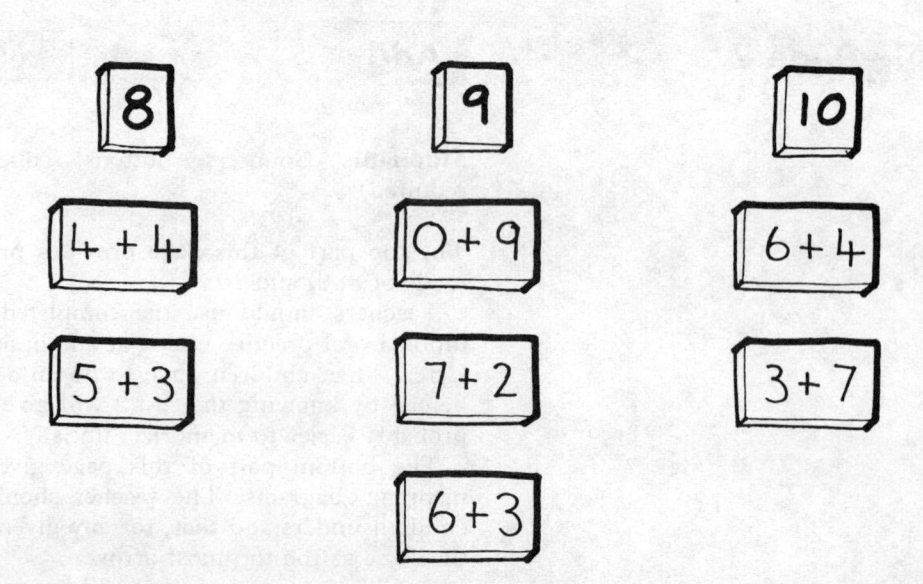

[family 8: 4+4, 5+3]
[family 9: 0+9, 7+2, 6+3]
[family 10: 6+4, 3+7]

Workbook 8: Addition to 10; Number names 141

3 Practice examples involving adding on 0, 1, 2, 3, ... Mapping-type diagrams on 'wipeable' plastic covered cards might be used.

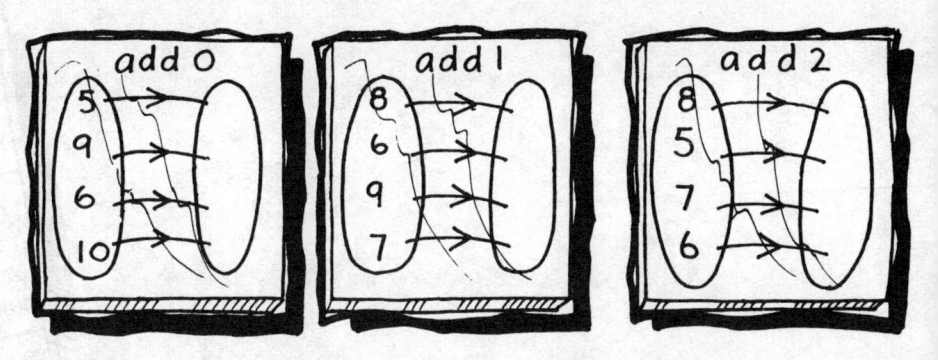

4 *Practice with twin facts* 'Window' cards would be useful for this activity.

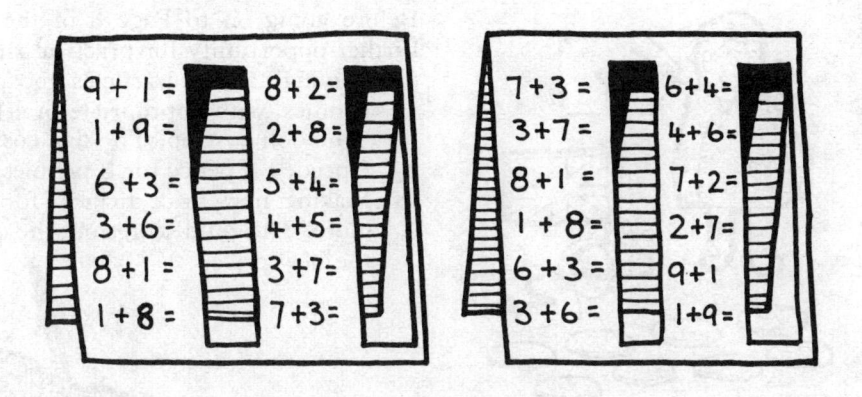

5 *Matching* Again, 'wipeable' cards would be convenient.

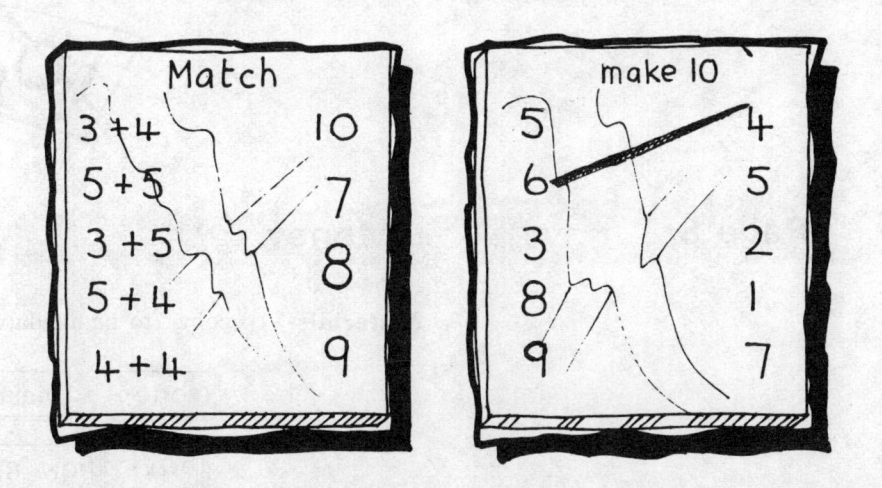

6 Miscellaneous additions with totals, say, 8, 9, and 10.
7 *Oral problems* The following is a typical example. 'Pam ate six sweets. Then she ate four *more*. How many did she eat altogether?'

142 Workbook 8: Addition to 10; Number names

8 *Word and picture problems* (Workcards with a clipped-on paper strip would do for this.)

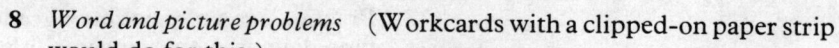

> 3 fish 6 fish
> How many altogether?
>
> 7 plums 3 plums
> How many altogether?

Class shop activities

Before going on to Page 8 of the Workbook, children should have further opportunity for practical shopping activities such as:

(a) 'Buying' 2 priced articles and paying with the correct number of pennies, with appropriate oral language work.
'The doll cost 6p. The flag cost 2p.
I needed 8 pence (or 8 pennies, or 8p) altogether.'

(b) Making new price tickets, for example, making each article 3p more. The child scores out the old price on an article and writes on the new price.

Page 8   Money   Totals to 10p

Materials   1p coins (to be available if required); flashcards

money | Make each | more
buy | How much altogether?

The work on this page is similar to work previously met. Children should be reminded that the old price must be scored out and the new price written on the blank 'ticket' underneath.

Workbook 8: Addition to 10; Number names   143

Children may also need to be reminded that they have to write over the dotted 'p' in each case when doing the examples on the bottom part of the page.

These points could be explained with blackboard illustration before the children attempt the page.

The teacher could provide additional work in the context of shopping. For example, worksheets, or 'wipeable' cards might be provided.

(a) The card could be filled in after the child had 'bought' articles at the class shop.

The shop
I spent ☐p and ☐p
Altogether I spent ☐p

The shop
I spent 6 p and 2 p
Altogether I spent 8 p

(b) As extra work after the completion of Page 8, the teacher could fill in the first two 'boxes' and ask the child to add them and write in the total.

The shopping cards from the **Teacher's Materials Pack** (Card 8) could also be used to give practice with addition of money. For example, pairs of 'articles' could be chosen which would require a total of 8p, 9p, or 10p, say:

Cards 25 to 38   Addition to 10

Materials Counters, beads, buttons, cubes, 1p coins, etc., should be available if required; flashcards.

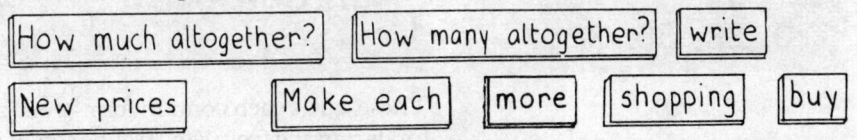

| How much altogether? | How many altogether? | write |
| New prices | Make each | more | shopping | buy |

At this point teachers may wish to use **Cards 25 to 38** to give further practice in addition to 10. All of the odd-numbered cards concentrate mainly on practice examples of the type $3+4=\square$. The even-numbered cards contain more difficult 'word and picture problems'. The cards may be done in any order and their use can be spread over a period of time. The children will need practice with examples like these which have to be copied and then completed.

Workbook 8: Addition to 10; Number names

Less able children may require counters, cubes, etc., to help them with some additions. The teacher may also feel that for some children it will sometimes be better to clip paper to the card on which the child writes the answer, rather than ask a slow child to copy and complete.

Cards 25, 27, 29, 31, 33, 35, 37

Addition to 10

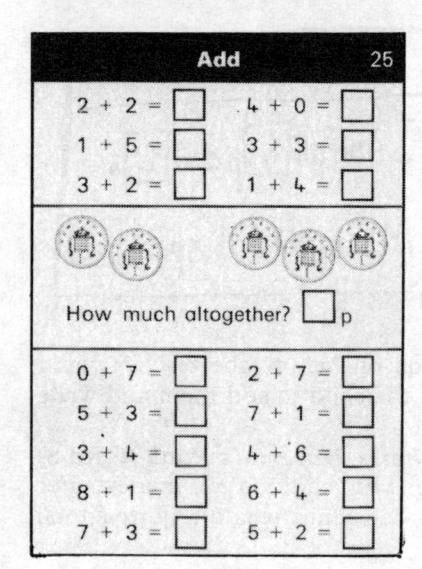

All of these cards have the same format. They are divided into three sections. The top section contains six examples of the type $2 + 3 = \square$ where the answers are 6 or less. The bottom section of each card contains ten similar examples but with totals up to and including 10.

The middle section contains a 'word and picture problem' where the answer can be obtained by counting the objects on the card. The answer to each of these problems is 6 or less. The teacher might also encourage some pupils to give an addition story (perhaps orally) to suit the drawings. For example, for Card 37

Cards 26, 28, 30, 32

Addition to 10

These cards each contain four 'word and picture addition problems' with totals ranging from 7 to 10. The sets of animals, etc., which have to be added cannot be counted from the drawings on the cards. Some children may well have to use counters to represent '3 sheep' and '4 sheep' and combine them to find the answer '7 sheep'.

Less able children will require help with the reading but they should be encouraged to try these problems and share in the experience of coping with this aspect of number work. The more able children will benefit from being 'stretched' a little while trying to cope with the extra reading and writing demands of these particular cards.

Workbook 8: Addition to 10; Number names

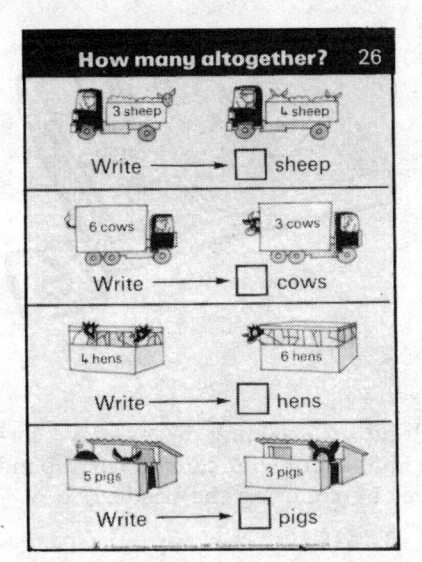

The foregoing remarks apply also to the Money Cards 34, 36, and 38, which have similar language difficulty.

Cards 34, 36, 38

Addition to 10p

These cards also contain 'word and picture problems' but in this case involving money with totals from 5p to 10p. The children have met activities about 'new prices' and 'buying' before in **Workbooks 7 and 8**. 1p coins should be available for those children who need them.

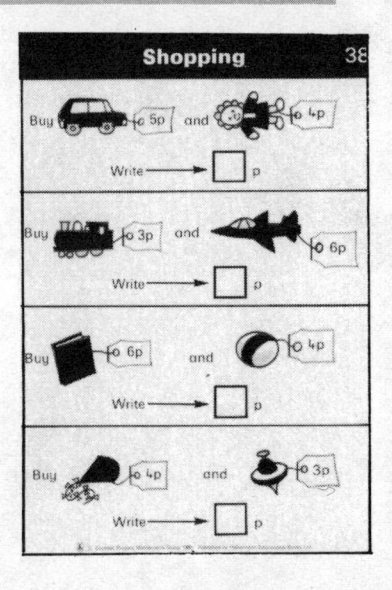

Addition of three numbers

Before children attempt Pages 9, 10, and 11 they should be given practical activities involving the addition of *3* numbers. Oral discussion with the teacher is important. Here are some suggestions:

1 Counting tray work

The teacher puts numeral cards beside each tray. The child puts small objects in the trays and finds the total which is recorded with a numeral card.

146 Workbook 8: Addition to 10; Number names

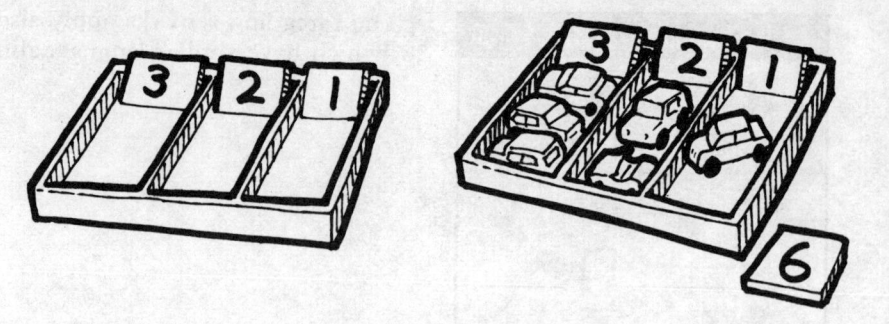

2 Labelled tubs

The child is given three labelled tubs containing beads, say, corresponding to the label. The child finds a numeral card to correspond with the total and checks the answer by counting the beads.

3 Beads

The child puts beads on a string to correspond to given numeral cards, and then finds the total. Interlocking cubes may also be used.

4 Pegboard and pegs

This is a similar activity to the previous one but in this case pegs are arranged in a row on a pegboard (pegs of 3 colours).

5 Squared paper work

The child colours squares (3 different colours) according to the given 'sum', and finally writes the answer.

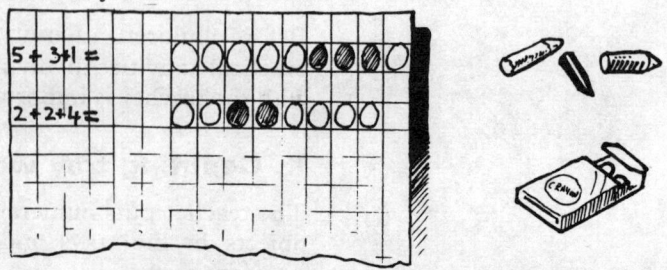

Workbook 8: Addition to 10; Number names 147

6 'Draw' workcards

These can be similar to the example below.

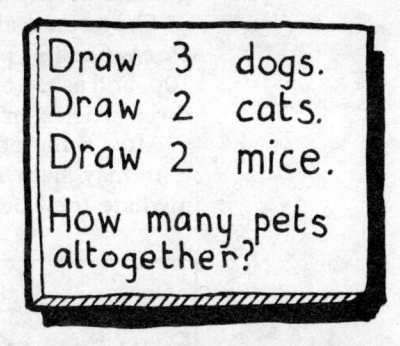

> Draw 3 dogs.
> Draw 2 cats.
> Draw 2 mice.
> How many pets altogether?

Page 9 | **Add** | Addition of 3 numbers

Materials Counters, buttons, cubes, etc. (if required).

Teachers should decide whether or not less able children should omit Pages 9, 10, and 11 for the moment.

Some preliminary blackboard explanation should be given. The teacher draws, say:

and invites a child to write the number corresponding to the dots in each part:

$4+1+2=$

The child should be encouraged to find the total without counting all the dots, but of course this can be done to check that the answer is correct.

It may help to allow children to write an *intermediate total* above the second numeral initially, before writing in the final total.

$$4 + \overset{5}{1} + 2$$

After sufficient work of this kind the children should be able to attempt Page 9. The additions at the foot of the page may cause difficulty but children should have access to counters, cubes, etc., if these are needed.

Page 10 | **Add** | Addition of 3 numbers

Materials 1p coins, counters, cubes, buttons, etc., should be available if required; flashcards.

| How much altogether? | How many altogether? |

148 Workbook 8: Addition to 10; Number names

Some class shop activity is desirable before children proceed to Page 10. They 'buy' 3 priced articles and count out the total number of pennies needed to 'buy' the three articles.

They could also be given 3 shopping cards (**Teacher's Materials Pack**, Card 8), provided the teacher ensures that the total does not exceed 10p, and asked to lay out the total number of pennies needed to 'buy' the three articles on the cards.

After some of this activity the children may attempt Page 10.

It may help some children if they are allowed to write an intermediate total beside the middle price label.

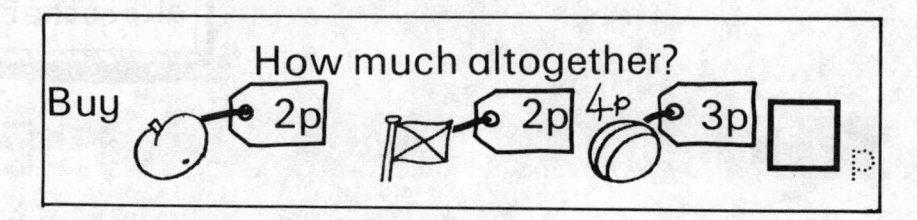

How much altogether?
Buy ⊙ 2p ⚑ 2p 4p ⊙ 3p ☐ p

Some children may need the help of 1p coins.

The 'word and picture problems' on the lower half of the page are similar to those met before, except that *3* numbers have to be added.

Again, it may help some children to allow them to write in an intermediate total beside the centre picture in each case. Some children may require counters, cubes, etc.

2 apples   4 apples   3 apples   ☐ apples
                             6

Page 11 At the fair Addition of 3 numbers

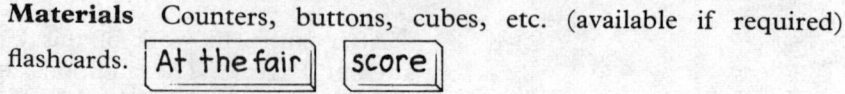

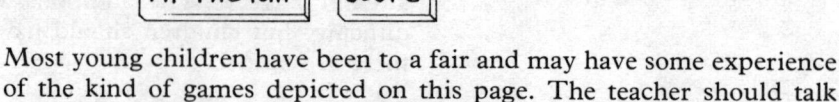

Materials Counters, buttons, cubes, etc. (available if required) flashcards. At the fair   score

Most young children have been to a fair and may have some experience of the kind of games depicted on this page. The teacher should talk about games where the idea is to score points and add up the points.

It would be highly desirable for the children actually to *play* one or two games of this kind. This might give them more incentive to add 3 numbers! Here are two suggestions.

'*Hoopla*' A 'hoopla' board with suitable numbers pasted on would be very useful. The numbers must be chosen so that adding any *3* of them does not result in a total exceeding *10*.

Workbook 8: Addition to 10; Number names 149

Skittles Widely-spaced skittles are set up. Each skittle bears a number, as shown. Each player has to knock down 3 skittles.

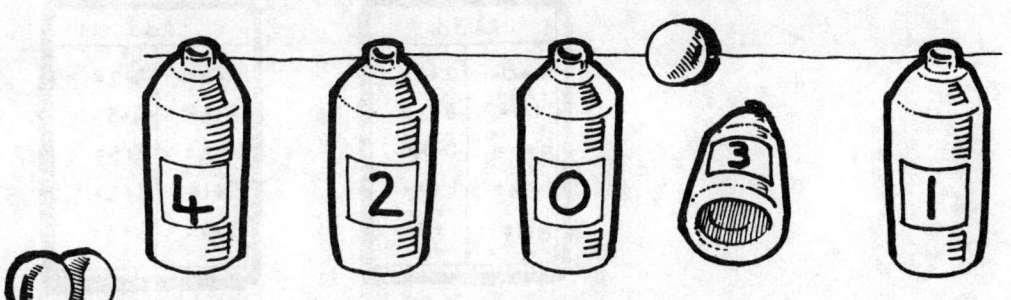

Other numbering is possible provided only 1 four is used so that totals cannot exceed 10; for example, 4, 3, 3, 2, 1.

Cards for the teacher to make

Teachers will no doubt wish to give children further practice with the addition facts with totals to 10. For less able children who take longer to copy and complete the work on cards, the teacher might provide cards with a paper strip attached, 'window' cards, or plastic-covered cards of the 'wipeable' type.

Here are some examples of work cards.

1 Cards which include all the 'twin' facts for totals of 9 and 10.

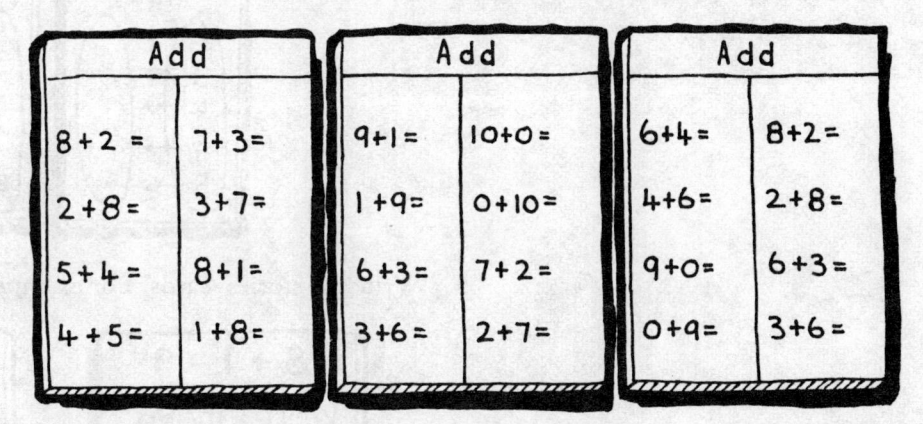

Add	
8+2 =	7+3 =
2+8 =	3+7 =
5+4 =	8+1 =
4+5 =	1+8 =

Add	
9+1 =	10+0 =
1+9 =	0+10 =
6+3 =	7+2 =
3+6 =	2+7 =

Add	
6+4 =	8+2 =
4+6 =	2+8 =
9+0 =	6+3 =
0+9 =	3+6 =

2 Here are four cards of miscellaneous examples with totals of 9 or 10.

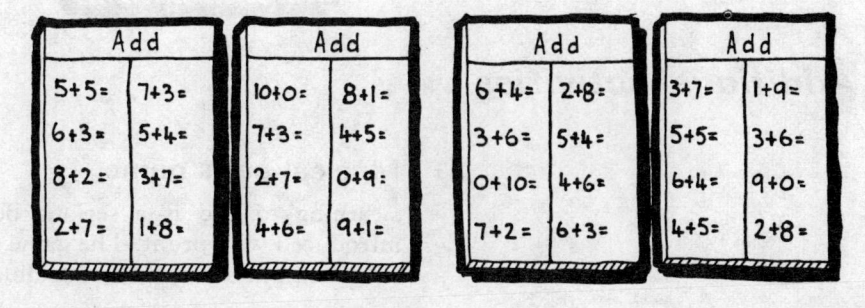

Add	
5+5 =	7+3 =
6+3 =	5+4 =
8+2 =	3+7 =
2+7 =	1+8 =

Add	
10+0 =	8+1 =
7+3 =	4+5 =
2+7 =	0+9 =
4+6 =	9+1 =

Add	
6+4 =	2+8 =
3+6 =	5+4 =
0+10 =	4+6 =
7+2 =	6+3 =

Add	
3+7 =	1+9 =
5+5 =	3+6 =
6+4 =	9+0 =
4+5 =	2+8 =

150 Workbook 8: Addition to 10; Number names

3 Here are six cards of miscellaneous examples with totals of 7, 8, 9 and 10.

Add	
10+0=	2+6=
1+6=	6+3=
6+4=	0+10=
4+4=	6+1=
8+1=	1+7=

Add	
5+5=	7+2=
5+3=	4+5=
4+3=	2+5=
9+1=	8+2=
3+7=	6+3=

Add	
5+4=	3+6=
0+8=	7+1=
2+8=	3+4=
7+3=	7+0=
4+5=	6+4=

Add	
7+3=	3+5=
5+4=	5+2=
5+5=	6+2=
9+0=	8+0=
4+6=	2+7=

Add	
3+7=	4+4=
4+6=	0+9=
5+3=	3+6=
0+7=	1+9=
1+8=	3+5=

Add	
5+5=	5+4=
3+6=	3+5=
4+4=	3+7=
3+4=	4+5=
4+6=	4+3=

4 Worksheets or 'wipeable' cards for addition of 0, 1, 2, 3, etc., using mapping diagrams. For example:

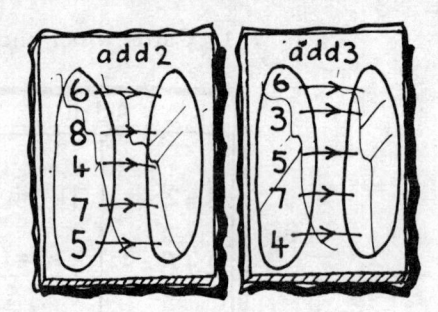

add 2: 6, 8, 4, 7, 5

add 3: 6, 3, 5, 7, 4

5 'Write the stories' cards. For example:

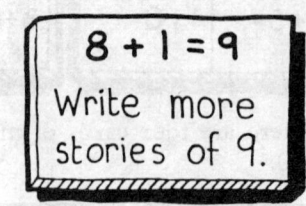

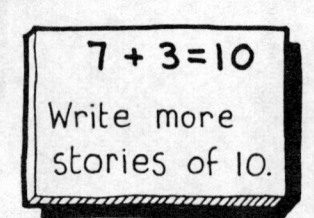

8 + 1 = 9
Write more stories of 9.

7 + 3 = 10
Write more stories of 10.

Additional activities

1 Musical pairs game

Learning to add is a serious business, but a little fun can be introduced with profit. The game of Musical pairs, or an adaptation of it, combines fun with consolidation of addition facts.

Workbook 8: Addition to 10; Number names 151

Six girls and six boys can play. Each girl has a placard round her neck with one of the numerals 0, 1, 2, 3, 4, 5 on it. The six boys have similar placards.

The girls join hands and form an inner ring. The boys form a ring to the outside of the girls (as in a 'Paul Jones' dance). When the music starts the two rings revolve in opposite directions. When the music stops each boy pairs with the nearest girl and they add their numbers. The pair, or pairs, with the lowest total are 'knocked out' and the game proceeds till only one pair is left.

Children wearing lower numbers are more likely to be knocked out so, for each new game, placards should be changed.

2 Knock-out dip

This is another very simple game which may be played by 3 children. It requires a box or bag containing numeral cards as follows:

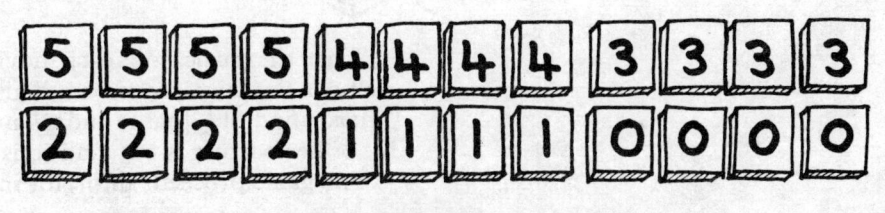

Each child in turn picks 2 cards out of the 'lucky bag' and adds the numbers together. The child with the lowest total is 'knocked out'. The game is quickly over and then all may start again.

3 'Musical chairs'

This is a variation of the usual musical chairs game. The aim of the game is to give children practice in the complements of ten which is also enjoyable. From 10 to 18 children may take part, depending on the numerals used. As in 'Musical pairs', there are two teams of equal size, seven in each, say.

Each team member has a numeral ticket round his or her neck bearing one of the numerals 2, 3, 4, 5, 6, 7, or 8. The numbers are the same for both teams, but are written in different colours. One team sits

152 Workbook 8: Addition to 10; Number names

on seven chairs and, while the music plays, the other team perambulates around them. The arrangement of the teams might be something like this.

When the music stops each moving team member has to keep going round *in this same direction* until his or her 'complement', is found e.g. 7 has to find 3; 2 has to find 8, and so on. The child who is last to find his or her partner is out, and so is the partner.

The game proceeds until, for instance, four children remain:

If the child with 2 finds the child with 8 first, then they form the winning couple.

Teachers may have their own preferred activities which help to consolidate addition facts. Any activity which achieves this aim and has an element of fun, is worth the time spent on it.

Workbook 8: Addition to 10; Number names   153

4 There are many games and activities provided in the *Teacher's Materials Pack* which would be useful for addition to 10. Some of these, which have been previously described, are:
   Counting to 4 cards (Card 1)
   Snake game (Cards 2 and 3)
   Counting to 8 cards (Cards 6 and 7)
   Shopping cards (Card 8)
   Animal jigsaws (Cards 11 and 12)
   Fishing game (Card 13)
   Window card (Card 14)
   Fair game (Cards 15 and 16)

5 Other useful cards from the *Teacher's Materials Pack* are
   Make 7 and 8 cards (Card 17)
   Make 9 and 10 cards (Card 18)

These cards give sets of cards with addition facts on them which are then sorted into those for a particular 'story' (say story of 9). The story of 9 cards are then put together jig-saw fashion to form a large numeral 9. Make a dinosaur (Card 19) is also about addition to 10. It uses a sequence of addition facts whose totals increase one at a time.

Number Names (Pages 12 to 15)

Development

This section introduces the reading and writing of the number names from one to five and then from six to ten. There is emphasis on the sequence of the number names counting from one to ten and back from ten to one.

Finally the concept of ordering into first, second, and third is introduced.

Practical activities and teaching

Number names one to five

This section of the work links up the numerals 1 to 5 with the number names one to five. The children should be able to
(a) associate a numeral with its appropriate number name, e.g. 5 and five, and *vice versa*;
(b) associate a set of objects with the appropriate number name, e.g.

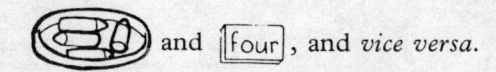

and four, and *vice versa*.

Workbook 8: Addition to 10; Number names

However, not all children will be ready for this work at this stage. It is left to the teacher's discretion which children should tackle it now.

For those children who can cope with this work, wall charts and flash cards similar to those shown below could be on display and used in some of the ways suggested. The actual writing of the number words is introduced after much practical activity and recognition of the number names.

Wall chart

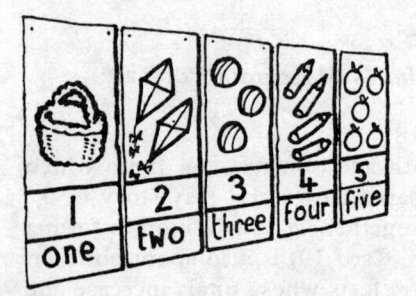

The teacher could extend the wall chart first mentioned in the Teaching Notes for **Workbook 2**, to include the number names one to five.

This should be a useful reference chart for the children in all of the following work.

Flashcards

The teacher could prepare several sets of flashcards for the children (and teacher) to use.

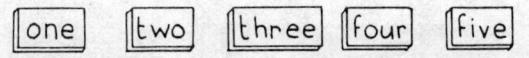

| one | two | three | four | five |

It is also assumed that the teacher has already made several sets of flashcards

| 1 | 2 | 3 | 4 | 5 |

for earlier work in number.

Introducing the number names one to five

The teacher should show an alternative way of displaying

| 1 | 2 | 3 | 4 | 5 |,

that is as

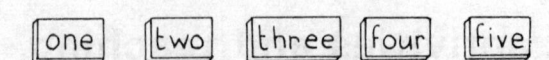

| one | two | three | four | five |

The teacher could do some of the following activities with the children.

1. Hold up [3]. Find the appropriate number name, i.e. [three].
2. Hold up [four]. 'What does it say?'
3. Hold up [two]. Put out the appropriate number of counters.
4. Put out 4 toys. Find the appropriate number name, i.e. [four].
5. Give out the five number names. Ask the children to put them in order.

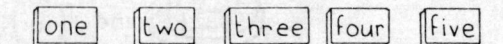

| one | two | three | four | five |

Workbook 8: Addition to 10; Number names   155

6 Put out [four]. 'Put out number names before and after this one'.
   [three] [four] [five]

Further practical work involving the number names one to five

1 Sorting box
Children could use and count material using sorting boxes or a box partitioned as shown.

2 Flashcards
(a) Children could pick a flashcard and string beads, e.g.
[five], string five red, five blue, five red; or
[three], string three red, three blue, three red;

(b) Children could take flashcards and match number names.

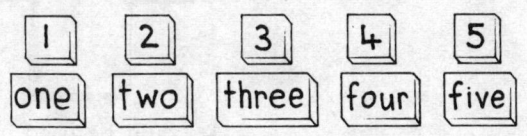

[1] [2] [3] [4] [5]
[one] [two] [three] [four] [five]

(c) Children could be given a card of the type shown on the left and cover each figure with the correct number name, e.g. [three] on top of [3].

(d) A child could deal out one number name flashcard to each child in a group of four. Each child then picks the appropriate number of counters from a box provided. This could be repeated several times.

156 Workbook 8: Addition to 10; Number names

3 Picture cards

Picture cards could be made by using commercially obtainable gummed cut outs, for example:

three   two   one   four   five

The number names could then be matched to each as shown.

Card 1 of the **Teacher's Materials Pack** contains cards with drawings on them (up to 4 objects) for this purpose. Cards with 5 objects on them could be selected from Cards 6 and 7 of the **Teacher's Materials Pack**.

4 Dice with numbers 1 to 5 or one to five

(a) Using a cube, each of the numbers 1, 2, 3, 4, and 5 could be put on a face, leaving one face blank. The die could be thrown and the appropriate number name flashcard, e.g. four, picked up.

(b) A cube could be made out of cardboard, thus:

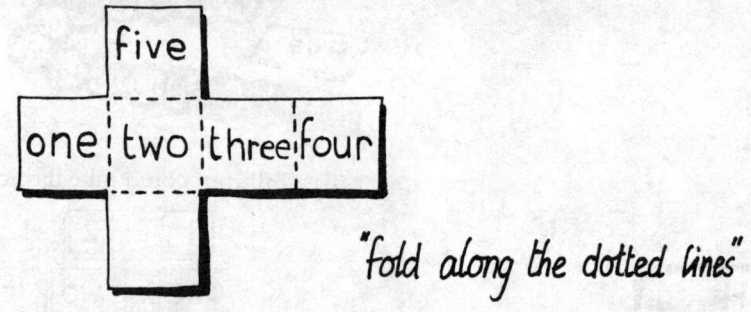

five
one two three four

"fold along the dotted lines"

It could be used in various ways:
  (i) Throw the die and put out the appropriate number of counters.
  (ii) Throw the die and pick up the appropriate numeral flashcard, e.g. 5.
  (iii) It could also be used in the Snake game mentioned below.

Games

1 Snake game

This game is suitable for 2 children. Make a track game using a snake.

Workbook 8: Addition to 10; Number names 157

Place two or three sets of number name flashcards (one to five) face down in a pile on the table.

One child picks a card, e.g. four, and moves a counter forward the appropriate number of places. The winner is the first person to reach the head of the snake.

The die mentioned previously could also be used instead of the cards.

Teacher's Materials Pack, Cards 2 and 3, contain a track for the Snake game.

2 Snap

This game is suitable for 2 children.
(a) 'Snap' could be played using numeral flashcards

|1| |2| |3| |4| |5|

and number name flashcards

|one| |two| |three| |four| |five|

It would be best if one child had the numeral flashcards and the other the number name flashcards.

(b) 'Snap' could also be played using the picture cards mentioned previously in conjunction with the number name flashcards.

Teacher's Materials Pack, Card 1, provides cards with sets of 1, 2, 3, and 4 objects. These could be used instead of making picture cards. **Teacher's Materials Pack**, Cards 6 and 7, would give some cards with 5 objects on them.

Writing the number names one to five

Practice in writing the number names could be attempted by some children
(a) by writing over dotted letters on a worksheet;

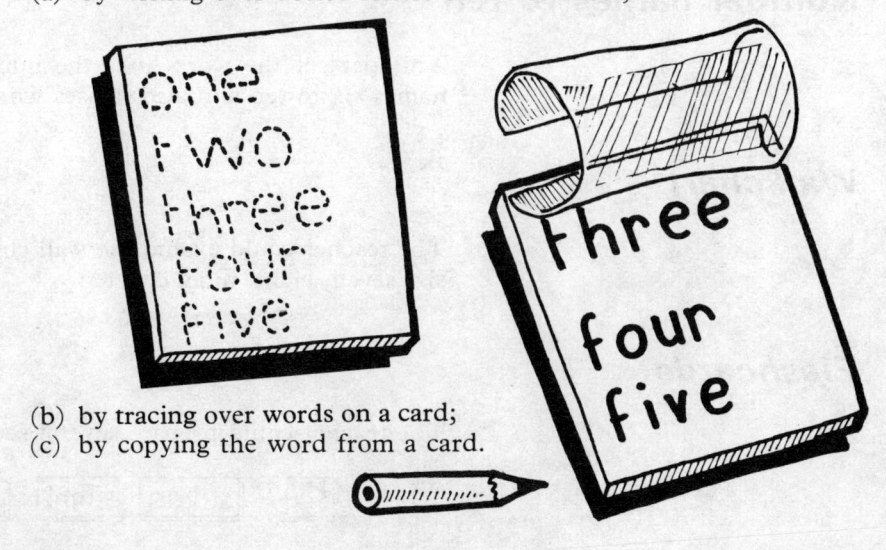

(b) by tracing over words on a card;
(c) by copying the word from a card.

Workbook 8: Addition to 10; Number names

Page 12 — Number names — Number names to five

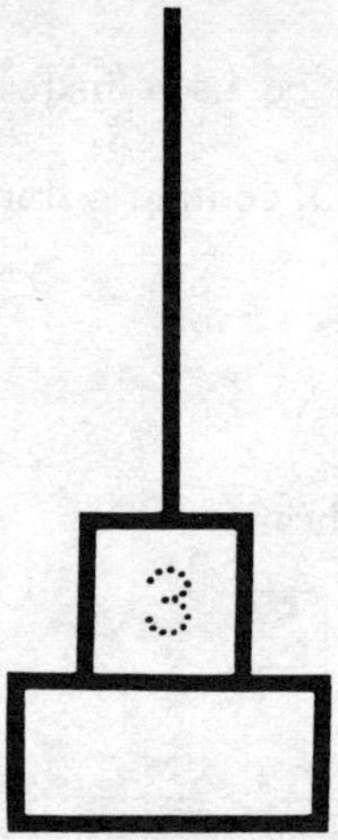

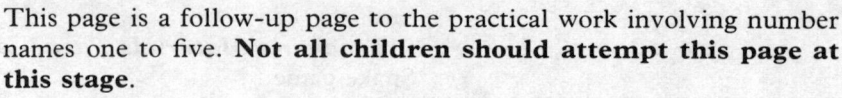

Materials None.

This page is a follow-up page to the practical work involving number names one to five. **Not all children should attempt this page at this stage**.

The children are asked to *write* the number names and, even though the number names are given at the top of the page for reference, this task could well be too difficult for many children.

The first task on the page involves the children in (a) going over the dotted outline numeral, e.g. 3; (b) drawing 3 beads on the wire; and (c) writing the number name underneath.

The second task on the page involves the children in matching a set of objects to the appropriate numeral and then writing the number name in the appropriate box. The children are meant to draw a line from the numerals or number names to the sets of objects as shown.

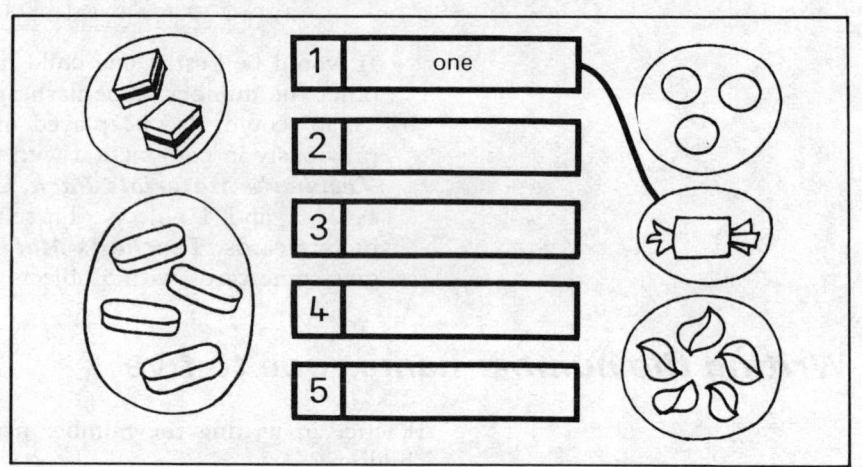

Number names to ten

This part of the work links the numerals 6 to 10 with the number names six to ten and also revises work on the number names to five.

Wall chart

The teacher could extend the wall chart to include the number names six, seven, eight, nine, and ten.

Flashcards

The teacher could prepare several sets of flashcards.

six   seven   eight   nine   ten

Workbook 8: Addition to 10; Number names

Introducing the number names to ten

This work should follow the same pattern as outlined in 'Introducing the number names one to five'.

Further practical work involving the number names to ten

1 Similar activities to those outlined in 'Further practical work involving the number names one to five' could be carried out, with number names to ten, using the sorting box, flashcards, and picture cards.

Teacher's Material Pack, Cards 1, 6, and 7, provide cards with sets of up to 8 objects on them.

Teacher's Materials Pack, Cards 20 and 21, provide a matching and ordering activity for horses numbered 1 to 10 with stables labelled one to ten.

2 **Dice activities**

This time the numerals 5, 6, 7, 8, 9, 10, or the names five, six, seven, eight, nine, ten, could be put on the faces of a die and the die used in a similar manner to that outlined previously for number names to five.

3 **Games**

(a) *Track Game* **Teacher's Materials Pack**, Cards 15 and 16, provide a track for a Fair game. This track could be used in conjunction with either (i) the number name flashcards

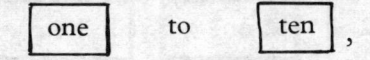

| one | to | ten |,

or (ii) a die with number names | six | to | ten |. The child would move a counter forward by reading the appropriate number name.

(b) *Snap* This game, as outlined previously, could be extended to include the number names to ten.

Writing the number names six to ten

Practice in writing the number names could be attempted by some children by writing over dotted letters, tracing, or copying, as outlined in 'Writing the number names from one to five'.

160 Workbook 8: Addition to 10; Number names

Page 13

Number names — Number names to ten

Materials None.

This page is a follow-up page to the practical work involving number names to ten.

The number names to ten are given at the top of the page for reference and the first task involves the children in a matching activity similar to that outlined in the Teaching Notes for Page 12 of the Workbook.

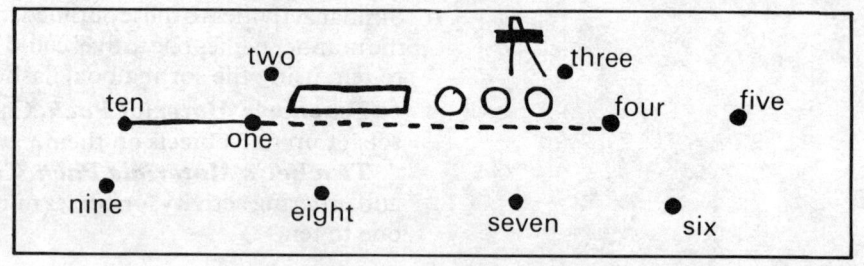

The second task is a dot-to-dot exercise involving joining the number names in sequence from one to ten to make a speedboat. The children may wish to colour their drawing after joining the dots.

Page 14

Number names — Number names to ten

Materials None.

This page emphasizes the writing of number names in a sequence, e.g.

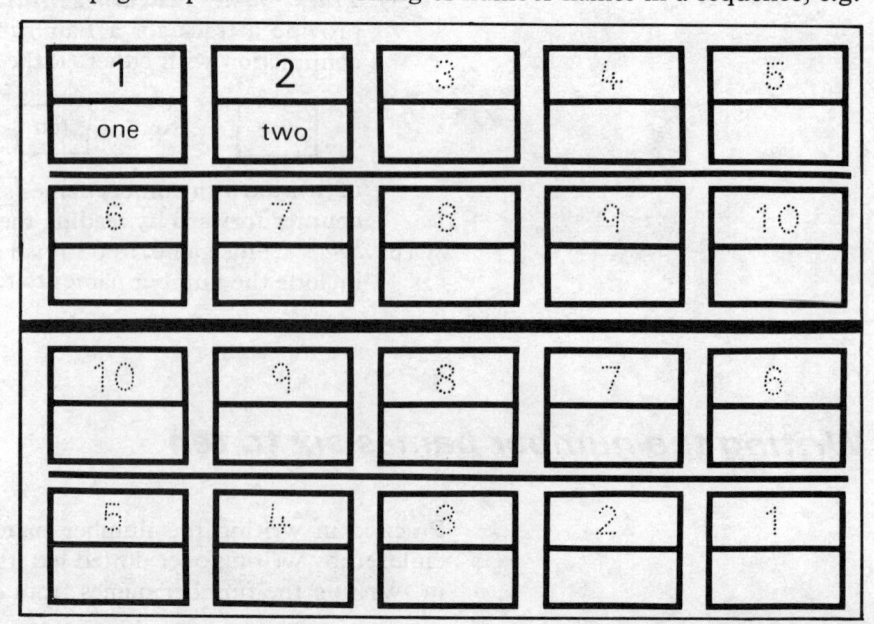

Workbook 8: Addition to 10; Number names   **161**

Other sequences include 10, 9, 8, 7, 6; and 5, 4, 3, 2, 1. Not all children should attempt this work.

The bottom part of the page gives further examples of dot-to-dot exercises involving joining the number names in sequence from one to eight. One drawing gives a star, the other a church.

Cards for the teacher to make

The teacher may wish to supplement the work on number names to ten by making cards similar to the following sample cards.

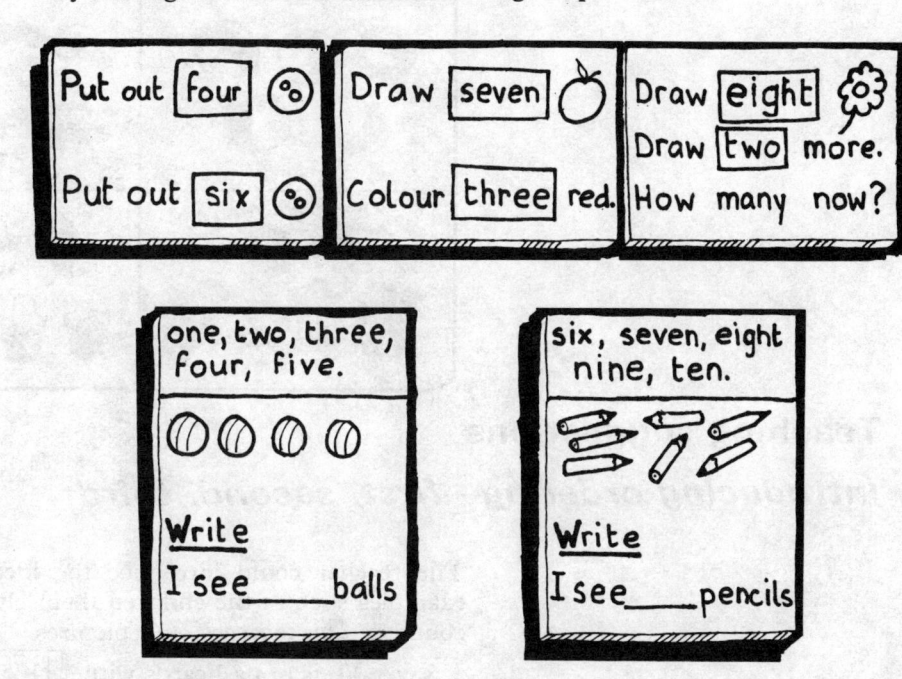

Worksheets for the teacher to make

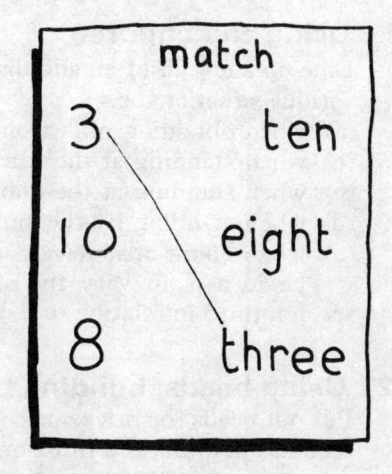

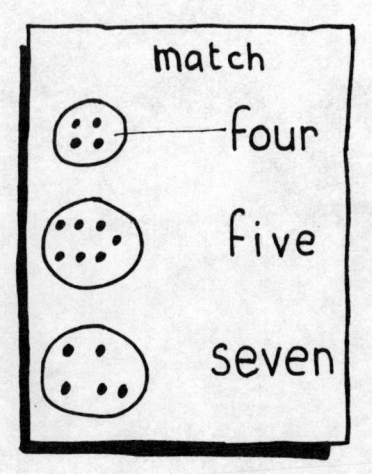

162 Workbook 8: Addition to 10; Number names

Additional activities

Workcards 1, 3, 5, 7, 9, 11, and **13,** which may have been used already in conjunction with **Workbook 4**, could be used again to give practice with number names. Flashcards one to ten could be placed on top of the appropriate set.

Some of the more able children may be able to *write* the correct number name for each set of objects.

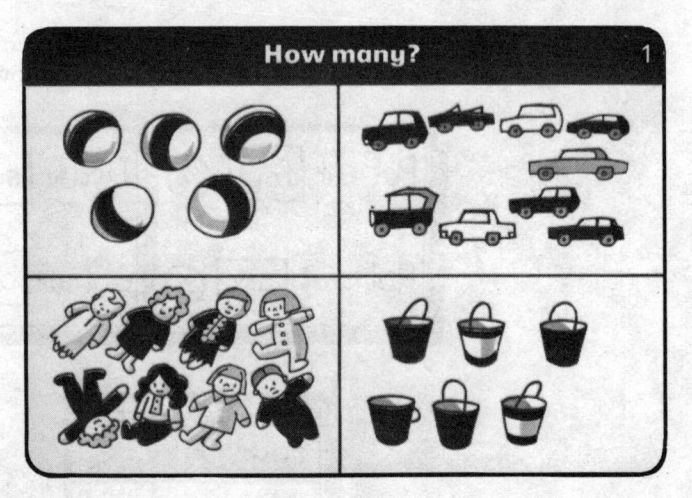

Teaching suggestions

Introducing ordering—first, second, third

The teacher could introduce the idea of first, second, third using examples such as the children themselves; beads or building bricks or counters, etc; toy-cars; and pictures.

Several sets of flashcards with first second third would be useful.

1 Using the children
Line up a few children and discuss who is first, second, and third in various situations, e.g.
(a) when obtaining milk from a central point;
(b) when standing at the teacher's desk;
(c) when standing at the door (going out, coming in);
(d) when standing by the sink or Wendy House;
(e) when going upstairs, or downstairs.
    The idea is to vary the situation so that the placing of first, second, third in relation to these points in the classroom changes.

2 Using beads, building bricks, or counters, etc.
Put out beads (or bricks or counters) so that the first one is red, the second one blue, the third one green.

Workbook 8: Addition to 10; Number names   **163**

3 Using toy cars
Line up toy cars at traffic lights or a pedestrian crossing. Point to the first, second, and third cars. Vary the position of the traffic lights and crossing.

4 Using pictures
Look at a picture of a street and discuss the first, second, and third things you would pass when walking along this street in a certain direction. Then discuss what would be the first, second, and third things you would pass if you walked *back* along the street.

The teacher may wish to place flashcards

| first | second | third |

by the appropriate object, though this is not essential.

Throughout all of this work, the teacher should discuss realistic situations where 'first', 'second', 'third' are used, for example
(a) in queues;
(b) in sport—running, swimming, horse racing, football (who scored the first goal), etc.
(c) in the family—first child in the family, first to get up in the morning, etc.

Page 15   **First, second, third** | Ordering |

Materials Red, blue, and green coloured pencils.

This page is a follow-up to much discussion and practical work.

Most children will need to have the instructions read to them and the teacher should demonstrate and discuss similar work with the children before they try this page.

Not all children should attempt this page. For some, the initial oral and practical work will be sufficient.

Workbook 9

Subtraction within 10

Cards 49 to 60 — Subtraction within 10

Cards 61 to 70 — Miscellaneous addition and subtraction

Contents

Revision—subtraction within 6	Pages 1 and 2
Subtraction within 10—taking away	Page 3
Subtraction within 10—crossing out	Pages 4 and 5
Taking from 7 and 8	Pages 6 and 7
Money—subtraction from 7p and 8p	Page 8
Taking from 9 and 10	Pages 9 and 10
Money—subtraction from 9p and 10p	Page 11
Subtraction within 10—miscellaneous examples	Page 12
Miscellaneous subtraction of money within 10p	Pages 13 and 14
Problems	Page 15
Subtraction within 10	Cards 49 to 60
Miscellaneous addition and subtraction	Cards 61 to 70

Materials

A selection from the following is required:
 counters, 1p coins, bricks, interlocking Unifix-type cubes, conkers, pebbles, toys, etc.
The following **Teacher's Materials Pack** cards may be helpful.
 Window card (Card 14) for extra examples
 Fair game (Cards 15 and 16) to be used in conjunction with flashcards
 Bingo players' cards (Cards 22 and 23)
 Money subtraction cards (Cards 24 and 25)
It would be worthwhile making flashcards of words and phrases:

|cross out| |a sale| |spend| etc.

Workbook 9: Subtraction within 10

Flashcards could also be made for all the subtraction facts for taking from 7, 8, 9, and 10:

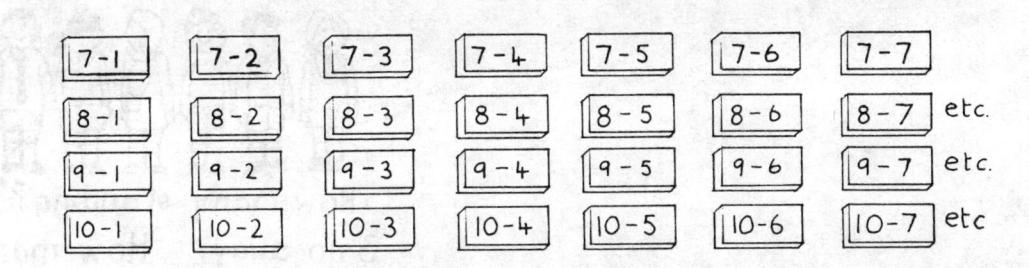

| 7-1 | 7-2 | 7-3 | 7-4 | 7-5 | 7-6 | 7-7 |
| 8-1 | 8-2 | 8-3 | 8-4 | 8-5 | 8-6 | 8-7 | etc.
| 9-1 | 9-2 | 9-3 | 9-4 | 9-5 | 9-6 | 9-7 | etc.
| 10-1 | 10-2 | 10-3 | 10-4 | 10-5 | 10-6 | 10-7 | etc

... and so on.

Subtraction within 10 (Pages 1 to 15 and Cards 49 to 60)

Development

In **Workbook 6** the 'take away' aspect of subtraction was introduced through the use of 'concrete' materials and all the facts up to 'taking from 6' were covered, with the exception of 'take away 0'.

In this Workbook 'take away 0' is introduced and the work is extended to include all the subtraction facts up to 'taking from 10'. The facts are first presented in a random way, and then systematized later. Take away situations involving 1p coins and amounts up to 10p are used to reinforce the basic number facts. Phrases such as 'I spend', 'Take off 4p', and 'How much left?' are used.

The 'adding on' and the 'difference between' aspects of subtraction are introduced in **Infant Mathematics: Second Stage**.

Preliminary activities and teaching

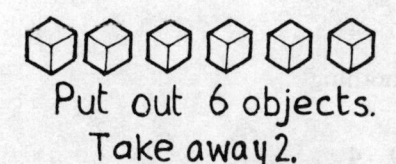

Put out 6 objects. Take away 2. "How many left?"

If the workbooks have been done in numerical order it will have been some time since the children last did subtraction. Many of the activities suggested in **Workbook 6** should be used to remind the children of the subtraction facts and the language. For example:-

1 *Physical removal* Put out 6 objects. Take away 2. 'How many left?'

166   Workbook 9: Subtraction within 10

2   Use the children themselves. 'How many standing?' Three go away. 'How many left?

"How many standing?"
3 go away. "How many left?"

3   *Drawings on the blackboard*   Draw six flowers on the blackboard. Rub out four. 'How many left?'

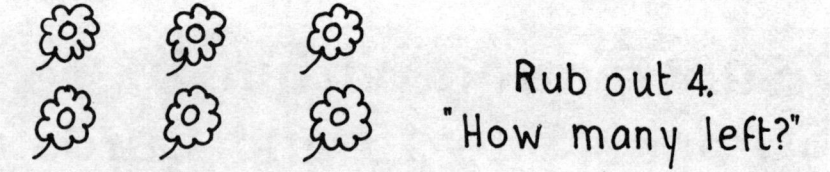

Rub out 4.
"How many left?"

4   Covering over either drawings or objects. The covering can be done by hand or using a piece of card.

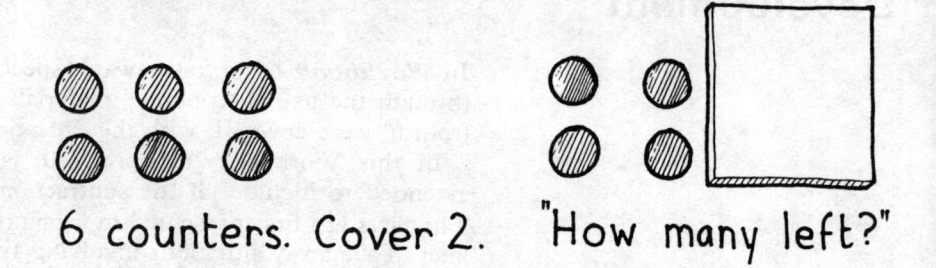

6 counters. Cover 2.   "How many left?"

5   *Take away '0'*   This Workbook starts by revising the subtraction facts within 6, and 'take away 0' is included. Many of the previous activities should be used again to illustrate this fact, for example:
(a) Four children come forward. 'None' are sent back.
'How many are left?'

$$4 - 0 = 4$$

(b) John has 4 sweets. He eats none.
'How many are left?'

$$4 - 0 = 4$$

(c) Put out 4 objects. Take away 'nothing'.
'How many are left?'

$$4 - 0 = 4$$

(d) Make up the stories including the zero facts.

Workbook 9: Subtraction within 10   **167**

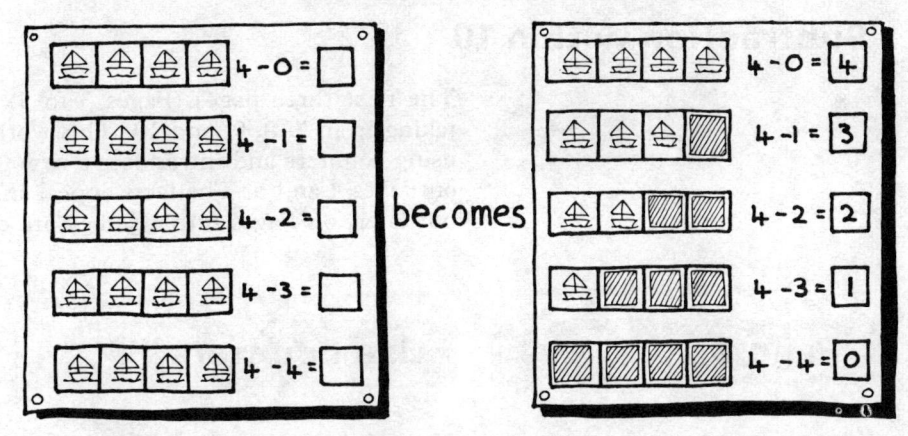

```
⛵⛵⛵⛵  4-0=☐              ⛵⛵⛵⛵  4-0=4
⛵⛵⛵▨  4-1=☐              ⛵⛵⛵▨  4-1=3
⛵⛵▨▨  4-2=☐   becomes    ⛵⛵▨▨  4-2=2
⛵▨▨▨  4-3=☐              ⛵▨▨▨  4-3=1
▨▨▨▨  4-4=☐              ▨▨▨▨  4-4=0
```

Pictures of objects covered with coloured gummed paper or 'coloured in' as shown above would make a suitable wall chart for this work.

6 Pushing over skittles or 'soldiers' could lead to further revision of the facts. The language is important. 'One falls over. Three are left standing, i.e., 4 − 1 = 3, but all four are still present. The question 'How many standing?' is important.

"How many standing?"

"4 − 1 = 3"

There are many other activities which are just as useful as the ones suggested above. It is important that children have considerable experience using concrete materials before attempting the Workbook pages.

It should be stressed at this stage that much oral work should be done to help children memorize the facts.

Pages 1 and 2   Stories   Revision—Subtraction within 6

Materials Counters, cubes, etc. (if required).

It is hoped that, after the revision of the practical activities discussed in the preceding notes, many children will be able to find the answers unaided. The pictures may be used to help some children and the covering technique is a convenient one here. Children who have difficulty with the abstract nature of the work should be shown how to use actual objects to obtain the correct answers.

Page 1 deals with taking from 3 and 4, while Page 2 deals with taking from 5 and 6. The top part of each page presents the facts in a systematic way while the bottom part gives a miscellaneous set of examples with repetitions.

Workbook 9: Subtraction within 10

Subtraction within 10

The next three pages (Pages 3 to 5) extend the subtraction work to taking from 7, 8, 9, and 10. This work revises the idea of taking away using counters and introduces a new taking away idea—crossing out—on Pages 4 and 5. The facts appear in a random order on these pages, but later, on Pages 6 to 10, they are dealt with in a systematic way.

Page 3 — Use counters — Subtraction within 10

Materials Counters.

Prior to doing this page children should have experienced 'taking away' from 7, 8, 9, and 10 using several different materials.

It is intended that the children lay counters on top of the circles on this page, and then take away the required number. If the counters available are too large for the circles an equivalent number will have to be put out on the desk. If counters are not available some other suitable objects such as cubes could be used instead. It would be possible for some children to colour in the pictures to get correct answers.

Pages 4 and 5 — Cross out — Subtraction within 10

Materials Crayons or pencils.

This is a new idea for subtraction and is probably best illustrated by blackboard examples.

Make drawings of objects on the board. Ask, 'How many?', and record the answer. Now cross out some objects and complete the recording for 'How many left?' Initially the teacher could cross out to show what is required. Later the children could do it.

$8 - 3 = 5$

Because of the larger numbers involved, crossing out should be easier than 'covering'. Children should be encouraged to count as they cross out until they have crossed out the required number. They may then count to find how many are not crossed. Children who are poor readers will be helped by oral explanations and by the repetition of phrases used on the pages.

Workbook 9: Subtraction within 10   169

| Page 6 | **Stories** | Taking from 7 |

Materials   Counters, cubes, etc. (if required).

The top part of the page systematizes the 'story of 7', including the zero facts. The drawings could be used by children employing the 'covering' technique to find the answers.

The bottom part of the page gives miscellaneous examples of taking from 6 and 7. At the bottom of the page is a written problem. Several similar examples should be done on the blackboard before doing the page example. Using a 'covering' technique on the picture might help some children. Less able pupils should be allowed to use cubes, etc., to find the answers.

This is the beginning of systematizing and, it is hoped of the memorizing of these facts. Much oral work requiring the children to find the answers mentally will be necessary. Again, the count-down type rhymes (see Appendix 2, page 231) should help children remember the subtraction facts contained in these rhymes. Flashcards giving the subtraction facts up to 'taking from 7' would be helpful.

| Page 7 | **Stories** | Taking from 8 |

Materials   Counters, cubes, etc. (if required).

The top part of the page systematizes the 'story of 8', including the zero facts. The 'covering' technique could be used by children on the drawings to find the answers. The bottom part of the page gives miscellaneous examples of taking from 7 and 8.

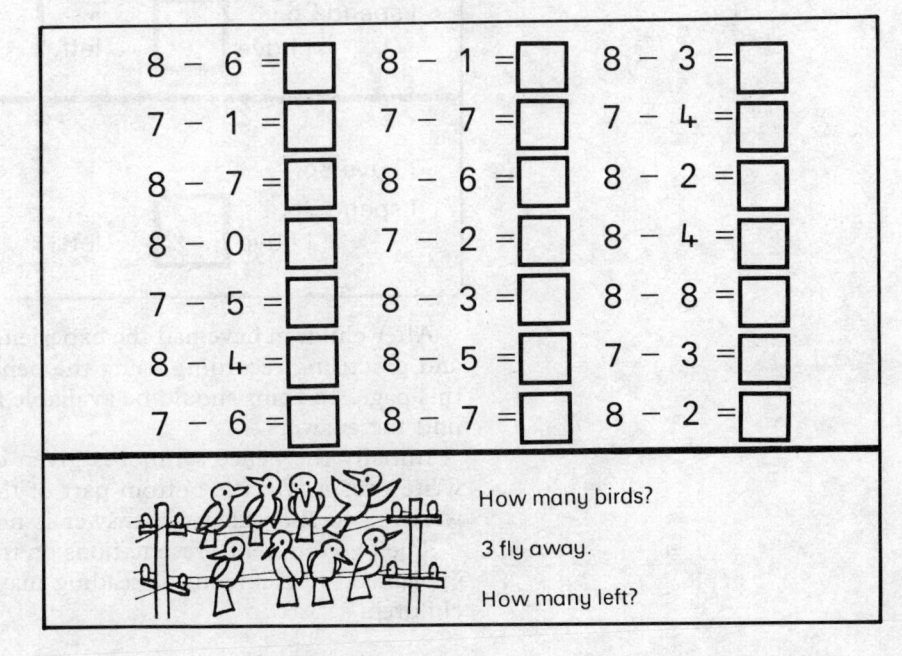

8 − 6 = ☐	8 − 1 = ☐	8 − 3 = ☐
7 − 1 = ☐	7 − 7 = ☐	7 − 4 = ☐
8 − 7 = ☐	8 − 6 = ☐	8 − 2 = ☐
8 − 0 = ☐	7 − 2 = ☐	8 − 4 = ☐
7 − 5 = ☐	8 − 3 = ☐	8 − 8 = ☐
8 − 4 = ☐	8 − 5 = ☐	7 − 3 = ☐
7 − 6 = ☐	8 − 7 = ☐	8 − 2 = ☐

How many birds?

3 fly away.

How many left?

170 Workbook 9: Subtraction within 10

At the bottom of the page is a written problem and again, several similar examples should be done on the blackboard before the page example is attempted. Using a 'covering' technique on the picture might help some children.

Children who find the work difficult because of its abstract nature should be allowed to use cubes, etc., to find the answers.

Again, much oral work requiring the children to obtain the answers mentally will be necessary. Some of the rhymes in Appendix 2 may be helpful. In addition, flashcards of the subtraction facts up to taking from 8 could be used. Ideas for games using such flashcards are given on page 176.

Page 8   Spending   Subtraction within 8p

Materials   1p coins.

Since this page is all about spending, the class shop activities (see Appendix 1) would be ideal preparatory work. Once again the language is important and this should be brought out in the questioning. 'How much money have you?' 'What do you want to buy?' 'How much have you left?' 'How much did John spend?' etc.

The child could take 7p to the shop, spend 3p, and then count what is left. This answer would be recorded in the 'box' as $\boxed{4}$ p

Use coins if you need to.

I have 7p. I spend 2p. I have ☐ p left.	I have 7p. I spend 4p. I have ☐ p left.
I have 8p. I spend 3p. I have ☐ p left.	I have 8p. I spend 6p. I have ☐ p left.

After children have had the experience of buying from the class shop and practising recording using the pence symbol 'p', they could tackle this page. 1p coins should be available for any child who needs them to find the answers.

Initially the pence symbol is given dotted and the children have to write over it. On the bottom part of the page they should continue to write 'p' to show that the answer is not just a number.

The two different presentations on this page will have to be carefully explained. The amount of reading may also make it difficult for some children.

Workbook 9: Subtraction within 10   171

This money work could be supplemented by more worksheets similar to Page 8, or by cards using a clip-on answer strip, or by money questions on a 'window card' like *Teacher's Materials Pack*, Card 14.

The shopping cards (*Teacher's Materials Pack*, Card 8), with articles costing less than 8p could be used by the children to discover what would be left from 8p if they bought the article pictured on the card.

| Page 9 | **Stories** | Taking from 9 |

Materials Counters, cubes, etc. (if required).

The top part of the page systematizes the 'story of 9', including the zero facts. The drawings could be used with the covering technique to find the answers.

The bottom part of the page gives miscellaneous examples of taking from 8 and 9 and includes a written problem about fish swimming away. Discussion and blackboard examples of this type would be helpful.

Again, these more difficult subtraction facts will need much more oral work to help children memorize them. Flashcards with the subtraction facts up to taking from 9 could now be used.

| Page 10 | **Stories** | Taking from 10 |

Materials Counters, cubes, etc. (if required).

This page has a similar layout to Page 9, with the systematized subtraction facts for taking from 10 appearing at the top. The picture is of 10 bottles and the well-known rhyme '10 green bottles' (see Appendix 2) could be introduced to give the count-down from 10 (although this rhyme is really about taking away one: 10−1, then 9−1, etc.). Again, the picture could be used to help children get the answers, but any child who finds this too abstract should be allowed to use counters or cubes or any other simple material. Much oral work will be required before children will memorize all these facts.

When a page is completed by the children it is worth asking questions about it. The answers on the page can be used. This repeated questioning should encourage the memorizing of facts.

Workbook 9: Subtraction within 10

Additional activities

The rest of the Workbook gives various examples to cover the facts to 'taking from 10' and is aimed at helping children to memorize them. At this stage teachers may wish to show the systematizing in the form of 'take away 1', 'take away 2', etc., which would give the following examples:

10 − 0 =	10 − 1 =	10 − 2 =	10 − 3 =	10 − 4 =	10 − 5 =
9 − 0 =	9 − 1 =	9 − 2 =	9 − 3 =	9 − 4 =	9 − 5 =
8 − 0 =	8 − 1 =	8 − 2 =	8 − 3 =	8 − 4 =	8 − 5 =
7 − 0 =	7 − 1 =	7 − 2 =	7 − 3 =	7 − 4 =	7 − 5 =

10 − 6 =	10 − 7 =	10 − 8 =	10 − 9 =	10 − 10 =
9 − 6 =	9 − 7 =	9 − 8 =	9 − 9 =	
8 − 6 =	8 − 7 =	8 − 8 =		
7 − 6 =	7 − 7 =			

Only the new facts for subtraction from 7, 8, 9, and 10 are listed here, but obviously children would have to know all the earlier ones as well.

Each fact could appear on a flashcard, or sets of examples could be provided on worksheets or workcards as shown below.

9 − 2 =	9 − 3 =	5 − 4 =	7 − 5 =	7 − 1 =
7 − 2 =	7 − 3 =	10 − 4 =	8 − 5 =	9 − 1 =
10 − 2 =	5 − 3 =	8 − 4 =	10 − 5 =	6 − 1 =
6 − 2 =	6 − 3 =	9 − 4 =	9 − 5 =	10 − 1 =
8 − 2 =	10 − 3 =	6 − 4 =	6 − 5 =	8 − 1 =

The less able children would be helped by clipping an answer strip of paper on to the card.

Further miscellaneous cards appear at the end of the Notes for this Workbook.

Page 11 — Spending — Subtraction within 10p

Materials 1p coins.

This page is similar to Page 8 and, as before, class shop activities should precede the page. 1p coins should be available for children who need them and teachers should stress the use of the pence symbol 'p' which shows that the answer is money. A careful explanation of what the children have to do should help the less able.

As with Page 8, the work could be supplemented by
(a) extra worksheets;
(b) extra workcards;
(c) **Teacher's Materials Pack**, Card 8, for items costing less than 9p;
(d) **Teacher's Materials Pack**, Card 14, using money examples.

Workbook 9: Subtraction within 10

Page 12

Take away `Subtraction within 10`

Materials Counters, cubes, etc. (if required).

This page contains miscellaneous examples on taking from 7, 8, 9, and 10. Two 'word problems' break up the page and give variety, but they may present reading difficulties for some children. The pictures, however, should help the less able.

Again, as suggested for Pages 8 and 11, the work could be supplemented to give the children much more practice.

Page 13

A sale `Subtraction within 10p`

Materials 1p coins (if required).

The idea of a sale giving cash reductions is used again. There are four different reductions—taking off 4p, 5p, 6p, and 7p. The items are named here and some of the words may be new to some children; the pictures should help. As on the previous occasion when this idea was used, the children should cross out the old price and write the new one on the other label. They will need to be reminded to use the pence symbol 'p'. Blackboard demonstrations would help here.

Prior to doing this page it would be worth doing class shop activities such as writing out new labels for articles, etc.

The shopping cards on **Teacher's Materials Pack**, Card 8, could be used once again for extra work of this kind by asking the children to make out new prices, say 2p off each, on pieces of paper clipped to the cards.

Page 14

Spending `Subtraction within 10p`

Materials 1p coins (if required).

As always, the practical activities are important and spending at the class shop should precede the written work. Some teachers may wish to provide the opportunity for class shop activities for different groups of children throughout the day.

The top part of this page is similar to Page 11. Piggy-banks are used this time. The bottom part of the page uses the mapping diagram idea. It would be worth reminding children that the first instruction in each case applies to all three examples. This can be shown on the blackboard by doing similar examples.

174   Workbook 9: Subtraction within 10

Take away 5p.	Take away 6p.
6p → ☐	10p → ☐
10p → ☐	7p → ☐
7p → ☐	9p → ☐

Less able pupils should be allowed to use coins as required.

Additional work could be provided on worksheets, workcards with answer strips attached, or the window-type card as in *Teacher's Materials Pack*, Card 14.

Page 15   How many left?   Problems

Materials   Counters, cubes, etc. (if required).

This page consists entirely of 'word problems' and so might prove difficult for some children. It is important that many similar problems are dealt with before doing the page. The problems fall into two categories. The first type has items which can be counted, the second type is more abstract. Examples of the countable type should be done first. Teachers should use blackboard drawings or picture cards to explain the work.

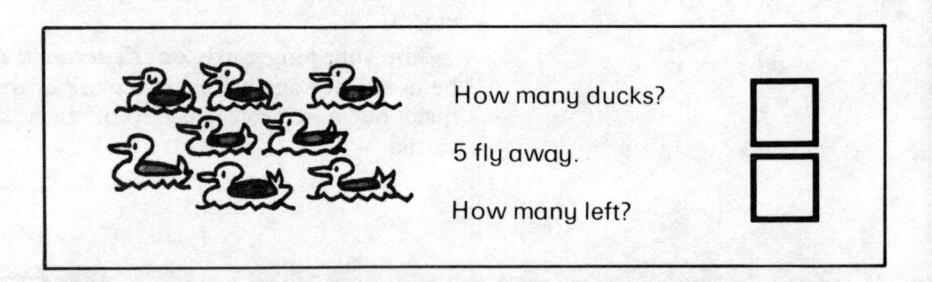

How many ducks?   ☐
5 fly away.
How many left?   ☐

In the other type of problem the articles are 'concealed' in a box. Children therefore need to recall a known subtraction fact to obtain the answer. Less able children might lay out material to represent the eggs.

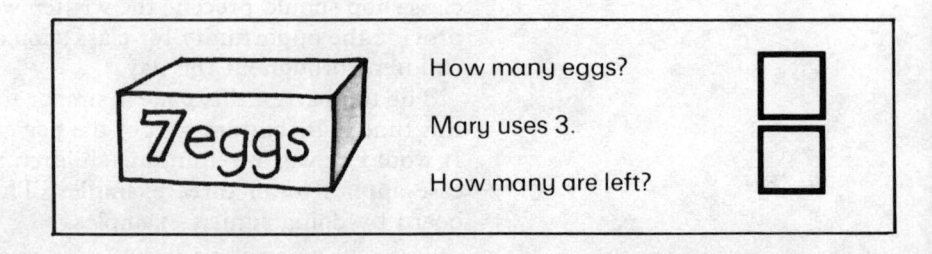

How many eggs?   ☐
Mary uses 3.
How many are left?   ☐

Workbook 9: Subtraction within 10   **175**

Again it would be possible to supplement the work by providing further worksheets or workcards similar to this page.

For children who find this work too difficult oral explanation and the use of materials, counters, cubes, etc., should help.

Some children may wish to tackle cards like this:

> Draw 7 apples.
> Put 4 in a box.
> How many are left?

> Draw 8 birds.
> Hide 3.
> How many are left?

Child draws [⚬⚬/⚬⚬] ⚬⚬⚬ and writes 7 − 4 = 3

Cards for the teacher to make

It is recommended that a set of subtraction flash cards are made to cover the new facts. A large set could be used for class or group work and a smaller set, about playing card size, could be used by individuals or by small groups when playing games.

The facts to be covered are:

10−0	9−0	8−0	7−0
10−1	9−1	8−1	7−1
10−2	9−2	8−2	7−2
10−3	9−3	8−3	7−3
10−4	9−4	8−4	7−4
10−5	9−5	8−5	7−5
10−6	9−6	8−6	7−6
10−7	9−7	8−7	7−7
10−8	9−8	8−8	
10−9	9−9		
10−10			

If the 'take away 0' cards were added to the set suggested for **Workbook 6**, this would give a complete set of subtraction facts within 10. Duplicates would be necessary for facts such as 10 − 0, 9 − 0, etc., to have approximately equal numbers of each answer.

Selections of these facts could also be used to make extra cards for children using the answer strip or the window-type Card 14 from the **Teacher's Materials Pack**.

Workbook 9: Subtraction within 10

Additional activities and games

1. *Teacher's Materials Pack*, Cards 22 and 23, can be cut up to give 8 bingo players' cards like the one shown. The bingo game can be played using the flashcards described above. It would be advisable to include duplicates of some facts to give roughly equal chances for the appearance of each number.

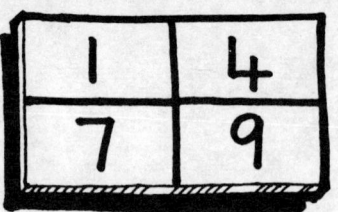

    In one form of the game the cards are placed face down. A child takes the top card, gives the answer, and places the card face up in a discard pile. The child checks his bingo card for the number answered and, if it appears, covers it with a counter. The next child then takes a turn, and so on until one player covers all the numbers on his card. If a child gives a wrong answer a counter could be removed.

    Another possibility involves all the players covering the number which is the correct answer to a card. This game would finish much faster as each player has a chance to cover a number each time an answer is given.

2. The substraction flash cards could be used to play the Fair game on *Teacher's Materials Pack*, Cards 15 and 16, which was mentioned in *Workbook 6* (page 107). A player should move forward the number of places which corresponds to the answer on the card.

3. The facts cards could be used by individual children for matching to numerals, objects, dot patterns, etc.

4. *Teacher's Materials Pack*, Cards 24 and 25, on subtraction of money, provided a game where each child has a picture of a cash register showing, for example, 6p, 5p, or 4p, etc. Other cards are also provided:

    The object of the game is for each child to collect cards like these to match his cash register card.

5. Oral work at this stage could try to link the addition and subtraction facts. The teacher might concentrate on a particular story, for example, the 'story of 7'.

Workbook 9: Subtraction within 10   177

4 and 3 make 7.   7 take away 4 is 3.
7 take away 3 is 4. etc.

This can be illustrated by a drawing, as shown. Ask children to tell this story. The subtraction can be done by covering.

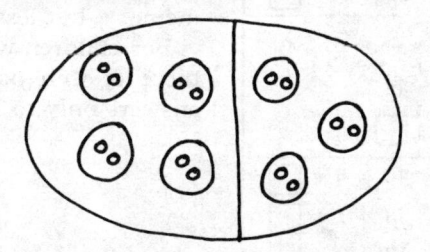

6 The children could write down the numbers

0 1 2 3 4 5 6 7.

The teacher could then ask questions about 'taking from 7,' e.g. 'Seven take away four', or show the flashcard $\boxed{7-4=}$ and the children cross off the correct answer. It is better not to ask all possible answers at any one time so that any error may be spotted.

Cards 49 to 60   Subtraction within 10

Materials   Counters, cubes, 1p coins, etc. (if required).

This set of cards covers all the subtraction facts within 10. They are presented in a way that should allow all children to attempt some of the work. The odd-numbered cards mainly contain straight-forward practice examples, with easier examples at the top. The even-numbered cards are 'word and picture problem' cards on number and money. The cards are all about the same order of difficulty and so could be used by, say, six different children at the same time.

It is not expected that all children complete both sides of these cards. Some children may do only the odd numbers and the less able pupils may only complete the top half of each card. With the problem-type cards some teaching should be done to ensure that as many children as possible can make a reasonable attempt at them. Flashcards of words such as $\boxed{\text{write}}$ would be helpful.

Cards 49, 51, 53, 55, 57, 59

The top part of these cards contains subtraction facts within 6. The first six examples need to be copied and the answer supplied. There then follows a

178 **Workbook 9:** Subtraction within 10

simple picture problem where the drawings on the card can be 'covered up' to find the answer. These subtractions are also within 6. This top part of each card should suit almost all children.

The bottom part of each card has ten examples of subtraction within 10. It is hoped that children will be capable of doing these from memory, but less able pupils may have to resort to concrete materials.

For children who would take too long to copy and complete a card a piece of thin paper or tracing paper could be clipped on to allow answers only to be written.

Cards 50, 52, 54

These cards contain four 'word and picture problems'. In the first two on each card the objects can be counted, but in the last two examples a representation of the number of objects is shown and it is hoped that most children will be able to complete these by recall of number facts. Children who find this work too abstract may be shown how to use material to simulate the problem. In recording the answers the children are asked to write words as well as numbers, e.g. **6 ducks left**. Flashcards of any words which are new to the children would be helpful.

Card 56

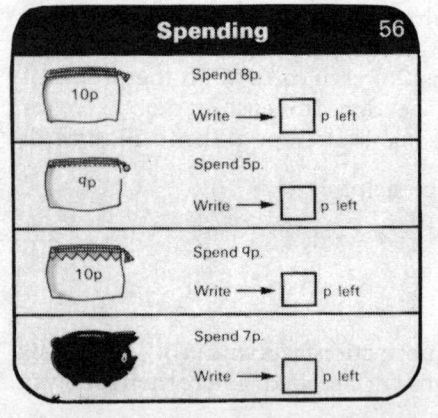

This is a spending card and is similar in layout to some examples on **Workbook 9**, Pages 8, 11, and 14. Purses and piggy-banks show the initial amount of money, and then some is spent. When recording, the children have to write '4p left'. 1p coins could be available for children who need them.

Workbook 9: Subtraction within 10　　**179**

Cards 58 and 60

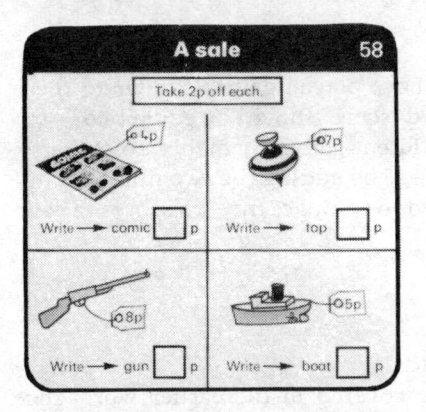

These two cards are of 'the sale' type. In Card 58 the prices are reduced by 2p and in card 60 they are reduced by 3p. In recording the answer the name of the article has to be written, e.g. 'boat 3p'.

Similar extra work could be done through the class shop activities.

Cards 61 to 70

Miscellaneous addition and subtraction

Materials　Counters, 1p coins, cubes, dice, etc. (if required).

This is a miscellaneous selection of cards covering addition facts to 10 and subtraction facts within 10. The odd-numbered cards contain mainly a mixture of addition and subtraction practice examples of the types

$5 + 4 = \boxed{}$ and $9 - 3 = \boxed{}$

The even-numbered cards contain 'word and picture problems' on addition and subtraction with 'games' and money work included for variety.

Cards 61, 63, 65, 67, 69

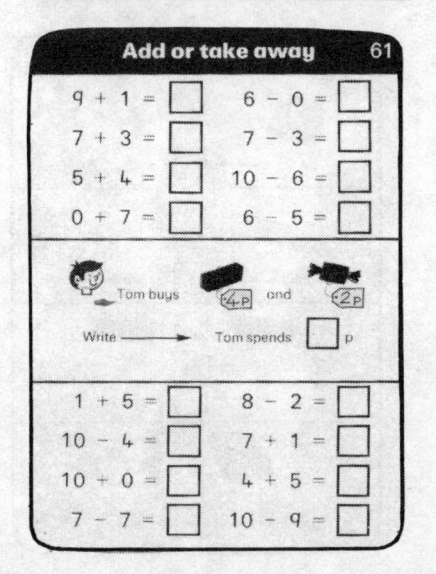

Add or take away

These five cards are all of the same type. A simple word problem separates the card into two parts and in some cases the problem concerns money. The top part contains a column of four additions and a second column of 4 subtractions. The bottom part of the card contains a mixture of addition and subtraction.

It is hoped that children will be able to do most of these without resorting to concrete material, but if it is required it should be made available. Again, clipping a piece of thin paper over the card would allow slow workers to give the answers without copying down the examples.

180 Workbook 9: Subtraction within 10

Card 62

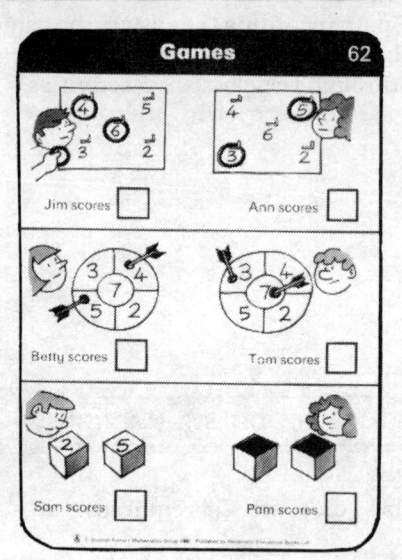

Games

It would be helpful for children to have played games similar to these before attempting the card. The word 'score' should be explained.

The card shows scores in three different games, namely quoits, darts, and dice. The total is found in each case by adding the two numbers but several other questions could be asked to compare the two scores in each game. For example,

'Who scored more, Jim or Ann?'
'How many more did Jim score?'
'Who had the highest score?'
'Who won and by how many?' etc.

Since the addition facts to 10 are covered in the earlier work, dice marked 0 to 5 would ensure that a total greater than 10 would not be available for children playing an addition game with two dice. Polystyrene cubes with the numbers written in 'marker pen' make very quiet dice!

Cards 64 and 66

Problems

These cards each contain four 'word and picture problems'. On Card 64 the pictures show individual birds, some of which could be 'covered' to give the answer to the subtraction.

Card 66 shows representative pictures but no countable objects, and on each card there are also two addition and two subtraction questions. The reading might make these cards too difficult for some children and oral explanation will be necessary.

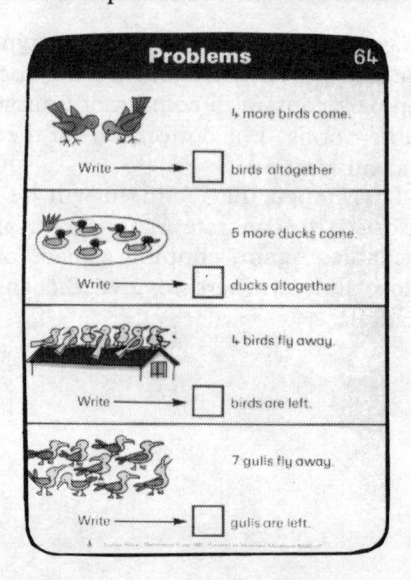

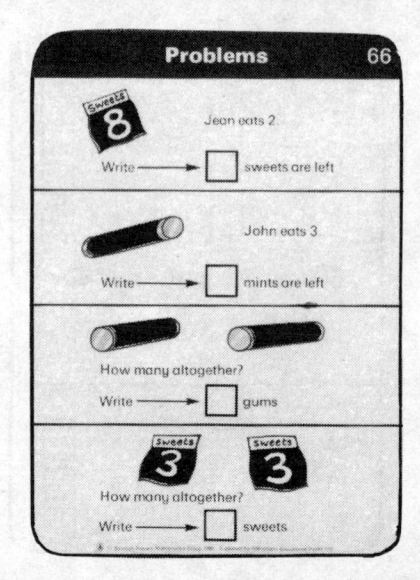

Workbook 9: Subtraction within 10 **181**

Card 68

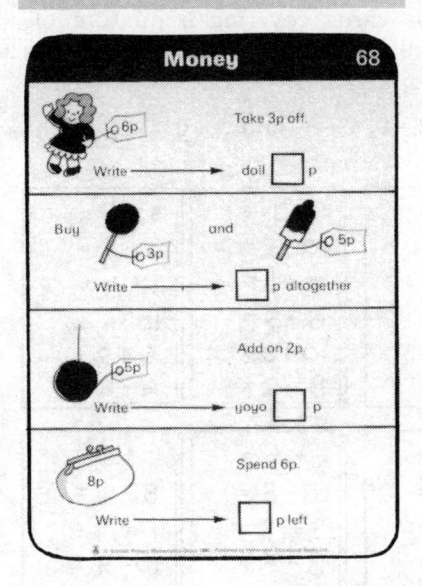

Money

As with the previous 'money' cards, the interpretation is important. Prices are increased or decreased and the phrases used must be understood. 'Take 3p off', 'buy', 'add on 2p', 'spend 6p' are all used on the card and, provided the children have met similar phrases in their practical work with the class shop, there should not be too many difficulties.

Card 70

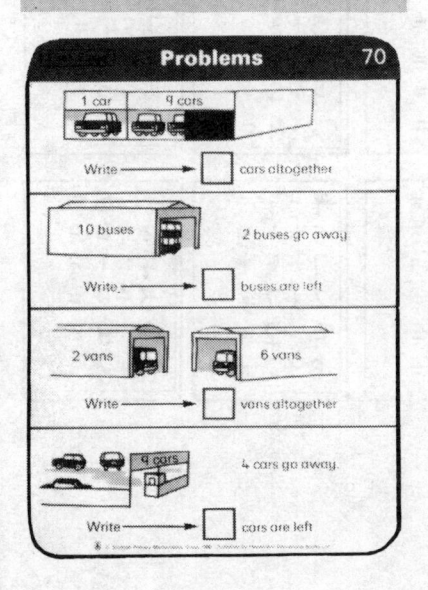

Problems

This card has representative pictures of objects and two addition and two subtraction problems are given. It is similar to Card 66 and again the answer should contain a number and words, e.g. '8 buses are left'.

182 Workbook 9: Subtraction within 10

Cards for the teacher to make

Here are some further miscellaneous cards covering a mixture of addition and subtraction facts. The only facts not included in this set of cards are:

$1+0, 2+0, 1-0, 1-1, 2-0, 2-1,$ and $3-0$

3 + 2 = 10 - 0 = 1 + 1 = 6 - 2 = 5 + 4 = 9 - 9 =	5 + 5 = 6 - 3 = 3 + 7 = 10 - 1 = 1 + 2 = 8 - 0 =	6 + 0 = 10 - 2 = 3 + 3 = 8 - 1 = 4 + 2 = 6 - 4 =	1 + 3 = 10 - 3 = 6 + 1 = 6 - 5 = 10 + 0 = 8 - 2 =	3 + 4 = 8 - 3 = 1 + 4 = 10 - 4 = 6 + 2 = 6 - 6 =
1 + 9 = 7 - 0 = 3 + 5 = 8 - 8 = 2 + 7 = 10 - 5 =	6 + 3 = 10 - 6 = 1 + 8 = 5 - 1 = 7 + 0 = 8 - 7 =	3 + 6 = 10 - 7 = 6 + 4 = 8 - 6 = 1 + 7 = 2 - 2 =	1 + 6 = 10 - 8 = 3 + 7 = 8 - 5 = 6 + 4 = 5 - 0 =	4 + 0 = 8 - 4 = 1 + 5 = 10 - 9 = 7 + 1 = 3 - 3 =
5 - 2 = 2 + 1 = 3 - 2 = 4 + 4 = 9 - 3 = 7 + 2 =	9 - 2 = 4 + 1 = 7 - 1 = 2 + 2 = 5 - 3 = 1 + 3 =	3 + 5 = 2 + 3 = 7 - 2 = 4 + 2 = 5 - 4 = 9 - 1 =	7 - 3 = 9 - 0 = 5 + 3 = 5 - 5 = 4 + 5 = 2 + 4 =	10 - 10 = 2 + 5 = 7 - 4 = 4 + 3 = 4 - 0 = 9 + 1 =
3 - 1 = 4 + 5 = 6 - 1 = 9 - 4 = 7 + 3 = 3 + 0 =	4 + 6 = 6 - 0 = 3 + 1 = 8 + 0 = 4 - 4 = 9 - 5 =	2 + 8 = 5 + 0 = 7 - 7 = 9 - 6 = 8 + 1 = 4 - 3 =	9 - 7 = 5 + 1 = 7 - 6 = 2 + 7 = 4 - 2 = 8 + 2 =	7 - 5 = 2 + 6 = 4 - 1 = 5 + 2 = 9 - 8 = 9 + 0 =

Workbook

Shape, Length, Time

Cards 15 to 24 — Solid shapes

Cards 39 to 48 — Flat shapes

Contents

Solid shapes

| Building models | Cards 15 to 24 |
| Sorting and matching | Pages 1 to 4 |

Length

| Long, short, thick, thin, tall | Pages 5 to 9 |

Flat shapes

| Making pictures with shapes | Cards 39 to 48 |
| Sorting and matching | Pages 10 to 13 |

Time

Reading o'clocks	Pages 14 to 16
Drawing hands on clockfaces	Pages 17 and 18
A time sequence	Page 19

Length

Longer and shorter	Pages 20 and 21
Thicker and thinner	Page 22
Taller and shorter	Page 23

The teaching notes on time also contain work on vocabulary, language, days of the week, etc.

184 Shape, Length, Time Workbook

There are no Workbook pages or Cards dealing with weight, area, or volume. Suggestions for informal activities which relate to these topics are given in Appendix 1 (page 221).

Using this Workbook

This Workbook is not part of the sequence of **Workbooks 1 to 9** which deal with number and money. It contains five *separate* sections of work on shape, length, and time topics which are intended for use at suitable times *throughout* the year. The workbook is likely to be 'lifted and laid', the teacher deciding when the time has come to attempt one of its units. It is intended that the individual units on shape, length, and time should be *interspersed* with number work from **Workbooks 1 to 9**. It is *not* recommended that all the number work be done first, or that this Workbook be attempted all at once at the end of the year.

The sections need not be done in strict order. However, the easier units appear in the earlier pages and the more difficult work is placed later. In particular, there are advantages in doing the 'solid shapes' section *before* 'flat shapes'. More importantly, the last unit on the comparative length words, 'longer' and 'shorter', should come *after* the section on 'long', 'short', etc. Apart from this, there is some flexibility about when exactly each unit is used.

Materials

Solid shapes

Cones, cylinders, cubes, and cuboids in the form of plastic or wooden shapes or empty cartons (detailed suggestions are given in the Teaching Notes for this section); coloured pencils or crayons; 'junk' materials for making models.

Length

Materials for comparing lengths, heights, and thicknesses, including pencils, ribbons, string, crayons, thread, straws, strips, etc. (detailed suggestions are given in the Teaching Notes for this section); coloured pencils or crayons; plasticine; flashcards.

|long| |short| |thick| |thin| |tall|

Flat shapes

A cone, a cube, and a cuboid; paper shapes to fit some faces of these solids (see Teaching Notes); plastic, wooden or cardboard circles,

Shape, Length, Time Workbook

triangles, squares, and rectangles; (detailed suggestions are given in the Teaching Notes); large cardboard shapes for teaching purposes; boxes or trays to contain sets of shapes; coloured pencils or crayons; gummed paper shapes.

Time

Cardboard, paper, etc., for making wallcharts, flashcards, etc., for work on time vocabulary and time sequences; a real clock with a simple face and/or a cardboard clock whose hands can be used one at a time;

flashcards |6 o'clock| |7 o'clock| etc.; clockface cards [clock image] for 2 o'clock, 3 o'clock, etc.; small individual clocks for some pupils; coloured pencils or crayons.

Length

Pairs of objects whose length, thickness, and height can be compared (more detailed suggestions are given in the Teaching Notes); flashcards

|longer| |shorter| |thicker| |thinner| |taller|;

coloured pencils or crayons.

The following items from the *Teacher's Materials Pack* would be useful for this part:
    Flat shapes (Cards 26 and 27)
    Shape game (Card 28)
    Time sequences (Cards 29 and 30)

186 Shape, Length, Time Workbook

Solid shapes
(Cards 15 to 24 and Pages 1 to 4)

Development

The children should have had an opportunity to build models from junk materials before starting this section which is an attempt to 'structure' such activities (see Appendix 1, page 221).

The cards suggest models which the children should build using the set of cartons described below. The Workbook pages provide further sorting and matching activities involving the same models.

Four types of shapes are used in this section—cones, cylinders, cubes, and cuboids. However, these names are not introduced in the cards or pages at this stage.

Cards 15 to 24

Solid shapes

Materials A set of packets similar to those shown below can be used for building all the models on the cards.

4 identical cylinders
These could be spice cartons or cores from paper rolls with circles stuck on each end.

2 identical cones
There are paper drinking cups of this shape.

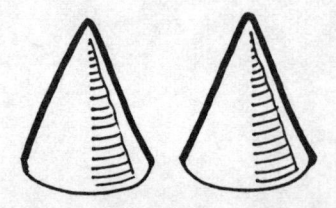

Shape, Length, Time Workbook

A selection of 6 cuboids.
Two of these should be identical. At least one should be a cube.

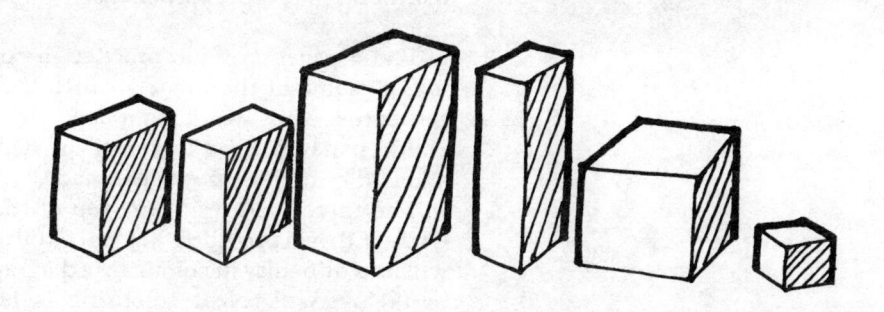

Other 'shapes and sizes' of these three types of shape should be included if available. Wooden or plastic shapes could also be used. One way of checking that the shapes will produce satisfactory models is by quickly building the following: the church (Card 21); the sleeping man and the aeroplane (Card 23); and the chair (Card 24).

If more than one set of cartons can be gathered together in a large box then a group of children can use the cards at the same time. The more shapes available the better, as this gives children experience of choosing the correct type.

The cards ask the children to build named models such as

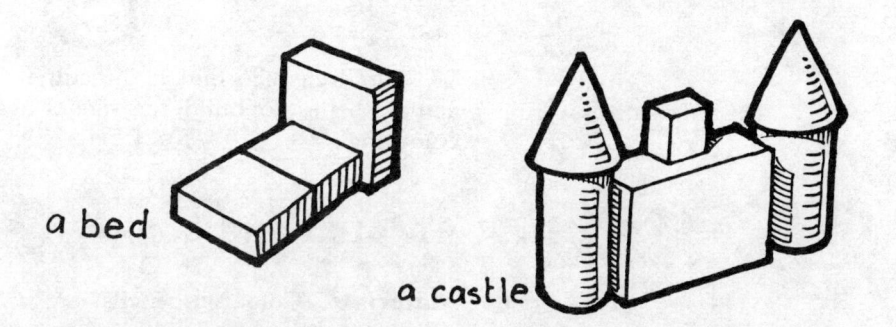

a bed

a castle

These names might be read out by the teacher to help the children to visualise what they are going to build. Also, models should be built up and discussed with the children *before* they start work on the cards. The cards need not be tackled in order, although the more difficult models appear on the later cards. The shapes should *not* be glued together.

The most important feature of this work should be discussion of the shapes used. This will include descriptions of 'size' as well as 'shape'. Words and ideas which might arise include:
- long, short, tall, thick, thin, wide, narrow, high and low;
- hollow, solid, heavy, light;
- face, flat, curved, edge, straight, round, point, corner;
- cylinder, cone, cube (see later note on 'naming shapes');
- inside, outside, on top, below;
- build, roll, etc.

188 Shape, Length, Time Workbook

| **Pages 1 and 2** | **Shape models** | Solid shapes |

Materials Coloured pencils.

These pages provide practice in sorting shapes by colouring drawings of some of the models which the children should have built from the cards. This work on paper should not be introduced until the children have had experience of handling actual shapes and talking about the models they have made.

The three pictures at the top of each page should be coloured first. They will then provide a 'key' to colouring the rest of the page. Some pupils will find difficulty in colouring a diagram like the one shown, in which the parts 'overlap'. Neat colouring is less important than an ability to distinguish shapes and talk about them.

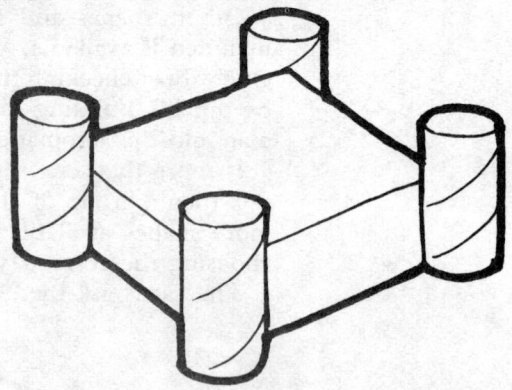

Children who find it difficult to sort out the shapes should use actual shapes to build the model again, and then refer to it when colouring.

| **Page 3** | **Match and colour** | Solid shapes |

Materials Coloured pencils.

The children should draw lines to show where each shape appears in the completed model.

The cylindrical legs of the robot may cause problems as one is 'standing up' while the other is 'lying down'. Once again, the use of actual shapes, which can be turned from one position to the other in making the model, should overcome these difficulties.

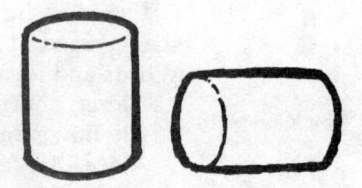

Once the children have drawn the matching lines the diagrams should be coloured in a similar way to Pages 1 and 2.

Shape, Length, Time Workbook 189

Teaching suggestions

Sorting

Cartons, including those used to make the models, should now be sorted into sets.

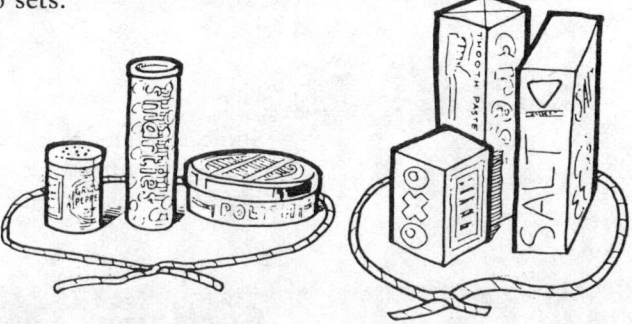

This should be repeated with other sets of shapes including cones. Two different types of shape are probably enough at first, but this could later be extended to three sets.

Naming solid shapes

The names—cone, cylinder, cuboid, cube—have not been used on the cards and pages of this unit. Reading and writing of these names will be introduced during **Infant Mathematics: Second Stage** for those pupils who are ready for it. However, teachers may wish to name shapes orally at this stage.

Cone
The name 'cone' for this type of shape can be associated with 'ice cream cone'. Knitting wool is often wound round a cardboard core which is nearly cone-shaped.
  Important features to be associated with the name are that a cone has a curved face but can sit on its flat face. It also 'comes to a point'.

Cylinder
'Cylinder' is a more difficult word to remember and pronounce than 'cone'. It is rarely used in everyday conversation. Teachers should make up their own minds whether to use this word or not this stage although there is no really good alternative.
  Important features are the curved face with flat 'ends'. It is like a closed tube.

190 Shape, Length, Time Workbook

Cube and cuboid

'Cube' and 'cuboid' might be left until a later stage, especially as it can be difficult for children to distinguish cubes from other cuboids. General terms such a 'box' or 'block' might be used at this early stage.

An important feature of these shapes is that all their faces are flat.

Some teachers may wish to use 'correct' names from the start and gradually to introduce written labels to place beside sets of shapes. Others may wish to use looser descriptions for some of the shapes.

Page 4 — Sorting — Solid shapes

Materials Coloured pencils. (Solid shapes should also be available).

This page provides follow-up work on paper to the sorting activities with 'real' shapes described above.

The top half of the page asks children to draw rings round shapes of the same type. They should have met this type of recording before in **Workbook 1:** Sorting, etc. If they use different colours to draw different rings, it will not matter so much if the rings overlap. The drawings should be discussed with the children to bring out what each drawing represents and then to discover which ones show the same type of shape. This could be done using an actual shape and asking 'Which shapes are the same kind as this one?'

The bottom half of the page uses colouring to sort shapes. In the first set of drawings the shapes are all of the same height. The second set is much more difficult since height and width vary. The important

Shape, Length, Time Workbook 191

idea is to distinguish between those which are like a 'tube' or 'tin' (the cylinders) and the others which are cuboids—'boxes', like a 'brick', etc. Some children should realise that 'Woof' and 'Purr' are fictitous dog and cat foods.

Additional activities

1. Cards 15 to 24 asked children to make particular models. They should also have the opportunity of making models of their own by sticking together cartons, egg boxes, cotton reels, etc. The models can then be painted. Commercial sets of wooden or plastic blocks can also be used to make models.
2. A class display of objects brought in by the children and sorted by shape can be built up over a period of time. It is probably best to stick to the types of shape introduced in this unit and to exclude other shapes. Alternatively, there could be a fourth set of 'other shapes'.  
3. Scrapbooks can be made using pictures of solid shapes cut from newspapers, comics, and magazines. The pictures could also be used to make wall posters for each kind of shape.
4. There are many other ways in which solid shapes can be sorted, for example:
       curved faces or flat faces;
       those which build towers and those which do not;
       those which roll and those which do not.

Teachers may wish to introduce these activites to some children at this stage, although work of this type appears at later stages of the *Primary Mathematics* course.

Length (Pages 5 to 9)

Development

This section describes sorting activities with materials which should help children to use the following words:

long, short, thick, thin, tall, wide, narrow, high, and low.

Children tend to use the words 'big' and 'small' to describe all lengths. This unit aims to refine that language so that an *appropriate* word from the list above is used instead.

The Workbook pages are intended to give further practice in the use of five of these words—long, short, thick, thin, and tall. Written work should not be attempted until the children have sorted and discussed actual materials.

The use of comparative terms, such as 'longer', 'taller', is dealt with in a later section (see notes for Pages 20 to 23).

Practical activities and teaching

Introducing 'long' and 'short'

1 Teachers might start this work by sorting out materials with the children. A set of pencils, rods, straws, or crayons, all of the same type and colour but of *two* clearly different lengths, could be sorted into 'long' ones and 'short' ones.

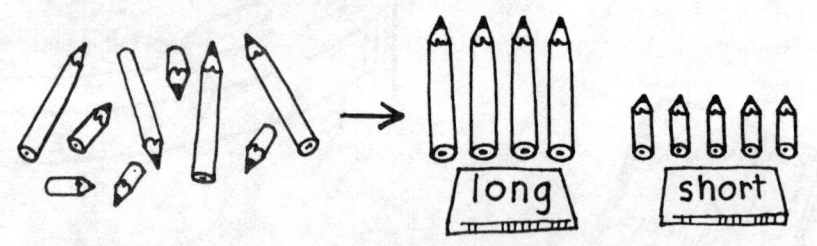

This should be repeated several times using other materials such as ribbons, lengths of string and wool, etc. (see 'Materials' list on page 184).

One method of sorting with a group of children would be to put a 'long' and 'short' object into each of two trays. The children could then be asked to sort out all the 'long' ones like this one and the 'short' ones like that one.

2 Discussion between the teacher and the children is most important. It may be necessary to start with the children's own language of 'big' and 'small' and use these words to introduce the more appropriate terms 'long' and 'short'; for example, 'All these big ones are *long*', and indicate 'length' by moving a figure along the object.

Shape, Length, Time Workbook

3 It would also be worthwhile sorting mixed sets of objects where there was one 'long' and one 'short' object of each kind. All the long objects should be of roughly the same length, as should all the short objects.

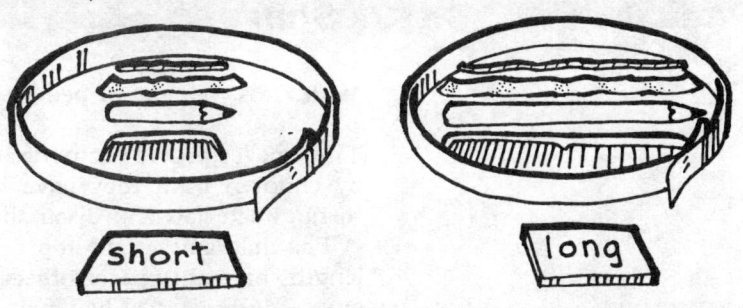

4 Children could also roll out plasticine to make long and short snakes and sausages.

Recording

1 Flashcards with the words long and short could be placed beside sets which had been sorted and left on display in the classroom.

2 Gummed paper shapes or pictures cut from magazines can be sorted and stuck on to a wall poster with the appropriate word beside each set.

3 A class book of long and short things could be created using pictures cut from magazines, comics, and newspapers.

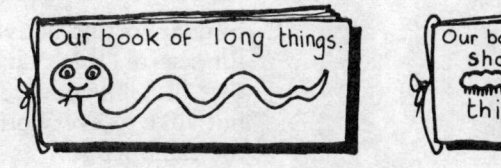

194 Shape, Length, Time Workbook

| Page 5 | Long | Language of length |
| Page 6 | Short | Language of length |

Materials Coloured pencils.

These pages provide activities on paper which should not be attempted by children until they have had plenty of practice in handling and sorting materials and discussing sets of 'long' and 'short' objects.

The diagrams at the top of the page show two distinctly different lengths of each type of object. The children should colour the 'long' ones as instructed. They may also wish to colour the short ones in the same diagram using a *different* colour.

When asked to draw a long snake and a long pencil on Page 5, the children should take the drawings on the page to represent a 'short' snake and a 'short' pencil. Their drawings should then be longer than the given ones.

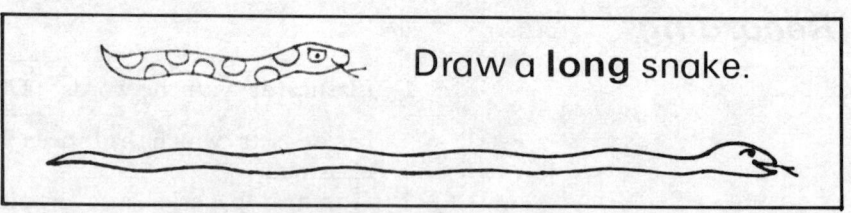

Draw a **long** snake.

The last part of Page 6 asks the children to count long and short tails on the mice. The other drawings on Pages 5 to 9 can also be used to give practice in *counting* small numbers of objects. For example (on Page 5), 'How many toothbrushes are there?'; 'How many long ones?'; 'How many short ones?'; etc.

Teaching suggestions

'Longer', 'shorter', 'same length as'

Although comparative terms such as 'longer than', 'shorter than', 'the same length as' are introduced in a later unit (Pages 20 to 23 of this Workbook), they are likely to arise in discussion of sorting activities and of the drawings on the Workbook pages. The oral use of these words should be encouraged as much as possible.

Introducing 'thick' and 'thin'

1 Similar sorting activities to those for 'long' and 'short' can be used for sets of 'thick' and 'thin' objects. It is most important, at first, that the objects used should be of *two* widely differing thicknesses but alike in every other respect and, particularly, they should be of the same length.

Shape, Length, Time Workbook

The word 'fat' is one which most children seem to know and it is useful to associate it with 'thick'. Feeling the objects with the fingers helps to put the ideas of 'thick' and 'thin' across to children.

The children should have experience of sorting a variety of objects. Suitable materials would include pencils, crayons, knitting needles, thread, short lengths of rope and wool, sticks, etc.

2. Discussion is particularly important: 'These pens are thick'. 'There are two thin pens'; 'Show me a thick knitting needle', etc. Recording of sorting activities can be done in a similar way as for 'long' and 'short'.

3. Other useful activities include
   (a) *making* thick and thin snakes with plasticine;
   (b) *counting* all the thick crayons;
   (c) *drawing* a thin worm on paper;
   (d) *finding* a thick rope; etc.
   (See later section on 'Cards for the teacher to make'.)

4. Comparative terms, 'thicker' and 'thinner', are likely to arise in discussion. Children could also be asked to 'Find things which are thicker than this crayon,' etc.

5. *Some* children may be able to deal with two length 'properties' at the same time. They could be asked to
   (a) find a long, thin, knitting needle;
   (b) draw a short, thick, worm and a long, thin, worm;
   (c) count the short, thick, pens;
   (d) sort out all the long, thin, ropes;
   (e) make a long, thin snake and a short, thick snake with plasticine; etc.

For some children this type of activity will be too difficult at this stage and should be left until much later.

Page 7	Thick	Language of length
Page 8	Thin	Language of length

Materials Coloured pencils.

These pages should only be used to follow up practical work with materials. They can be used in the ways suggested for the 'long' and 'short' Pages 5 and 6.

Introducing 'tall' and 'short'

1. Sorting activities could start with the pupils themselves who can be sorted into groups of 'tall' and 'short'. A large 'graph' or poster could be made by 'drawing round' the tallest and shortest pupils in the class and cutting their silhouettes out of paper. Comparative phrases such as 'taller than' should arise naturally from such work.
2. Building towers of bricks or interlocking cubes would help to put over the idea.
3. Pupils could also stick pictures from magazines or comics to make a wall poster showing tall things and short things. A tall picture of a giraffe could be contrasted with a short ape; a tall factory chimney with a short house chimney; and so on.
4. Stories could be told about dwarfs and giants followed by drawing a giant taller than the classroom door, etc.

Page 9 — Tall and short — Language of length

Materials Coloured pencils.

This work on paper should follow practical work of the type described above. Most of the examples ask the children to count, 'How many tall robots?' etc. They may also wish to colour over the cartoon drawings using different colours to show 'tall' and 'short'.

The tree and man which they draw at the foot of the page should be distinctly taller and shorter than the given drawings.

Discussion of the objects on the page is once again the most important feature of the work.

Cards for the teacher to make

Teachers may wish to use cards to give some of the children additional activities involving the words introduced so far—long, short, thick, thin, tall. *A few examples* of possible cards are given below.

Shape, Length, Time Workbook 197

1 *'Find'* cards

| Find a long / a short | Find a thick / a thin | Find a tall / a short |

2 *'Draw'* cards

| Draw 3 long | Draw 4 short | Draw 2 thick |
| Draw 6 thin | Draw 5 tall | Draw 3 short |

This 'draw' idea might be extended to 'Draw a long, thick ✏,' for the most able children.

3 *'Make'* cards. These would be used with plasticine, clay, or dough.

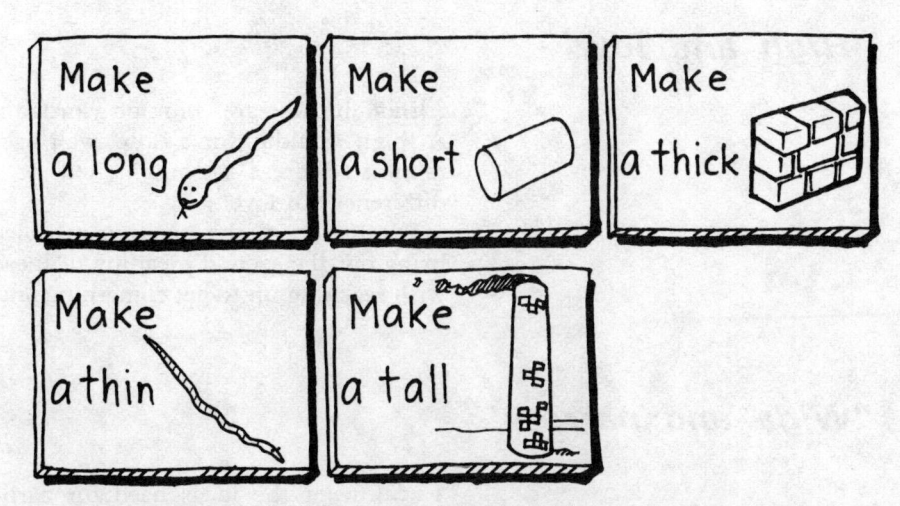

| Make a long | Make a short | Make a thick |
| Make a thin | Make a tall | |

This idea could also be extended for able children, 'make a short, thin sausage', etc.

Shape, Length, Time Workbook

Additional activities

1. A group of children could be given several flash cards with length words on them `tall`, `long`, and so on. They could then be asked to place each word beside an appropriate object in a display of materials on a table in the classroom.
2. Scrap books of tall, short, thick, or thin things could be made in the same way as for long and short things.

Further length words

It may be that for some children the vocabulary which appears on the Workbook pages—long, short, thick, thin, tall—represents quite enough in the way of new words and ideas to cope with at this stage. Such children might only meet the further words—wide, narrow, high, low—in an informal way in the course of other work.

However, teachers may wish to introduce activities to give some of the more able children experience of these ideas. Brief descriptions of such work are given below. There are no Workbook pages dealing with these words at this stage.

'High' and 'low'

Although these are common words they are used in two distinct ways. A 'high' building or a 'low' wall use the words to describe height or tallness whereas a 'high' shelf or a 'low' window really indicate differences in level.

Discussion of the position of objects in the classroom can help to bring out the second meaning of these words. 'High' can be associated with reaching up to get something and 'low' with bending down.

'Wide' and 'narrow'

1. Some of the ideas used for earlier length words are appropriate here.
   (a) Sorting using a variety of materials. Suitable materials include

ribbons, strips of card, belts, and other objects which have very little 'thickness'. Children tend to confuse the ideas of 'wide' and 'thick'. Flashcards could be used to label sets but the word 'narrow' is difficult for some children.

(b) Making posters, displays, scrapbooks, of 'wide' and 'narrow' things.

2 Discussion of objects in the classroom can also help—a wide window, a narrow corridor, a wide cut-out footprint, a narrow belt, a wide watchstrap, etc.

3 Worksheet or card activities similar to those for 'long', 'short', etc., could also be used for 'wide' and 'narrow'. These could include sorting, making, counting, drawing, and colouring activities.

Flat shapes
(Cards 39 to 48 and Pages 10 to 13)

Development

The aim of this unit is to make children familiar with the following shapes—circle, triangle, square and rectangle. These shapes might be introduced from the faces of the three-dimensional shapes which the children have already met.

The cards give children an opportunity to handle flat shapes and to fit them into outline pictures. The pages contain sorting and matching activities involving the same 'pictures' as the cards and are intended as a follow-up to work with actual shapes.

The names of the shapes do not appear on the cards and pages at this stage although they would probably be used in discussion.

Shape, Length, Time Workbook
Practical activities and teaching

Introducing the shapes

1 One of the main problems in introducing work on two-dimensional shapes is that children confuse their names with the three-dimensional shapes they have already met. It is important that they realise the difference between a square which is 'flat' and a 'box' or cube which is not but whose faces can be squares. This difference will not be appreciated by all children at this stage.

One way of helping to establish this distinction might be to introduce three of the shapes from the faces of solid shapes.

Circle
A prepared cardboard or paper circle can be laid on top and then 'removed' from the appropriate face of a cylinder and a cone to introduce the name and shape 'circle'.

Square
A square can be 'removed' from one face of a cube (children may call it a 'box' or 'brick').

Rectangle
A rectangle (oblong) can be taken from one face of a 'box' or 'cuboid'.

Triangles may have to be introduced by showing the children cardboard or paper triangles. The important point is that all of these shapes are flat—not 'thick' like cones, cylinders, and 'boxes'.

Alternatively, some teachers may wish to introduce these flat shapes as cardboard or paper shapes without reference to solid shapes. Inappropriate use of names such as 'cube' for 'square' would then be dealt with as it arose.

2 Examples of these shapes in and around the classroom can be discussed. The window panes, table tops, and doors are likely to be rectangles. The light switch and wall sockets will probably be square. Wheels, lids, coins, etc., are circles. It should be made clear that it is the *surfaces* of these objects which are flat shapes called squares, circles, etc.

3 It is important that children see *different sizes* of shapes such as circles and squares.

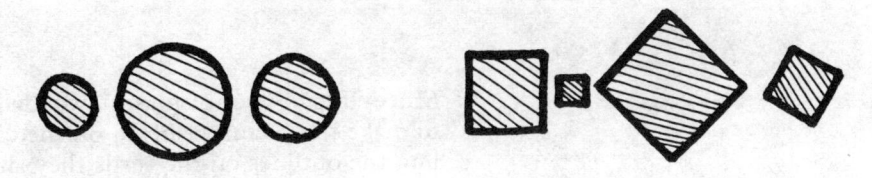

In the case of triangles and rectangles (oblongs), it is useful to show children a *variety of types* of each of these shapes.

Squares and rectangles

1 The name 'rectangle' can be applied to shapes which are

square   *or* oblong

The idea that a square is a special type of rectangle is a sophisticated one which is not really appropriate to very young children. One way of avoiding this problem would be to use the names 'square' and 'oblong' only until pupils were old enough to appreciate the true meaning of the word 'rectangle'. Alternatively, and this is the practice in **Infant Mathematics: Second Stage**, one might use the terms

'square' for this shape

and 'rectangle' for all the other rectangles

until the full sophistication can be revealed at a much later stage.

Names of shapes do not appear on the Workbook pages but should certainly be used *orally*.

2 Some children may find it difficult to distinguish between squares and other rectangles. One method which can help is to turn the shapes round. A square will 'look the same', whereas a rectangle (oblong) is 'longer' and looks 'different'.

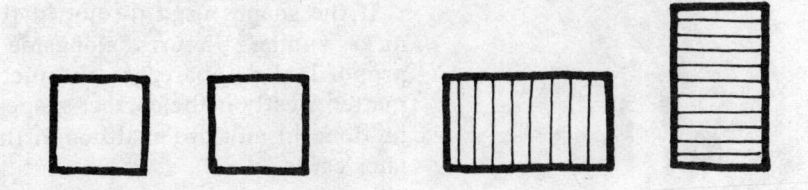

202 Shape, Length, Time Workbook

Cards 39 to 48

Flat shapes

Materials A set of plastic, wooden, or cardboard shapes is required to make the pictures shown on the cards. If the shapes are to be fitted into the outlines on the cards they should be of the sizes shown below.

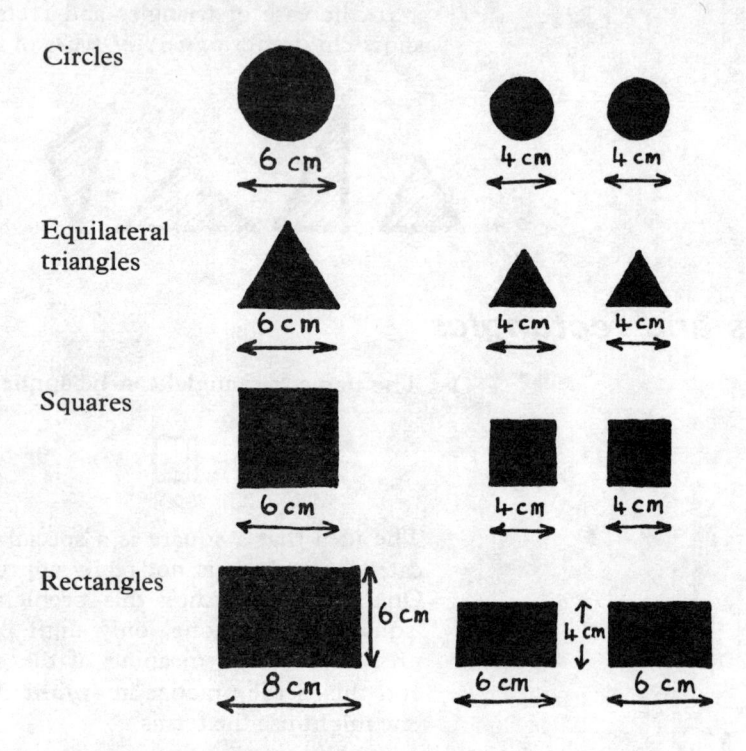

Circles — 6 cm, 4 cm, 4 cm

Equilateral triangles — 6 cm, 4 cm, 4 cm

Squares — 6 cm, 4 cm, 4 cm

Rectangles — 8 cm × 6 cm, 6 cm × 4 cm, 6 cm × 4 cm

Four sets of shapes like this are contained in Cards 26 and 27 of the *Teacher's Materials Pack*.

Other shapes which are similar to those above but not necessarily of these sizes could also be used to imitate rather than cover the pictures on the cards.

Shapes could be sorted into sets before being used for the cards. The teacher could start off the sorting into trays of 'small triangles', 'large circles', and so on. A group of children could then share the shapes while making the pictures on the cards.

If the shapes used are of the sizes shown above, teachers should show pupils how to fit them *on top of outlines* on the cards to make pictures. The names on the cards are intended to be read out by teachers to describe the pictures.

If the shapes used do not fit the pictures then the children should make similar pictures alongside the card. These may be 'out of proportion' compared to the pictures on the cards but this will not matter greatly if the correct shapes have been used. Cards 39 to 46 can be done in any order although the more difficult pictures are on the later cards.

girl

Shape, Length, Time Workbook 203

Cards 47 and 48 have no lines to show where the shapes fit and are intended as puzzles for more able pupils. They are more easily done by fitting shapes of the correct size *on top* of the outlines.

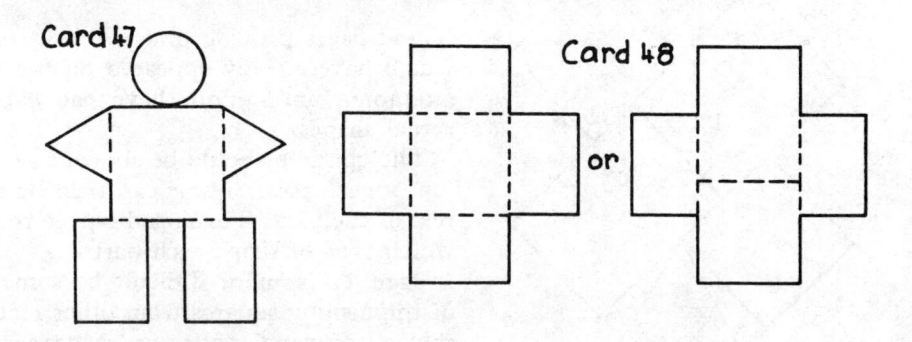

The most important feature of this work should be discussion of the shapes used and the pictures. Vocabulary and ideas which might be covered include:

long, short, longer than, shorter than, large, small, round, curved, straight, flat, edge, corner, same shape, circle, triangle, square, rectangle, next to, on top of, etc.

Sorting and naming shapes

After the children have used some of the cards there could be some more formal sorting work before they attempt the Workbook pages. The shapes could be sorted in many different ways as follows:
(a) into large shapes and small shapes;
(b) into four different types of shape—circles, squares, triangles, rectangles.

Teachers may wish to use written labels for these sets, although the names do not appear on the Workbook pages. Reading and writing of names will be introduced in **Infant Mathematics: Second Stage.**
(c) into eight possible sets—large squares, small triangles, etc.;
(d) into shapes with curved and straight edges.

204　Shape, Length, Time Workbook

Pages 10 and 11 | Shape pictures | Flat shapes

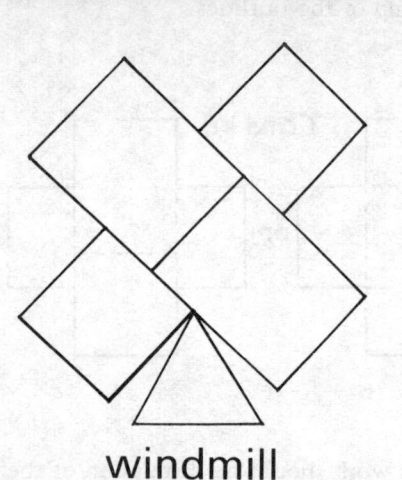

Materials Coloured pencils.

These pages provide practice in sorting shapes by colouring pictures which have already appeared on the cards. This work should not be attempted until pupils have had experience of handling and fitting actual shapes.

The children should be shown how to colour the three shapes at the top of each page. These can then be used as a 'key' for colouring the rest of the page. Turning the page round may help children to decide which type of shape each part is.

Page 11 is more difficult as some pupils may have problems in distinguishing squares from other rectangles. At this stage they might think of a rectangle as 'longer'. More accurate ideas can be developed later.

windmill

Pages 12 and 13 | | Flat shapes

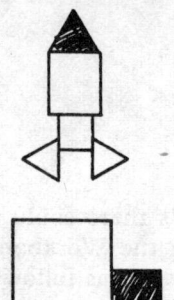

Materials Coloured pencils.

These pages use the idea of matching. Once the matching lines are drawn the shapes can be coloured in a similar way to Pages 10 and 11.

The children should be encouraged to talk about the shapes, for example,

'I used a triangle for the top of the rocket'.

'What shape is the front of the car?'

Additional activities

1　The children could be encouraged to make more pictures for themselves.

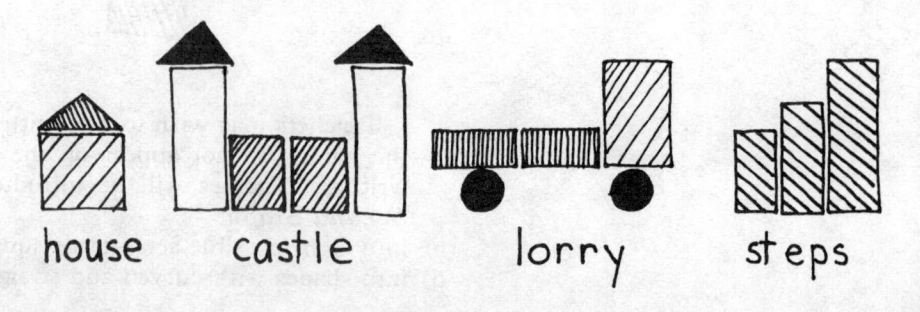

house　castle　lorry　steps

Shape, Length, Time Workbook

Coloured gummed paper shapes could be used to make a record of the pictures they make.

2. Gummed paper shapes and pictures of shapes cut from magazines could be used to make class books or posters for the classroom wall. Paint 'prints' using lids could also be used to make different sizes of circle, etc.

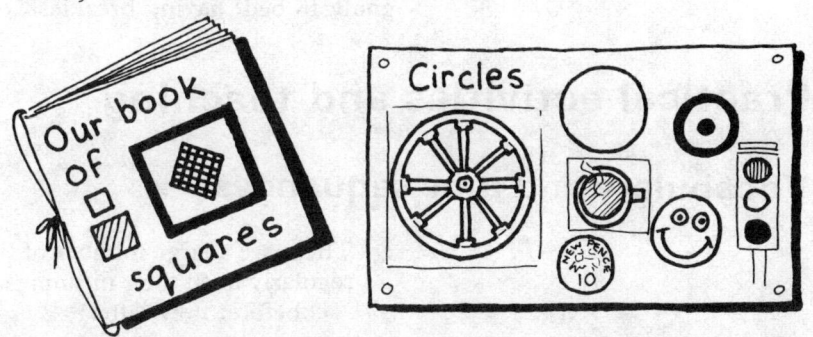

3. A classroom display of objects brought in by the children could be arranged in four sets. It would be important to ensure that only flat objects with little 'thickness' were used to try to avoid confusion with names of three-dimensional shapes.

    Possible objects include:

    Triangles Pictures of road signs, a set square, folded paper napkin, etc.

    Circles Coins, lids, wheels, table mats, etc.

    Rectangles Pictures, envelopes, post cards, sheets of paper, rulers, table mats, empty crisp packets, wafers, stamps.

    Squares Lids, handkerchiefs, photographs, table mats, napkins, tiles, etc.

4. Card 28 of the **Teacher's Materials Pack** contains a simple shape game which might be played by children who have completed this section.

Time (Pages 14 to 19)

Development

Two different types of work about time are described in this section. The first part of these notes deals with vocabulary and time sequences. This work will for the most part be done orally. There are no Workbook pages about it, although Cards 29 and 30 of the **Teacher's Materials Pack** contain sorting activities for time sequence work.

The second part of this section introduces clockface work. It deals with reading such times as 7 o'clock from a clockface, and with the more difficult and less important idea of drawing or setting hands to show times. There is also some attempt to give children an understanding of times at which particular events take place, for example going to bed, having breakfast, etc.

Practical activities and teaching

Vocabulary and time sequences

1 There are a large number of time words which children should hear regularly until their meanings become established. They include
　　before, now, after;
　　names of days of the week, seasons, months;
　　yesterday, today, tomorrow;
　　first, next, fast, slow, late, early, ago;
　　morning, afternoon, evening, night;
These words should be dealt with orally and, to some extent, incidentally during the course of the year.
2 Some of these words form time sequences which repeat over and over 'in a loop':
　　morning, afternoon, evening, night, ...
　　days of the week ...
　　seasons ...
　　breakfast, lunch or dinner, tea, supper ...
Others form a sequence with a 'beginning and end':
　　yesterday, today, tomorrow.

The days of the week

1 The children might be helped to learn the names and their correct sequence by the use of rhymes and songs (see Appendix 2, page 231.
2 Most of the work would be done orally, but later, when children can read the words, flashcards could be used. A classroom chart could be displayed and changed daily with the help of the children.

Shape, Length, Time Workbook 207

Folded and stapled to make a pocket to hold cards →

yesterday **today** tomorrow

| Tuesday | Wednesday | Thursday |

3 Later in the year flashcards might be sorted out in order:

| Monday | Tuesday | Wednesday | Thursday | Friday | Saturday | Sunday |

It is important for children to realise that this sequence keeps on recurring and so the sorting could be extended using a second set of cards.

Another activity would be to start with a different day; for example | Thursday | | Friday | 'What comes next?'

4 Many teachers keep a type of calendar chart which includes the date and is changed every day.

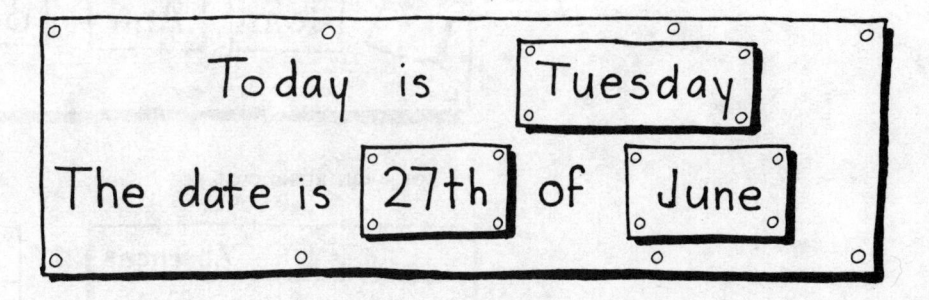

Today is | Tuesday |
The date is | 27th | of | June |

Some teachers keep simple weather records:

Yesterday it was ☀ | Thursday |
Today it is 🌧 | Friday |

208 Shape, Length, Time Workbook

5 A series of pictures of events which take place on particular days could be displayed: singing, football, church, etc.:

| Sunday | Monday | Tuesday | Wednesday | Thursday | Friday | Saturday |

or perhaps

Things we do on Saturday.

swim   watch T.V.   go to Gran's

6 Other possible displays might show classroom 'duties':

| Monday | Tuesday | Wednesday | Thursday | Friday |
| John | Ann | Brian | Gillian | Alan |

or even absences:

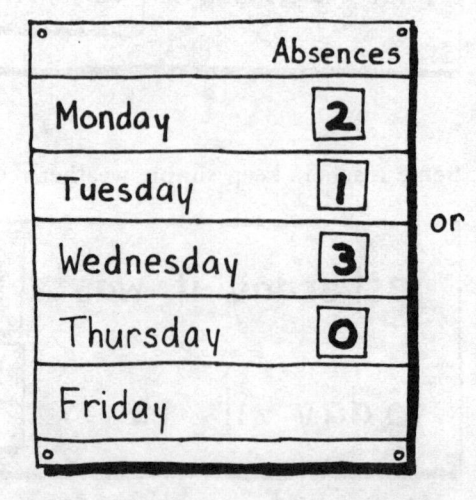

	Absences
Monday	2
Tuesday	1
Wednesday	3
Thursday	0
Friday	

or

	Absences
Monday	♀♀
Tuesday	♀
Wednesday	♀♀♀
Thursday	
Friday	

Shape, Length, Time Workbook 209

These displays are early examples of pictorial representation which will be developed further at later stages of the course. There are no specific worksheets or cards on graphs in *Infant Mathematics: First Stage.*

Morning, afternoon, evening, night

1 This is another important sequence which is continuous or 'forms a loop' by constantly repeating. This idea might be helped by arranging pictures of events which happen at these times.

| morning | afternoon | evening | night |

The sequence should be extended to repeat again ... night, morning ...

2 Mealtimes form a sequence which can be linked to ideas of morning, evening, etc.

| breakfast | lunch | tea | supper |
| | dinner | | |

Names for meals will vary from one area to another.

Before and after

Wall friezes might be made for the following events:

Things we do <u>before</u> breakfast.

Things we do <u>after</u> school.

210 Shape, Length, Time Workbook

Sequences of events

Picture cards which show a sequence of events could be used, even before the children can read, to give experience of arranging events in order. Some children might manage a sequence of only 3 or 4 cards while others will manage to order many more.

The *Teacher's Materials Pack* provides such sequences. One shows 'five ages of man'—baby, small boy, school boy, man, old man.

Another shows sandpit scenes which can be ordered as two small sets or one complete set.

The seasons and months

1 The *Teacher's Materials Pack* contains four pictures of seasonal scenes which can be cut out and arranged in sequence. At a late stage in the year the scenes might be matched to the appropriate words.

Spring   Summer   Autumn   Winter

The children should realise that this sequence repeats to 'form a loop'. This idea might be helped by starting with a different season, for example: Autumn 'What comes next?'

2 The poem 'A Tree' in Appendix 2 on page 244 might be given as a puzzle: 'What am I?' The children might be asked which season is not named and which line tells them about the missing season.

3 With some children it might be possible to start linking the names of the months with seasons using wall pictures or flashcards.

March   April   May   June

Spring

Shape, Length, Time Workbook

There are further poems in Appendix 2 which deal with the months.
4 Some of the more able children might cope with the order of the months, charts of birthday months, etc.
5 Class events could be added, as they occur, to a poster showing what happens in one particular month.

Introducing clockface work

A great deal of time work at this stage is best done orally and practically using a large clock with a simple face. It is best if the two hands are 'geared' to move together. Alternatively, a large cardboard clock could be used where *one* hand at a time might be used. A few suggestions about introducing such work are given below. Teachers will no doubt have their own favourite methods.

One way of starting might be to establish the placing of the numerals on a clockface. This could be done using a large blackboard drawing or a clockface drawn on a large sheet of cardboard with separate number cards stuck on as the lesson progresses.

The lesson might build up numbers in stages as shown.

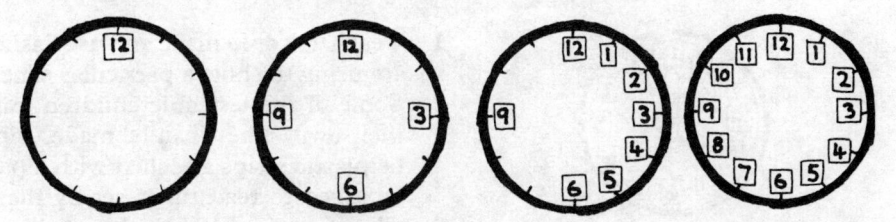

Some teachers might invent a 'story' to go along with placing the numbers. Alternatively, the numbers could be built up from 1 to 12. If two of the numeral cards are interchanged, children will find this difficult to spot.

The next stage might be to introduce the hands.
1 The children might be shown the 'long' minute hand and the 'short' hour hand moving round a real clock. The 'long' hand moves further and faster.
2 The short hand 'tells us which o'clock it is'. Point it to 4 and point the 'long' hand to 12 to introduce 4 o'clock.

Shape, Length, Time Workbook

3   It is good idea to show the children several o'clocks by winding the hands round from 4 o'clock to 5 o'clock, 6 o'clock, and so on.

4   Two important ideas might be established for any o'clock:
    'The **short** hour hand shows which o'clock it is.'
    'The **long** hand points to 12.'

An alternative method would be to use a clock with the 'long' hand temporarily removed to show the hour alone. This might prevent confusion between the two hands. The long hand would eventually be added pointing to 12 in each case.

"4 o'clock"   "5 o'clock"   "6 o'clock"

It would still be worthwhile showing the children how the hands of a real clock move, pointing out the o'clocks when they are reached.

There should be plenty of oral work in reading times from a clock before any attempt is made to do the Workbook pages.

Additional activities

8 o'clock

1   Teachers could make and use flashcards to place under the clock they are using to show a particular time.
2   Some of the less able children might use little cardboard clocks of their own. These can be made using a clock 'stamp.' The hands can be plastic strips attached with a paper fastener. The children would be asked to read times set by the teacher.
3   Clockface cards might be made using a stamp. The teacher could draw in the hands to show 12 different o'clocks. These cards can then be sorted in order or matched to the flashcards.

9 o'clock   10 o'clock   11 o'clock   12 o'clock   1 o'clock

4   Some attempt might be made to relate classroom events to particular times, for example, 'School starts at 9 o'clock'; 'Dinner time is 12 o'clock'; etc.

Shape, Length, Time Workbook 213

| Page 14 | **What time is it?** | Time |

Materials None (reference to a real or cardboard clock might help).

This page provides straight-forward practice examples in reading clockface times. The children should not attempt such written work without previous oral practice. 12 o'clock, the last time on the page, is likely to prove difficult as one hand lies on top of the other.

| Pages 15 and 16 | **Write the times** | Time |

Materials As for Page 14.

These two pages provide yet more practice in reading clockface times. However, on Page 15 each clock is associated with a cartoon of an event which might happen in a school day. This might help children to associate times with particular events: 'Dinner time was at 12 o'clock'. It should also allow teachers to talk about the page and ask questions after it has been completed: 'When did he get up?', 'What were they doing at 11 o'clock in the morning?', etc. If the times are read from left to right going down the page they are 'in order' for one day. This might lead to discussion of when the children in 'our' class do these things.

Page 16 is similar but with an animal cartoon and a rhyme associated with each time. The times are not in any order. Most of the children will be unable to read the rhymes. They may be amused if the teacher reads them out and uses them to discuss the times: 'What happened at 2 o'clock?' 'At what time was the dog in a fog?'

Teaching suggestions

'Drawing' clockface times

The next two pages deal with the more difficult task of drawing hands on clockfaces to show times. This is less important than the earlier work of reading clocks. Less able pupils might omit some of this work or use individual clocks to set the hands and show the times.

Oral practice, from which all the children have experience in moving the hands to show a time, would make a good introduction to Pages 17 and 18. This could be done by 'telling a story' about events happening at certain times:

'At 6 o'clock one morning the doorbell rang ...'

It is worthwhile emphasizing once more that for an o'clock time
'The **short** hour hand tells us which o'clock'.
'The **long** hand is at 12'.

214 Shape, Length, Time Workbook

Pages 17 and 18 — Draw the hands — Time

Materials   As for Page 14.

The top half of Page 17 asks the children to draw in the 'long' hand for o'clock times. This should allow teachers to emphasize that it will point to 12. The children should make the long hand *much* longer than the other one. They might also draw it in colour.

In the bottom half of the page the hour hand should be drawn to show *which* o'clock it is. Once again, colour might be used. The dotted coloured circle is intended as a guide to prevent children from drawing too long an hour hand.

Page 18 asks children to draw both hands. Using different colours, making a really 'long' hand, and sticking to the dotted circle for the length of the hour hand, will all help to produce better results.

The bottom half of the page uses cartoons for the same reason as on Page 16. If the rhymes are read to the children then the times can be discussed: 'What happened at 8 o'clock?'

Teaching suggestions

Time sequences

1   Teachers may wish to make charts, friezes, etc., to relate events to clock times and to build up time sequences. For example

Shape, Length, Time Workbook 215

Flashcards ⟨9 o'clock⟩ and clockface cards ⟨clock⟩ can be associated with drawings of events which happen at these times.

2 Flashcards can also be arranged in sequence:

⟨9 o'clock⟩ ⟨10 o'clock⟩ ⟨11 o'clock⟩ and so on.

An important sequence is what 'happens' around 12 o'clock:

⟨12 o'clock⟩ ⟨1 o'clock⟩

where the number of hours changes from 12 to 1, 2, and so on. It can help to establish the sequence by asking questions such as, 'What is the o'clock *before* 7 o'clock?'; 'What is the next o'clock *after* 12 o'clock?'

Clockface cards can also be used for such activities.

3 A difficult but worthwhile relationship is that between clock times and morning, afternoon, and evening.

There are *two* 9 o'clocks each day.

9 o'clock *in the morning* is a suitable time to start school.

9 o'clock *in the evening* or *at night* is a time when you are in bed.

Typical events are:

The postman comes at 7 o'clock *in the morning*.

School closes at 3 o'clock *in the afternoon*.

And so on.

4 Mealtimes can make a useful sequence:

breakfast — 8 o'clock; lunch — 12 o'clock; tea — 5 o'clock; supper — 8 o'clock

5 The concept of long times passing is a difficult one for young children. It may be that some are not yet ready for activities on time sequences extending over several hours.

Page 19 — Jill and Tom ⟨Time⟩

Materials As for Page 14.

This page shows a time sequence of incidents in one day for Jill, Tom, and the dog. The cartoons could be discussed before or after the children write the times. A good way of doing this would be as a 'story' of Tom getting up, breakfast, and so on.

The captions are too difficult for most children of this age to read. The teacher might read over the whole page after they have completed it. The captions rhyme, which might interest the children and help when discussing the times.

Length (Pages 20 to 23)

Development

The aim of this section is to give children experience of comparing directly the lengths, thicknesses, and heights of two objects. The Workbook pages give practice in the use of 'comparative' length words—'longer', 'shorter', 'thicker', 'thinner', 'taller'. Teachers might also wish to introduce 'wider', 'narrower', 'higher', 'lower', for some children.

Practical activities and teaching

Introductory activities

1. The children should be presented with *pairs* of objects whose lengths can be compared directly by placing them side by side. This should be repeated with a variety of materials—string, ribbon, rope, straws, crayons, rods, etc.

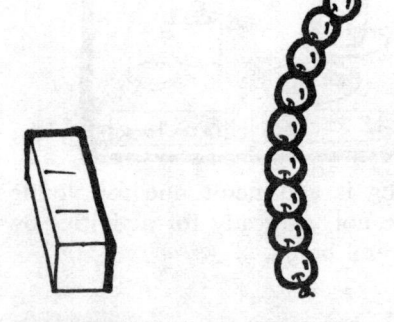

2. Flashcards can be placed beside the objects as the appropriate language is developed:

    'This knitting needle *is longer than* this one.'

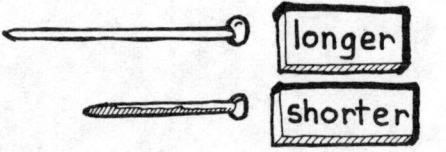

    'The red needle *is shorter than* the yellow one'.

3. Objects of two different types could also be compared.

4. Pictures of objects can be cut from magazines and stuck on to paper or cardboard to make a poster.

Shape, Length, Time Workbook 217

5 Teachers may wish to record in the form of a relationship using 'is longer than' and 'is shorter than.'

is longer than

This type of statement should certainly be used orally at this stage, but written recording of this type can cause problems with young children who tend to confuse the order of the two objects. This type of recording has *not* been used on the Workbook pages at this stage. Oral work with pupils might also lead to placing a card with the relation written on it when comparing actual objects:

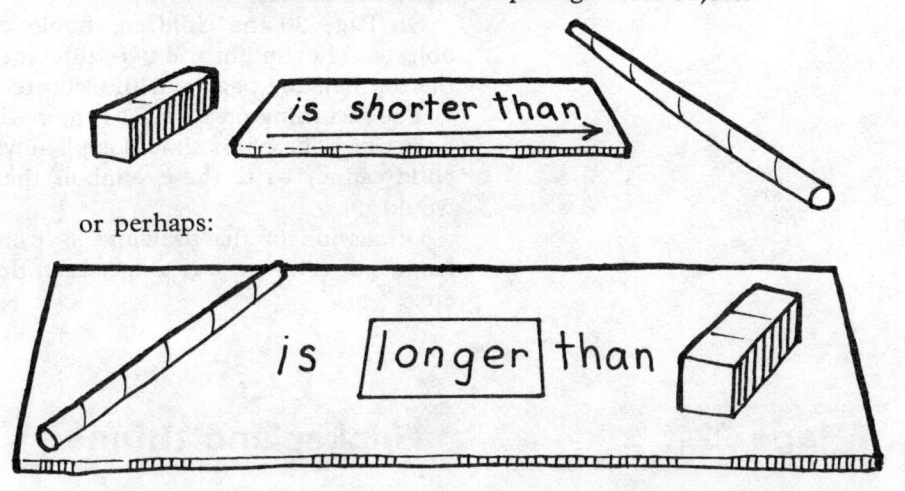

is shorter than

or perhaps:

is longer *than*

6 The children might make comparisons involving more than one object. They could be given an object such as a crayon and asked to 'Find *four* things which are longer than that crayon'. Some children will only pick objects very much longer than the given one. They should be encouraged to find ones which are closer in length but still 'longer'.

7 The children should also meet pairs of objects of roughly equal length. Discussion should lead to language of the type:

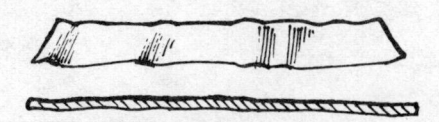

'The ribbon is *about the same length as* the string'.

This sort of comparison is much more difficult for young children and should come later than the longer/shorter comparisons described above. There is no written work of this type on the Workbook pages.

218 Shape, Length, Time Workbook

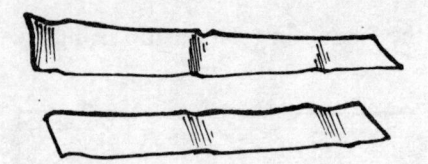

8   At a later stage the objects might have less of a difference in length. This could lead to more 'refined' use of the comparative words. For example:
'The two ribbons are *nearly* the same length.'
'This ribbon is *a little bit* longer than that one'.

Pages 20 and 21 — Longer and shorter [Language of length]

Materials Coloured pencils or crayons.

These pages provide written work on the words 'longer' and 'shorter' which is intended to follow experience in comparing real objects as described above.

On Page 20 the children should colour only one of each pair of objects. They might use two different colours for the 'longer' ones on the top half the page and the 'shorter' ones in the bottom half.

The recording on Page 21 is more difficult since both objects should be marked. Teachers should explain why 'l' and 'sh' are to be used. If a child cannot write these symbols then any marks such as × and ○ would do.

Discussion of the drawings is worthwhile to reinforce the use of language. 'This nose is longer than this one'; 'This feather is shorter'; etc.

Page 22 — Thicker and thinner [Language of length]

Materials Coloured pencils or crayons.

The recording on this page should be preceded by considerable oral work and comparison of actual objects. Activities similar to those described for longer and shorter are appropriate here also. At first the objects being compared should be the *same length* and type to present as few distracting features as possible. Later objects of different types and lengths might be compared.

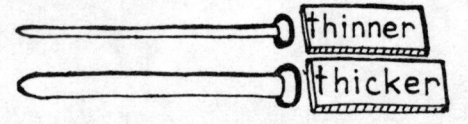

The recording on Page 22 is by colouring or marking *both* objects. This should be accompanied by discussion: 'Which snake is thicker?'; 'This nail is thinner than that one'; etc.

Some of the children may be able to cope with two 'length' ideas at once: 'This nail is longer *and* thinner than this one'.

Shape, Length, Time Workbook

Page 23 — Taller and shorter — Language of length

Materials Coloured pencils or crayons.

There should be oral work and comparison of actual objects before this page is attempted. Activities similar to those for longer and shorter are again appropriate.

Comparison of the heights of the children themselves is a worthwhile activity which can be recorded as a wallchart. Solid shapes or 'towers' built with Unifix-type cubes are also suitable for height comparisons.

The drawings of the chimney and flagpole at the foot of Page 23 are 'middle-sized' in that there is room for children to make drawings 'taller' or 'shorter' than the given ones. They will need to *read* the instruction carefully or have it read to them. The quality of their drawings is not as important as an obvious understanding of the meaning of the words.

Other comparative words

Teachers who have introduced the ideas of wide, narrow, high, and low earlier (see Teaching Notes for Pages 5 to 9, page 198) may wish to use the comparative forms of these words with some more able pupils at this stage.

Ribbons, strips of card, belts, ties, etc., are suitable materials for wider/narrower comparisons as they have little 'thickness' to confuse the children.

Items in the classroom which stand side by side might be discussed to give one meaning to the words 'higher' and 'lower'; for example 'The top of the cupboard is higher than the door'. The other meaning of these words refers to position: 'The light switch is higher than the door handle'. There are no Workbook pages about these words.

Cards and worksheets for the teacher to make

Some teachers may wish to provide further activities for some children.

1 *Sorting* The children could be given a *card* with a length word or relationship written on it and an object stuck to it. They could be asked to find 3 or 4 things which can be placed on the card as shown below.

220 Shape, Length, Time Workbook

This idea can be extended to cover the other comparative words.

2 *Drawing* Worksheets can be used to ask children to draw objects longer and shorter than a given one. This would also be possible for taller/shorter, thicker/thinner, wider/narrower. Workcards, with a sheet of paper clipped to one edge to take the child's drawing, could also be used.

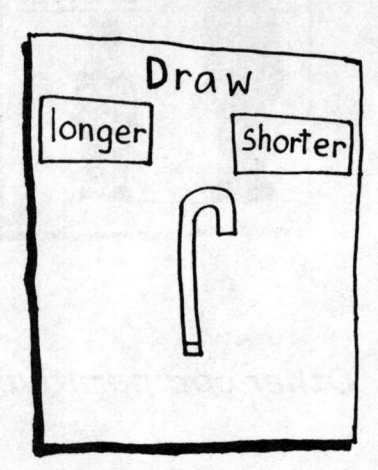

3 *Making* Children could use plasticine to make a shorter 'sausage' than the one shown on the card. This idea could be extended to other 'length words'.

Appendix 1

Free play

Play is an essential element in the educational development of children. It provides an environment in which the child acquires, in an informal but very important way, the beginnings of understanding of number, measurement, and spatial concepts. Forms of play which are rich in mathematical potential include: sand play, water play, art/craft activities, the home corner, games and jig-saws, class shop, weighing activities, plasticine, play with bricks, string, and so on.

Not all of these activities should be available at the one time. It is easier to organize a few at a time and change them, perhaps twice each term, to give variety. Another important variation is, say, at the sand or water play, to change the containers and other objects to give a wide range of experiences.

It should always be borne in mind that the essential nature of each activity is 'free play' and that no attempt at formal teaching of vocabulary or mathematical concepts is appropriate at this stage. However, if children are to benefit from the full range of experiences, they should be encouraged to spend a reasonable time at each activity and any incidental vocabulary and ideas should be introduced in a meaningful context.

Sand play

Materials Large tray or shallow bath containing clean, washed, river or sea-shore sand; containers of various shapes and sizes, buckets, cartons, bowls, pots; filling funnels; spades; spoons; toy animals; cars; houses; trees; . . . .

Activities

Most children enjoy the physical experience of sinking their hands in sand and letting it trickle through their fingers. They could fill containers and pour out the sand; fill one container from the other; fill a large container by using a small one several times. They could use a funnel to fill a bottle or narrow-mouthed container. They could pour sand to make volcano-style conical hills.

Sand is also a convenient base for setting out farmyards, villages, road systems, and so on.

Damp sand, although more messy, is very good for modelling and tunnelling.

Mathematical potential

Children gain experience of volume, weight, and 3-D shapes. The teacher's role is to talk to the child about the activities and to encourage the use of relevant vocabulary, e.g. fill, full, empty, pour, large, small, heavy, light, more, less, etc., and phrases like 'Is it full?: 'Is it heavy when it's full?'; and so on.

Water play

Materials Large plastic tray-type water container or baby bath on stand; containers of different shapes and sizes: cups, tea-pot, kettle, egg-cups, mugs, cartons; dolls' crockery; funnels; plastic tubes; ladles spoons; strainers; toy boats; squeezee bottles; mopping-up cloths; waterproof aprons, etc.

Activities

Pouring, filling, emptying, floating, and sinking objects. Sailing boats, blowing bubbles, squirting water. A tall plastic container could have holes made at several different heights so that different water jets are seen.

Appendix 1: Free Play

Mathematical potential

As with the sand play, the teacher should encourage the use of vocabulary such as fill, spill, full, empty, pour, squirt, jet, holds a lot, holds a little. The child should gain experience of volume, capacity, and even horizontal water level. Water play also provides valuable practice in pouring and filling skills involving hand and eye co-ordination.

Art/craft activities

Materials Crayons, felt pens, paint, brushes, sugar paper, cardboard, newsprint, wall-paper, newspaper, corrugated paper, silver paper, foil, cellophane, old Christmas cards, calendars, empty cartons, boxes, egg boxes, toilet roll or kitchen roll tubes, bottle tops, scraps of material, paste, glue, polycell paste.

In fact, virtually anything can be used to make something!

Activities

These are numerous and include painting (brush or finger), potato printing, paint blots, gummed paper pictures, simple collage, modelling with plasticine-type material, threading necklaces.

Children can make cars, engines, ships, aeroplanes, houses, rockets, trains, churches, castles, and so on, using junk material such as cartons, tins, tubes, round boxes, cardboard boxes, bottle tops, paper cups, etc.

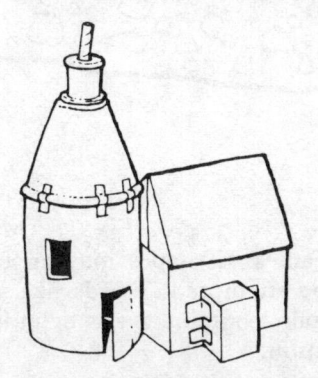

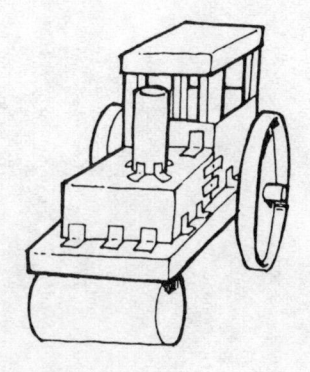

Appendix 1: Free Play

Mathematical potential

The above activities are very valuable in laying the foundations of many mathematical concepts.

Concept	Related activity
Area	Covering a surface with paint, foil, or gummed coloured paper.
Tiling and Pattern	Potato printing; repeated use of a simple stencil.
Order	Stringing beads could involve colour, size, shape, and number of beads. 'Make a string like this': Vocabulary might include: first, next, large, small, long, round, names of colours, etc.
Matching	Drawing and collage work should give one-to-one matching, e.g. hat to head; flower to stem; etc.
Symmetry	Paint blots; paper folding and tearing; balanced models; and drawings.
Shape and size	Choosing suitable objects and shapes for models; plasticine work.
Weight and volume	Filling and pouring; comparing weights by lifting or handling tins, cartons and boxes; plasticine work. Vocabulary might include: light, heavy, empty, full, hollow, solid, etc.

Again it is stressed that although these experiences are quite informal, the teacher should take the opportunity to use simple mathematical vocabulary with the children, e.g.

'What colour will the next bead be?'
'Cover your fish with small pieces of gummed paper.'
'You need more pieces to cover the bigger fish.'

The names of shapes may arise but no formal teaching of names should be attempted. Words like square, circle, triangle, and the fact that certain containers are cylinders or cubes may arise in general conversation.

Home corner

Appendix 1: Free Play   **225**

Materials   A screened-off corner with table and chairs; dolls' crockery and cutlery including cups, saucers, plates, pots, pans, kettle, tea-pot, jug, bowl, knives, forks, spoons. Cooker, rug, telephone, brush, etc., are particularly valuable.

Activities

Make-believe simulations of home life such as having a meal; having visitors (friends, relatives, nurse, doctor, milk-man, newspaper boy or girl); making a phone call; tidying, dusting, and washing up.

These activities provide many opportunities for role playing and realistic language development.

Mathematical potential

Putting out sufficient chairs, place settings, cups, saucers, knives, forks, spoons, etc., gives practice in the exercise of one-to-one matching (correspondence). Counting and sharing of plasticine cakes, biscuits, cupfuls in a tea-pot, and so on, would occur during these activities.

Games and jig-saws

Materials   Ludo, bagatelle, skittles, quoits, giant dominoes, dice, happy family cards, simple large-piece jig-saws, shapes and their outline holes, self-correcting types of jig-saw pieces.

226　**Appendix 1:** Free Play

Activities

Playing games (by themselves or with a partner); sorting out cards, shapes, etc.; fitting shapes into matching holes.

Sequences of shapes could be laid out (or drawn on cards) for the children to copy, e.g.

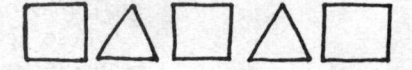

Cards with simple sequences could be made and given to the children to trace and copy—or even continue.

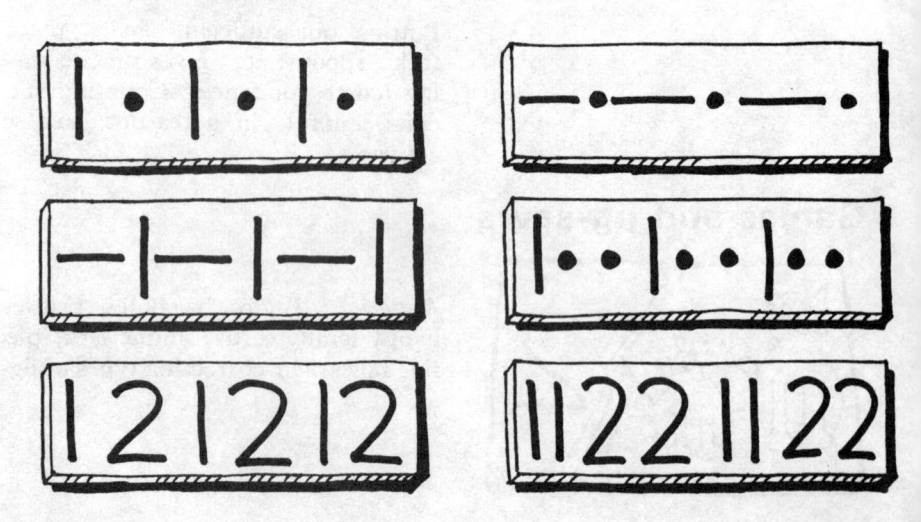

Appendix 1: Free Play 227

Mathematical potential

These activities give children experience of sorting objects by colour, shape, pattern and picture. Matching dot patterns and pictures to numerals. Recognition of dot patterns (dominoes, dice), numerals (quoits, bagatelle). Counting moves and scores towards the end of the year. Continuing a given pattern.

Shop play

Materials Empty cartons, packets, tins, boxes, comics, wrappers from sweets, coloured pictures from catalogues, toy cars, animals; plasticine sweets, ices, and cakes; old commercial display material; coloured counters and plastic coins.

Activities

Making things for the shop, sticking on prices; buying and selling; Preparing different types of shops (even a poster shopping list with coloured pictures of items).

Toy shop   Cars, plastic animals, train set, dolls' set, etc.

Baker's shop   Packets, plasticine cakes, doughnuts, etc.

Sweet shop   Wrappers, smartie tubes, boxes, plasticine sweets, etc.

Fruit and vegetable shop (greengrocer)   Artificial fruits, plasticine fruits and vegetables.

Supermarket   Cartons, boxes, tins, etc.

Initially coloured counters could be used in a simple barter system in which a red counter would buy an item marked with a red disc. Later

228 Appendix 1: Free Play

in the year simple prices might be used and plastic coins tendered to make a purchase.

These shopping activities are rich in language work. Words such as buy, sell, cost, price, value, worth, names of items, etc., should occur naturally.

Mathematical potential

Matching involving coloured counters and later numbers of coins. Counting of tokens and coins to make a purchase. Ideas of value or worth and notions of something being cheap or dear. Possibly some coin recognition and even some idea of relative value.

Towards the end of the year perhaps simple addition of money and even ideas of subtraction involving giving and receiving change can be included.

Weight table

Materials Objects for weighing including things made of plasticine; jars; boxes: cartons, packets; snappy bags; sand, pebbles, sawdust, marbles, beads; see-saw type balance.

Activities

No actual quantitative weighing at this stage. Lifting and handling different objects to find the 'heavy' or the 'light' one in a set of packages. The see-saw balance could be used to show the heavy side going down and the light side going up. In conversation with the children words such as heavy, light, weighs more, weighs less, empty, full, balances, weigh, would probably occur.

Mathematical potential

The heaviness of an object made of a material like plasticine depends on its size. Large pieces are heavier than small pieces. Large packages

Appendix 1: Free Play

(cornflakes) can be light while small things (ball-bearings) can be heavy. Identical jars or cartons filled with different materials (sand, sawdust, peas) have different weights. The see-saw (or two-pan balance) principle of heavy side down and light side up may be experienced.

Plasticine play

Materials Board or shallow plastic tray; coloured plasticine; Play-doh or any modelling clay; baking cutters, pieces of hardboard or rulers for patting or rolling into shape.

Activities

Modelling objects like animals, people, snakes, houses, tents, cakes, biscuits, sweets. Making solid shapes like a ball, a pencil, a box, and flat shapes using the baking cutters.

Words like pat, roll, cut, flat, long, thin, fat, round might be used in conversation with the children.

Mathematical potential

Children should obtain a valuable introduction to ideas involving volume, weight, solid, and flat shapes.

Building play

Materials Building bricks and blocks of different shapes, sizes, and colours; cubes, cartons, tins, boxes, and other empty containers.

Activities

Building towers, walls, houses, trains, bridges, rockets, castles, churches. Filling boxes. Repacking articles in their box.

Vocabulary for this work might include words such as build, balance, on top, underneath, fall, topple, and so on.

Appendix 1: Free Play

Mathematical potential

Early ideas on pictorial representation are gained from towers or rows of coloured building bricks. An awareness of shapes suitable for models including roofs and steeples should be acquired; stability in building should be experienced. Ideas about volume and 3-D shape are likely to occur.

String play

Materials Lengths of string, cord, wool, laces, tape, ribbon; lacing shoes or cards, e.g.

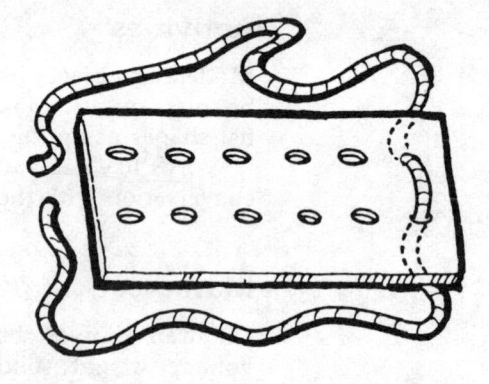

Activities

Sorting out by colour and kind of material. Ordering by length (finding the longest, shortest). Tying knots. Different ways of lacing shoes.

Mathematical potential

These activities should give ideas on sorting and ordering together with an experience of pattern in the lacing work.

Appendix 2

Number and time rhymes

Introduction

This section contains a selection of rhymes about number and time which have been gathered from many sources. The appendix is intended as a resource which teachers might dip into from time to time. Alongside some of the rhymes there are notes suggesting actions, games, finger plays, dramatization, illustrations, wall friezes, and apparatus. Many teachers will have better ideas of their own about how to use the rhymes with children.

Acknowledgement of permission to reproduce these rhymes has not been included here. The majority are traditional; all of the remainder are in common use, and it has been assumed that reproduction in this educational context is uncontroversial.

Contents

The rhymes are roughly classified by topic, but are not in any order of difficulty.

1 to 3	Rhymes involving 1 and 2
4 to 8	Rhymes about 3
9 to 12	Rhymes about 4
13 to 14	Rhymes about 5
15 to 17	Counting up to 5
18 to 20	Counting down from 5
21 to 25	Numbers from 6 upwards
26 to 32	Counting up in ones
33 to 38	Counting up in ones—counting objects
39 to 40	Counting up in ones—further rhymes
41 to 42	Counting down in ones
43 to 46	Counting down in ones—counting objects
47 to 49	Counting up and down in twos
50 to 52	Addition and subtraction
53 to 60	Time

Appendix 2: Number and time rhymes

Rhymes involving 1 and 2

1 Two little dicky birds

Two little dicky birds sitting
        on a wall,
One named Peter, one named Paul.
Fly away Peter,
Fly away Paul.
Come back Peter,
Come back Paul.

Line 1 Hold up two thumbs.
Line 2 Bring forward right thumb, then left thumb.
Line 3 Put right hand behind head, then bring forward with thumb hidden in clenched fingers.
Line 4 Ditto for left hand.
Line 5 Put right hand behind head then bring forward with thumb held up.
Line 6 Ditto for left hand.

2 Two fat gentleman

Two fat gentlemen met in a lane,
Bowed most politely, bowed once again.
How do you do? How do you do?
How do you do again?
Two thin ladies met in a lane . . . .
Two tall policemen . . . .
Two little babies . . . .

Line 1 Children hold up two thumbs
Lines 2 and 3 Bend thumbs so that they 'bow' to each other
Repeat using the forefingers for the thin ladies, middle fingers for the tall policemen, and little fingers for the babies.

3 Me and you

I've got one head,
One nose, too,
One mouth, one chin,
So have you.
I've got two eyes,
Two ears too,
Two arms, two legs,
And so have you.
I've got two hands,
Two thumbs too,
(Four fingers on each hand),
And so have you.

Children point to head, nose, mouth, and so on, using two hands for pointing to the two eyes and ears, holding up arms as appropriate, and so on. The second to last line could be omitted at this stage if desired and the rhyme finished off with 'And so have you'.

Rhymes about 3

4

There once was a sow,
Who had three piggies,
And three piggies had she.
And the old sow always went
  'Umph, Umph, Umph',
And the piggies went
  'Wee, Wee, Wee'.

Each time the rhyme is recited, one child is chosen to be the sow and three others to be the piggies. The 'sow' says 'Umph, Umph, Umph' at the appropriate time and the three 'piggies' say 'Wee, Wee, Wee'. Repeat the rhyme with four new children.

Appendix 2: Number and time rhymes

5

Three bowls of porridge,
Three kitchen chairs,
Three white beds,
Had the three brown bears.

This little rhyme would follow naturally after the story of Goldilocks and the Three Bears.

6

Three black crows sat on a tree
   Billy McGhee McGaw,
And they were black as black could be,
   Billy McGhee McGaw.
They flapped and flapped their wings and cried
   Caw, caw, caw,
And then they flew away again,
   Caw, caw, caw.

Line 1 Children hold up 3 fingers

Line 5 Children 'flap' hands close to their heads.
Line 7 Children 'flap' hands and 'fly' them away to arms length.

7

Three black kittens climb up a tree
See them jump down again ...
One, two, three.

This little rhyme brings in cardinal and ordinal aspects. Again, 3 children could act the parts of the kittens, climbing up on a bench and jumping down one at a time on the words 'One, two, three'.

8

Clap your hands ... One, two, three
Place them down upon your knee.
Nod your head, once and twice.
Keep as quiet as little mice.

This rhyme emphasizes ordinal number and is very suitable for hand and head actions by all the children, either standing or sitting.

Rhymes about 4

9

Four fat gentlemen
Fishing by the sea,
Four fat fish
Caught for tea.

Suggested hand-actions Children seated in pairs with four fingers of the right hand of one child laid beside four fingers of left hand of the other child to represent the fat gentlemen and the fat fish respectively. On reciting last line the right hand of one child pounces on the left hand of the other child.

10

Four potatoes in a pot,
Lift the lid and see if they're hot
If they're hot, eat the lot.
Four potatoes in a pot.

Children may do lid-lifting actions and potato-eating actions at the appropriate lines.

234 Appendix 2: Number and time rhymes

11

Here are my fingers side by side.
How many are there? Let's decide.
   One, two, three, four.

Line 1   Child puts four fingers flat on the table.
Line 3   Child counts the fingers, pointing to each one in turn with the other hand.

12 Fingers

One little finger, one little finger,
One little finger, tap, tap, tap.
Point to the ceiling, point to the floor,
And lay them in your lap.
Two little fingers, two little fingers,
Two little fingers, tap, tap, tap, etc.
Three little fingers, etc.
Four little fingers, etc.

This is a suitable rhyme for children to recite while seated, tapping on the desk with 1 finger, then with 2 fingers, and so on to 4 fingers. This rhyme incorporates both cardinal and ordinal aspects of numbers 1 to 4.

Rhymes about 5

13

Five plump peas in a pea-pod pressed.
One grew, two grew, and so did all the rest.
They grew, and grew, and grew, and grew,
   And grew and never stopped,
Till they grew so plump and portly
   That the pea-pod—popped!

Line 1   Five children crouch down to represent the peas.
Line 2   They rise a little.
Line 3   They keep rising slowly.
Lines 4 and 5   They stand right up.
Line 6   Each jumps off the ground, throwing arms into the air.

14 Five little ladies

Five little ladies standing in a row,
Five little gentlemen bow down low.
Five little ladies will not play,
So five little gentlemen walk away.

Line 1   Each child holds up the fingers (and thumb) of the left hand.
Line 2   The right hand is held up and the fingers bent over.
Line 3   The left hand 'backs off'.
Line 4   The five fingers of the right hand 'walk off'.

Counting up to 5

15

One red engine, puffing down the track.
One red engine, puffing, puffing back.
Two red engines, etc. [... up to five].

Line 1   One child moves across the floor with small steps.
Line 2   Child turns and comes back.
Line 3   Child is joined by a second child and the actions are repeated till there are 5 children acting the parts of the engines.

Appendix 2: Number and time rhymes

16

I like trees that grow
Tall and straight.
I can see one from my
Garden gate.
[Repeat for two, three, four, and five.]

Line 3, 7, etc. One child stands on floor with arms stretched upwards. He is joined by another, and another, ..., till there are five.

17 The bees

Here is the bee-hive,
Where are the bees?
Hidden away where nobody sees.
Soon they come creeping out of the hive,
One, two, three, four, five.

Line 1 Cup hands to form arch with fingers pointing upward.
Line 2 Open hands and leave them outspread.
Line 3 Clench hands to hide fingers.
Line 4 Move fingers of one hand individually to simulate creeping.
Line 5 Count fingers one by one.

Counting down from 5

18 Five little ducks

Five little ducks went swimming one day,
Over the pond and far away.
Mummy duck said 'Quack, quack, quack, quack'
But only four little ducks came back.
Four little ducks went swimming one day, etc.
Three little ducks went swimming one day, etc.
Two little ducks went swimming one day, etc.
One little duck went swimming one day, etc.
No little ducks went swimming one day,
Over the pond and far away.
Daddy duck said 'Quack, quack, quack, quack'
And five little ducks came swimming back.

Teachers could devise suitable actions for children to dramatize the rhyme, different groups of children being chosen each time.

19 Five fat sausages

Five fat sausages frying in a pan,
All of a sudden one went 'BANG'.
Four fat sausages, etc.
Three fat sausages, etc., etc.

Five children are seated in a ring on the floor. On the word 'bang' one child jumps up and goes quickly to his seat and so on till there are no children left on the floor.

20 Five currant buns

Five sticky buns in a baker's shop,
Big and brown with a currant on top.
A boy came along with a penny one day,
He paid one penny and took a bun away.
[Repeat for 4, 3, 2, and 1.]

This one lends itself to obvious actions. As well as the five 'currant bun' children, there may be a baker to take the pennies and the 'boy' who leads off the buns one by one.

Appendix 2: Number and time rhymes

Last verse
No sticky buns in a baker's shop,
Big and brown with a currant on top.
A boy came along with a penny to pay.
'Sorry' said the baker, 'We have no buns
  left today'.

Numbers from 6 upwards

21

Six yellow ducklings,
Waddling down the lane,
Paddling in the puddles,
Splashing in the rain.

22

Eight brown sparrows,
Looking for crumbs.
They're often very hungry,
When winter time comes.

23

Ten busy brown bees,
Buzzing in the heather.
Ten brown bumble bees
humming altogether. [Buzz, buzz, ...]

Each of rhymes 21 to 23 mentions a number of animals. The number is shown in **bold type** to suggest that it can be changed to whatever number the teacher wishes to deal with on a particular occasion.

These rhymes could be used with cardboard animals or drawings to give practice in counting. For example, the teacher could pin up or stick up eight cardboard sparrows, and then make use of the rhyme to ask,
  'How many brown sparrows are looking for
    crumbs?' etc. .....
Several children could be asked to answer, and then the rhyme repeated with the number included.
  'Eight brown sparrows,
    etc. .....'
Some sparrows could be added or removed and the whole thing repeated for a different number.
  Another possible use is along with a frieze showing six yellow ducklings, seven brown sparrows, etc. each rhyme would then become 'our' rhyme about six, or whatever.

24 Ten little men

Ten little men lying quite still
Ten little men climb the hill.
Ten little men curl up small.
Ten little men stand straight and tall.
Ten little men run away.
Ten little men come home to stay.

This could be used for a finger game.
Possible actions are:
Line 1 Hands resting on lap.
Line 2 Fingers waggling as hands move up
          to 'climb' to face level.
Line 3 Make two fists.
Line 4 Fingers spread out pointing upwards,
          palms facing out.
Line 5 Fingers waggle as hands 'crawl'
          outwards.
Line 6 Reverse of line 5.

Appendix 2: Number and time rhymes 237

25 Eight big fingers

Eight big fingers standing up tall
Two little ears to hear mummy call,
One little nose that I can blow,
Ten little toes, all in a row,
Two short thumbs that wriggle up and down,
Two little feet to stand on the ground.
Hands to clap and eyes to see
Oh, what fun to be just me!

There are obvious hand actions
for this rhyme.

Counting up in ones

26 Magpies

One for sorrow, two for joy,
Three for a girl, four for a boy,
Five for silver, six for gold,
Seven for a secret never to be told.

27 One, two, three, four

One, two, three, four,
Mary at the cottage door.
Five, six, seven, eight,
Eating cherries off a plate.

Possible actions are:
Line 2 Children knock on imaginary door.
Line 4 Children use fingers to pick up imaginary cherries from plate and 'eat' them.

28 One, two, three, a leerie

One, two, three a leerie,
Four, five, six a leerie,
Seven, eight, nine a leerie
Ten a leerie, 'postman'.

This rhyme is often used by children playing ball.
'*One, two, three*' Ball bounced 3 times.
'*A leerie*' With right leg lifted, the ball is bounced under the leg from behind and then caught in front. (Sometimes the ball is bounced against a wall.)
Last line Turn right round before catching the ball.
A possible classroom version is 3 claps followed by lifting leg and putting forearm under it. For last line, one clap and then jump in the air at 'postman'.

29 One, two, three, four, five

One, two, three, four, five,
Once I caught a fish alive.
Six, seven, eight, nine, ten,
Then I let it go again.
Why did you let it go?
Because it bit my finger so.
Which finger did it bite?
This little finger on the right.

Line 1 Cup both hands together to catch fish.
Line 3 Spread open hands wide to let it go.
Lines 6, 7 Hold little finger of right hand with fingers of left *or* stick right hand in air with little finger pointing up.

Appendix 2: Number and time rhymes

30 Come on board

One is one and two is two.
I'm a spaceman. Who are you?

Three is three and four is four.
Listen to my spaceship's roar.

Five is five and six is six.
Come on board, we must be quick.

Seven is seven and eight is eight.
Wouldn't you like to be my mate?

Nine is nine and ten is ten.
You will not see earth again.

Verse 1
I'm a spaceman. Point to self.
'Who are you? Point to someone else.
Verse 2
Cup hand around ear to listen to the 'roar'.
Verse 3
Run on spot to 'be quick'.
Verse 4
Point to someone to be your 'mate'.
Verse 5
The 'again' at the end could be repeated and the rhyme re-started from the beginning.

Some children may be able to hold up 1 finger for 'one is one', 2 fingers for '2 is 2', and so on.

The game could be played in a ring, walking round on the first line of each verse and stopping to do the actions on the second line.

31 In the cupboard

I went to the cupboard,
And what did I see?
    One lemon,
    Two oranges,
    Three apples,
    Four pears,
    Five peaches,
    Six plums,
    Seven bananas,
    Eight cherries,
    Nine gooseberries,
    Ten raspberries ....
And up on the shelf,
All by itself, A BIRTHDAY CAKE FOR ME.

This rhyme could be used with a large illustration (perhaps made up of children's drawings) showing a cupboard with one lemon on the bottom shelf and so on up to a large birthday cake at the top.

The same drawing could also be used with numeral cards. For example, the child could place [6] card alongside the plums.

The birthday cake could be for a pupil who has a birthday that day, instead of for 'me'.

32 Housewives

1 busy housewife sweeping the floor,
2 busy housewives polishing the floor,
3 busy housewives washing baby's socks,
4 busy housewives winding up the clocks,
5 busy housewives scrubbing out the sink,
6 busy housewives giving pussy a drink,
7 busy housewives tidying the room,
8 busy housewives shaking out the broom,
9 busy housewives stirring the stew,
10 busy housewives with nothing left to do.

This can be played as a 'ring' game by repeating the last half of each line three times. One child stands in the middle and then 2, 3, and so on up to 10. Everybody does the actions.

Appendix 2: Number and time rhymes

Counting up in ones—counting objects

33 Counting stones

Here are **stones**
All in a ring.
We will count them,
While we sing,
1, 2, 3, ...

The **stones** could be replaced by beads, counters, etc., without affecting the rhymes.

34 A chimney pot

I'm going to build a chimney pot,
Very, very, high.
I'll build it with my bricks,
And I'll make it touch the sky.
1, 2, 3, 4, ... **10**.
Here's the wind and here's the rain,
To knock my chimney down again.

Bricks could be built up to any number by changing **10**. They are knocked down at the end and the rhyme repeated.

35 The train

I'll make a train,
And go for a ride.
Here are the carriages,
Side by side.
One, two, three . . . .
Choo, choo,
Off we go.
Ten little carriages,
All in a row.

Similar to rhyme 34, but with the bricks placed in a 'snake' perhaps along a desk or the floor. Alternatively, children could be counted in one by one to form the train and go chuffing round during the last part. There could be any number of carriages.

36 Posting letters

The pillar box is fat and red,
Its mouth is very wide.
I'm going to take some letters,
And pop them all inside.
1, 2, 3, ...

'Real' letters could be used with perhaps a red cardboard post box with a slot in it to post the letters. An old cardboard box could be adapted and painted for the purpose.

37 Counting steps

How many steps shall I have to take
To get from here to the door?
Please count how many steps I take
Walking across the floor.
1, 2, 3, ...

The teacher could take the steps while the pupils count out loud (or silently).

38 Counting claps

One, one,
All clap one.
[Class or group clap once.]
Two, two,
All clap two.
Etc. . . . .

This rhyme could be built up in sequence as shown here. It would, however, be more difficult for children to count numbers which were not in sequence—7 claps, then 4 claps next time, and so on.

Appendix 2: Number and time rhymes

Counting up in ones—further rhymes

39 John Brown had a little Indian

Verse
John Brown had a little Indian,
John Brown had a little Indian,
John Brown had a little Indian,
One little Indian boy.

Chorus
There was one little, two little, three little Indians,
Four little, five little, six little Indians,
Seven little, eight little, nine little Indians,
Ten little Indian boys.

Second verse
John Brown had two little Indians,
Etc. . . .

This rhyme can be sung to a well-known tune.
   It could be dramatized in the following manner. Ten children in a row could wear 'indian headresses'.

First verse   The first one stands; the others squat.
Chorus   They pop up one by one at 'two little, three little', etc. until all are standing.

At the end of the chorus all but two squat again for the start of the second verse, and so on. . . .

   A simpler 'ring' game could also be played. Everyone moves round in a ring with '1 indian' in the middle. At the chorus everyone stops and counts 'one little, two little', etc. on fingers. Another child is 'called in' to make two in the middle for the next verse.

40 One elephant

One elephant went out to play,
Upon a spider's web one day.
He found it such enormous fun,
That he called for another elephant to come.

[*Possibly:*
Two elephants went out to play,
etc.]

There is a tune for this rhyme.
One possible set of actions is as follows:
Line 1   One child points both arms 'straight out'.
Line 2   Draw web in air with circular motion.
Lines 3, 4   Another child chosen by first joins him and they wiggle bottoms.

The song is then repeated with the second elephant chosing a third, and so on.

   Another method of playing is to move round in a ring with 'one elephant' lumbering about it the middle. He chooses another to join him at the end of the verse, and so on.

   A possible variation is to allow *each* elephant inside the ring to choose another to come in each time (giving 1, 2, 4, 8, etc. elephants).

   Another possibility is to change the words each time
e.g. *second verse*
Two elephants went out to play
. . . .
They found it . . . .
That they called . . . .
(and so on).

Appendix 2: Number and time rhymes

Counting down in ones

41

8, 7, 6, 5,
First I'll catch a fish alive.
4, 3, 2, 1,
I'll cook my fish till it's done.

These rhymes could be accompanied by actions or counting down on the fingers.

42 Blast off!

A long shiny rocket,
Standing on the ground,
Spaceman starts the engines,
Listen for the sound:
10, 9, 8, ... 1,
BLAST-OFF!

Counting down in ones—counting objects

43

Eight tin soldiers in a row,
Knock them down as you go,
8, 7, 6, ...

The **eight tin soldiers** could be replaced by any other objects and knocked down one by one to correspond to the counting.

44 Counting balloons

I've **six** balloons to sell today,
Come pay a penny and take one away.
[Repeat with other numbers.]

Real balloons or cardboard circles on sticks could be used. The number of balloons remaining would be found after each transaction. Real pennies or token coins could also be used. The rhyme can be repeated until *no* balloons are left.

45 Counting apples

On the farmer's apple tree,
Ten fine apples I can see.
Some for you and some for me,
Eat **one** apple from the tree.

Cardboard apples on a tree drawing might be one way of using this rhyme.

46 Ten fat sausages

Ten fat sausages frying in the pan,
Ten fat sausages frying in the pan,
And if all of a sudden one went 'bang!',
There'd be nine fat sausages frying in the pan,
Nine fat sausages frying in the pan.
Etc. ......

This can be sung to the tune of 'ten green bottles'.

When using this tune the first line should be repeated twice as shown.
   Possible actions are:
Lines 1, 2 Hold up correct number of fingers.
Line 3 Clap hands at 'bang'.
Line 4 Hold up 'new' number of fingers.

   This rhyme (and some of those which follow) involves the idea of 'none'.

Appendix 2: Number and time rhymes

Counting up and down in twos, etc.

47 Ten fat sausages (again)

Ten fat sausages frying in a pan,
Ten fat sausages frying in a pan,
And if one went 'POP!' and another went 'BANG!',
There'd be eight fat sausages frying in the pan
Etc.

This can be sung to the tune of 'ten green bottles'.

Possible actions are as for rhyme 46 with the addition of 'snapping fingers' at 'pop!'.

48

Under a web beside our gate,
A spider hangs, his legs are eight.
Above him flies the busy bee,
Six black and furry legs has she.
The pussy cat goes leaping past,
Her four legs carry her so fast.
I've only two, that isn't many
But Mr Worm, he hasn't any.

This rhyme could be illustrated as a frieze with the appropriate lines of the verse written as captions alongside the appropriate parts of the drawing.

49

One red { bicycle / tricycle passes me, / motor car
How many wheels do I see? [repeat]

This rhyme could be illustrated by drawings or models to allow counting up in 2s, 3s, and 4s.

Addition and subtraction

50 Here comes the bus

Here comes the bus,
It's going to stop.
Hurry up children,
In you pop.
Four inside
And **six**, on top.

How many altogether?

A large drawing of a bus, with cardboard children who can be placed 'inside' or 'on top', could be used.

Alternatively, a table could be used for the bus and the children sit under it or on top of it.

Different numbers could be placed 'on top' and 'inside' each time and children asked to count. Later practice with addition facts e.g. $4 + 6 = 10$ would be possible.

Another possible use is with a particular 'story'. For example use 10 children. If 4 go inside, how many on top? If 3 go inside .... and so on.

Appendix 2: Number and time rhymes

These rhymes might be used to add a bit of variety to the teaching or revision of addition 'stories'. The numbers in bold type can be changed each time to deal with all the facts in the 'story'.

A possible method of use is to set up, say, 4 cardboard men and use rhyme 52 to ask 'How many more to make up to ten'?

51 Eight are late

Two little schoolboys
Going to be late.
How many after them
To make it up to eight?

52 A happy green crocodile

A happy green crocodile,
Eats **four** men.
Then he has another—**How many?**
To make up to ten

The rhyme can be repeated with the answer 'six' inserted rather than the 'How many?' For some of the other Rhymes the answer would have to be 'six more' or 'another six'.

Time

53 Birthdays

Monday's child is fair of face,
Tuesday's child is full of grace,
Wednesday's child is full of woe,
Thursday's child has far to go,
Friday's child is loving and giving,
Saturday's child works hard for its living;
But the child who is born on the Sabbath day
Is bonny and blithe and good and gay.

54 Sneezing

Sneeze on Monday, sneeze for danger;
Sneeze on Tuesday, meet a stranger;
Sneeze on Wednesday, get a letter;
Sneeze on Thursday, something better;
Sneeze on Friday, sneeze for sorrow;
Sneeze on Saturday, see your sweetheart tomorrow.

Appendix 2: Number and time rhymes

55 Solomon Grundy

Solomon Grundy,
Born on Monday,
Christened on Tuesday,
Married on Wednesday,
Took ill on Thursday,
Worse on Friday,
Died on Saturday,
Buried on Sunday,
So that was the end of Solomon Grundy.

56

Monday is our washing day,
   Scrub, scrub, scrub.
Tuesday is our ironing day,
   Rub, rub, rub.
Wednesday is our mending day,
   Sew, sew, sew.
Thursday is our calling day,
   Off we go.
Friday is our sweeping day,
   Sweep, sweep, sweep.
Saturday is our baking day,
   Beat, beat, beat.
Sunday hear the churchbells chime,
   Ring, ring, ring.
Saying 'Children come to church',
   Ding, dong, ding.

57

Friday night is my delight,
And so is Saturday morning.
But Sunday night—it gives me a fright:
There's school on Monday morning.

58 A tree

In Spring I look gay,
Decked in comely array,
In Summer more clothing I wear;
When colder it grows,
I fling off my clothes,
And in Winter quite naked appear.

59 Cuckoo

Cuckoo, cuckoo,
Pray what do you do?
In April, I open my bill.
In May, I sing night and day.
In June, I change my tune.
In July, away I fly.
In August, away I must.

60 The garden year

January brings the snow,
Makes our feet and fingers glow.

February brings the rain,
Thaws the frozen lake again.

March brings breezes, loud and shrill,
To stir the dancing daffodil.

April brings the primrose sweet,
Scatters daisies at our feet.

May brings flocks of pretty lambs,
Skipping by their fleecy dams.

June brings tulips, lilies, roses,
Fills the children's hands with posies.

Hot July brings cooling showers,
Apricots and gillyflowers.

August brings the sheaves of corn,
Then the harvest home is borne.

Warm September brings the fruit,
Sportsmen then begin to shoot.

Fresh October brings the pheasant,
Then to gather nuts is pleasant.

Dull November brings the blast,
Then the leaves are whirling fast.

Chill December brings the sleet,
Blazing fire and Christmas treat.